KU-022-898

CONTENTS

5

Some parts of this book have appeared in *PMLA*
and *The Quarterly Review of Literature*

PREFACE

THE major assumption of this book is that George Herbert, the parson-poet of seventeenth-century England, is one of the best lyric poets who has written in the English language. I have not attempted the hopeless task of 'proving' such an assumption; rather, I have tried to assume an ideal reader of taste and availability to literary experience who will recognize a good poem once he is given the materials which enable him to understand it. I have hoped also for a reader interested in the relations of a work of art to its conceptual framework and to history. Such considerations help our understanding of most poetry. They are essential to an understanding of George Herbert's *The Temple*.

Although Herbert has been the subject of a number of recent essays, there was no book-length study of his work between George Herbert Palmer's essay of 1905 and Rosemond Tuve's fine *A Reading of George Herbert* of 1952. That gap of nearly half a century is largely responsible for the organization of this volume. In my first three chapters I have considered the past and present myths concerning Herbert's poetry, his life, and his religion, and I have tried to correct them. Chapters IV and V concern Herbert's theories of form and language, both basic to his poetic and religious practice; and in the final section I have attempted to relate those theories directly to the poems.

I determined to undertake this study in 1941, when Kenneth B. Murdock first introduced me to *The Temple*. Since that time I have acquired an enormous indebtedness to many individuals as well as to many printed volumes. I have attempted to indicate the latter in my notes, but the former is more difficult to acknowledge precisely: many students as well as faculty members of the English Department and of History and Literature at Harvard and Radcliffe have contributed more than they know. I owe particular debts to Mr Douglas Bush and the late F. O. Matthiessen and Theodore Spencer, with whom I worked closely on specific subjects related to George Herbert. My study of Herbert has also profited from the instruction, conversation, or generous correspondence of the following individuals: Miss Elizabeth Bishop, Miss Margaret Church, Mr Leonard Dean, Mr Lloyd Frankenberg, Mr Walter Houghton, Mrs Pearl Kazin Kraft, Mr Paul De Man, Mr James I. Merrill, Mr Charles Owen, Mr John B. Rackliffe, Mr Richard B. Schlatter, Mr Geoffrey Tillotson, Miss Rosemond Tuve, Mr Andrews Wanning, and Mr Theodore Weiss. The officers of the Harvard and Radcliffe College libraries have been most helpful, and some sections of my study would have been impossible without access to Houghton Library's fine Herbert collection, organized around the original gift of George Herbert Palmer. I am particularly grateful to Miss Gladys Brownell and Miss Jane Rollins of the Bard College Library, who granted me unusual courtesies. My largest debts are to Kenneth Murdock and my wife, who care for style as well as content and who have been long-suffering.

I

Time and *The Temple*

GEORGE HERBERT is one of the best English lyric poets. To our attempts to see his poetry today, the past images of it formed by Laudians, Puritans, neo-classicists, Evangelicals, Romantics, Transcendentalists, Anglo-Catholics, and modern apostles of Donne bring partial if valuable illumination. With certain notable exceptions, those who have admired the poems in the immediate as well as in the distant past can be roughly divided into two groups: the religious readers who bowed to Herbert's piety and the literary men who praised the 'wit' and 'ingenuity' or perhaps the form and the language. Each group often had strong reservations: the *dévot* could sometimes ignore the wit for the sake of the piety; and the *littérateur* might be able, reluctantly, to do the reverse. In either process both the poetry and the religion suffered, for they are intimately and inextricably interrelated in *The Temple*.

Herbert wrote just before the conflict which changed the English world—and the religious and literary 'interpretations' of his poetry began almost immediately. His English poetry had probably been known to a distinguished circle of friends before the posthumous publication of *The Temple* in 1633, and he had published one Latin poem as early as 1612. In 1625, moreover, Francis Bacon had dedicated his *Translation of Certaine Psalmes* to Herbert and thus furthered Herbert's reputation as a poet. But Herbert's literary stature depended upon the English poems in *The Temple*. The number of editions of *The Temple* indicates that Herbert was the most popular religious poet within his own century aside from the voluminous Francis Quarles; and except for John Cleveland, he was the most popular of the so-called 'metaphysical poets,' sacred or profane.[1]

Within seven years after the publication of *The Temple*, Herbert had already received the dubious flattery of uninspired imitation. Christopher Harvey clearly stated his debt in the title page of *The Synagogue: Or, The Shadow of The Temple . . . In Imitation of Mr George Herbert*. Harvey may have understood that art and wit and grace were inextricable in *The Temple*,[2] but the understanding did him little good. Despite his close imitation of Herbert in subjects, language, stanza forms, and rhythms, most of his poems are very bad. But *The Synagogue* is significant because its organization and the tone of many of its poems indicate how the rapid course of history from 1633 to 1640 could change a reading of *The Temple*. At Herbert's death in 1633 Laud had not yet become the highest dignitary of the English Church, and despite increasing tension every religious work was not then necessarily implicitly political in its import. To Harvey at the outbreak of the Civil War, however, Herbert seemed a latter-day partisan and his poetry a potential bulwark against the Puritan attack. Harvey's popularity, even among such readers as Izaak Walton, is a sign that many men of that time and later considered the piety and the politics of religious verse more important than the poetry. From 1641 until the latter part of the nineteenth century *The Synagogue* was often bound with *The Temple* as an inevitable second part. The title on the binding was nearly always simply, 'Herbert's Poems.' Anyone who cared for the first volume was assumed to desire the second.

Henry Vaughan's imitation of *The Temple* was another matter. In the preface to the 1655 edition of *Silex Scintillans*, Vaughan called himself the least of George Herbert's 'many pious *Converts*.'[3] Vaughan was excessively humble, but he did not exaggerate his discipleship: F. E. Hutchinson has justly remarked that no other English poet of any significance has ever borrowed so much from another.[4] Vaughan seems to have read Herbert so much that his borrowings were often unconscious: he introduced Herbert's phrases and images with surprisingly unrelated meanings and applications. Yet Vaughan's response to Herbert was also partial. Although occasionally he wrote a poem in such exact imitation of Herbert that it might be mistaken for one of his master's minor poems,[5] he seems rarely to have perceived the relationship of logical structure to Herbert's success. At his best Vaughan is the English 'poet of light,' and the images of light, felt symbols of God's immanence, give the intensity to his finest lines. Those lines differ from Herbert's not in degree but kind. For a poet such as Vaughan the superficial elements of Herbert's technique were often more of a burden than an aid.

To Vaughan, as to Harvey, Herbert appeared a prophetic figure who, as the chief example of pre-revolutionary piety, had somehow anticipated the struggle and had firmly and unhesitatingly declared for Charles and Laud. Barnabas Oley and Izaak Walton completed the image of Herbert as a Laudian of the primitive Christian era. Oley, who presented *Herbert's Remains* in 1652 as a weapon in the ecclesiastical warfare, seems to have given the title *A Priest to the Temple* to the volume which Herbert had called *The Countrey Parson.*[6] In his preface to *Herbert's Remains* Oley saw the triumph of the Commonwealth as the just punishment for the sins of the clergy; King and Church would triumph if the clergy imitated Herbert's life and his writings. Oley's essay provided the outline for Walton's biography of 1670. Walton's *Life of Mr George Herbert* is so successful as a work of art that it has influenced decisively—if often unfortunately—almost every subsequent reading of Herbert's poems. One's misgivings (if one is permitted to have misgivings about one masterpiece in defence of another) stem from the fact that Walton's primary aim was to present Herbert's life as the quintessence of 'all' the 'examples of primitive piety.'[7] In pursuit of that aim, Walton freely constructed 'conversations' and occasionally either invented incidents or accepted them on the basis of unreliable reports.[8] The resulting 'saint's life' established for the general reader of later ages the view of Herbert as a lovable and naïve Laudian.

Within a year after the appearance of Walton's *Life*, Oley published the second edition of *A Priest to the Temple*. His new preface indicates that a new age had already begun. Although Oley referred to 'the Myracle of our Happy Restauration,' he was hardly happy with the new Church.

His real alienation from that Church and that age is signalized by his long attack on a 'scandalous book,' John Eachard's *The Grounds and Occasions of the Contempt of the Clergy and Religion* (1670). Eachard's volume was one of the first as well as one of the wittiest attacks on the then outmoded 'conceited' language of the early seventeenth century. Eachard wished the clergy to avoid 'contempt' by adopting the new language and the new manner of the Restoration gentleman. But Oley was incensed by Eachard's manner—'Sceptice, Sarcastice, with wit Satyrical . . . Like one *puffed up*, and not like a *Mourner*.' As Eachard later protested,[9] the attack was mistaken: he and Oley did not differ drastically in ecclesiastical positions. Yet their differences in language and attitude were really more divisive: Eachard was as firmly of the new age as Oley was of the past. The differences between the new age and the past in the 1670's included fundamental assumptions as well as attitudes and language. Just at the time when Herbert's hagiologists had constructed a 'pattern of primitive piety,' an image of sincere and naïve faith, the developments in society, philosophy, religion, and poetry had reached a point at which the most important talents and intellects found such an image either irrelevant or ridiculous.

Eachard's essay was a fairly conservative example of the literary appeal to a new 'nature' and a new 'reason.' With more than a glance at Herbert, Dryden ironically assumed that appeal in the closing lines of *Mac Flecknoe* (1682):

> Thy genius calls thee not to purchase fame
> In keen iambics, but mild anagram.
> Leave writing plays, and choose for thy command
> Some peaceful province in acrostic land.
> There thou may'st wings display and altars raise,
> And torture one poor word ten thousand ways;
> Or, if thou wouldst thy diff'rent talents suit
> Set thy own songs, and sing them to thy lute.

Herbert's subject aside, his manner was unsuited to an age of 'clear and distinct,' albeit abstract, ideas. Joseph Addison's six essays on 'false wit' (*Spectator*, Nos. 58-63,

May 7th-12th, 1711) spell out Dryden's assumptions and conveniently summarize a literary attitude which had been developing for over fifty years and was not to be challenged for almost a century more. In his condemnation of the pattern poem Addison mentioned Herbert by name,[10] and although he did not refer to the poet in his discussion of other 'aberrations' (such as 'the conceit of making an echo talk sensibly, and give rational answers,' anagrams, acrostics, and puns), Herbert was guilty on almost every count. To Addison true wit consisted only in the 'resemblance and congruity of ideas,'[11] and it was genuine only if it could be translated effectively into another language. Language, denied intrinsic interest, was reduced to the function of the transparent glass; the realm of general laws was the ultimate reality for 'wit' as for Newton's universe. It did not occur to Addison that, all considerations of 'wit' aside, the devices which he criticized might more truly have imaged to a former 'monkish age' the secret, hieroglyphic nature of God's universe than could any number of translatable ideas. Addison's formulations provide the major clue as to why Herbert's poems were held in such low esteem by the eighteenth-century literary critics. Not until Coleridge's influence began to be felt did the official literary attitude toward Herbert change. There were no editions of *The Temple* from 1709 until 1799.

Such a rapid summary of the most important attitudes of two centuries gives only a partial view: every age has more than one 'spirit,' and we are here concerned with more than one age. Herbert's poetry continued to be enormously popular throughout the seventeenth century, and it possessed its ardent admirers in the eighteenth century. One has only to read the religious anthology pieces from the earlier periods to perceive how general was the sincere, if often uninspired, imitation of Herbert.[12] As the century wore on, however, the praise and even the occasional borrowings from *The*

Temple tended to betray a lack of understanding of Herbert's achievement. The pattern poems of Joseph Beaumont and Edward Benlowes are closer to Quarles or Harvey or Crashaw than to Herbert. Although he may have been influenced by *The Temple*, Traherne had a totally different conception of poetry. A poem such as Daniel Baker's 'Pindarique Ode,' 'On Mr *George Herbert's* Sacred Poems, Called, The Temple,' shows how far separated the reputation and actual influence of Herbert could be.[13] But the individuals who read Herbert with the greatest care and affection during the later seventeenth and the eighteenth century did not share in the 'official' views of Herbert's poetry. Most of them valued the poems in *The Temple* chiefly for the piety, but that piety was not related to any specific political settlement or religious form: it was the communicated record of recognizable religious experience. As early as 1650 Richard Baxter quoted Herbert's 'Dotage,' 'Home,' and the final stanzas of 'The Glance' in *The Saints Everlasting Rest*, the most popular of his many volumes in both England and America. *The Saints Rest* undoubtedly helped to secure 'low' and non-Anglican readers for Herbert, yet even without Baxter's quotations *The Temple* would probably have been known and admired by such distinguished nonconformists as Peter Sterry, John Bryan, and Philip Henry.[14] The reason for Herbert's popularity in those circles was expressed most memorably by Baxter in the preface to his *Poetical Fragments* (1681): '*Herbert* speaks *to* God like one that *really believeth* a *God*, and whose business in the world is most *with God. Heart-work* and *Heaven-work* make up his Books.'

Although the Puritans recognized 'Heart-work' in *The Temple*, few of their poets profited by Herbert's example. Like Baxter, they might sometimes use Herbert's phrases or imitate a few simple devices, but with their lack of interest or ability in technique, most of their poems failed to communicate their sincerity to an audience larger than their immediate like-minded contemporaries.[15] The most interesting of the New England poets, however, was an exception. While the body of Edward Taylor's work is unique in quality, his debt to Herbert is enormous. He imitated Herbert's stanza forms[16] and borrowed ideas, metaphors, and cadences. Despite his weaknesses (in general he is notable for lines rather than for entire poems), Taylor's personal use of Herbert's poetry helps to place him firmly in the best tradition of seventeenth-century religious verse.[17]

But Edward Taylor, who continued writing until 1725, was an anachronism even in New England—and his poetry was not published until the twentieth century. The work of John Reynolds (1667-1727), a moderate dissenting English minister, is more of its time. Reynolds's unbounded admiration for Herbert is particularly notable in a man who believed that 'never was the Christian law of love so well evinced and establish'd as in the *newtonian* philosophy.'[18] His 'To the Memory of the divine Mr *George Herbert*, Author of the *Temple*,' one of the most eulogistic as well as most interesting of the memorial pieces on Herbert, shows in detail how *The Temple* could be read as every Christian's autobiography:

> Strange! how each fellow-saint's surpris'd
> To see himself anatomiz'd!
> The *Sion*'s mourner breathes thy strains,
> Sighs thee, and in thy notes complains;
> Amaz'd, and yet refresh'd to see
> His wounds, drawn to the life, in thee!
> The racer, almost out of breath,
> Marching through shades and vale of death,
> Recruits, when he to thee is come,
> And sighs for heav'n, and sings thy *Home*;
> The tempted soul, whose thoughts are whirl'd,
> About th' inchantments of the world,
> Can o'er the snares and scandals skip,
> Born up by *Frailty*, and the *Quip*;
> The victor has reward paid down,
> His earnest here of life and crown;
> The conscious priest is well releas'd
> Of pain and fear, in *Aaron* drest;
> The preaching envoy can proclaim
> His pleasure in his *Master*'s name;

A name, that like the grace in him,
Sends life and ease to ev'ry limb;
Rich magazine of health! where's found
Specific balm for ev'ry wound![19]

Reynolds's longest poem is *A View of Death*. Despite its title, it is neither a medieval *memento mori* nor a predecessor of the graveyard school; it is, on the contrary, inspired by the optimistic conviction that 'death may well be studied, when it will open our eyes and lead us into the regions of philosophy.'[20] Reynolds furnished his poem with ample annotations on difficult or doubtful points, and his cited authorities are numerous and impressive: Locke, Descartes, Henry More, Dampier, Boyle, Bacon, Lucretius, Cowley, Derham, Huygens, Kepler, 'Lowenhoek,' Hooke, and Aristotle. The authorities referred to most frequently, however, were Newton and George Herbert. The thirty-fourth stanza of Herbert's 'Providence' showed the construction of the 'Great Chain of Being.'[21] 'The Pulley' showed the theological necessity for the deviation of nature from its original 'paradisiacal' form.[22] But 'Man' was the poem which prophetically celebrated the extraordinary providence of man's central position in the complicated universe.[23] The heavens, Reynolds insisted, *did* declare the glory of God and His amazing care for man:

> Great God! what pow'r, and prudence to the full
> Are scatter'd thro' th' expanded whole!
> Stupendous bulk, and symmetrie,
> Cross motion, and clear harmonie,
> Close union, and antipathie,
> Projectile force, and gravitie,
> In such well-pois'd proportions fall,
> As strike this artful mathematic dance of all.[24]

If 'More servants wait on Man, Then he'l take notice of' at present, Reynolds's purpose was to increase man's attention through the study of the new science.

Any eighteenth-century reader who wished could learn

from Reynolds how to read *The Temple* and the new science
in each other's reflected light. Most of the eighteenth-
century readers of Herbert, however, learned of him through
John Wesley rather than through John Reynolds. F. E.
Hutchinson has ably summarized Wesley's interest and
influence: 'He quotes him familiarly in letters from his
twenty-fourth to his eightieth year; he reads aloud to his
disciples the *Temple* poems and *The Country Parson*; he
prints in his seventieth year the only considerable body of
Herbert's poems reprinted between 1709 and 1799, and he
adopts or re-writes for his various volumes of *Collections* no
less than forty-seven of the poems. He includes Walton's
Life of Herbert in his popular series, *A Christian Library*
(1753).'[25] Wesley's 'adaptations,' which regularized the
metres as well as 'purified' the diction, must have substantiated Herbert's general reputation as a pious man but
inferior artist. Yet, whatever he felt proper for congregational singing, Wesley was a man of literary discrimination,
and it may have been with a sense of joyful penance that he
published *Select Parts of Mr Herbert's Sacred Poems* in their
original form in 1773.

Despite their personal joy in the poems, a number of
these seventeenth- and eighteenth-century admirers were
sufficiently influenced or intimidated by the literary standards of their time to feel apologetic for Herbert's art. Even
Baxter added, in the midst of his praise, 'I know that *Cooly*
and others far excel *Herbert* in Wit and accurate com-
posure.'[26] And William Cowper, who could echo Herbert
and who had found his poems of immense comfort, believed
them to be 'gothic and uncouth.'[27]

Coleridge was the first important critic who praised *The
Temple* on literary grounds. In his remarks in his *Biographia
Literaria* and *The Friend*, his emphasis was firmly on
style. In the *Biographia*, after a discussion of the approxima-
tion of natural speech in poetry, with citations of Charles .

Cotton and *Troilus and Criseyde,* Coleridge turned to Herbert:

> Another exquisite master of this species of style, where the scholar and the poet supplies the material, but the perfect well-bred gentleman the expressions and the arrangement, is George Herbert. As from the nature of the subject, and the too frequent quaintness of the thoughts, his *Temple; or Sacred Poems and Private Ejaculations* are comparatively but little known, I shall extract two poems. The first is a sonnet, equally admirable for the weight, number, and expression of the thoughts, and for the simple dignity of the language. Unless, indeed a fastidious taste should object to the latter half of the sixth line. The second is a poem of greater length, which I have chosen not only for the present purpose, but likewise as a striking example and illustration of an assertion hazarded in a former page of these sketches: namely, that the characteristic fault of our elder poets is the reverse of that, which distinguishes too many of our more recent versifiers; the one conveying the most fantastic thoughts in the most correct and natural language; the other in the most fantastic language conveying the most trivial thoughts.[28]

After more than a century of emphasis on the piety, Coleridge nearly reversed the balance with the few comments published during his lifetime.

Soon after the publication of the *Biographia,* however, Coleridge's emphasis seems to have changed. In a letter to W. Collins, dated December 1818, he wrote: 'To feel the full force of the Christian religion it is perhaps necessary, for many tempers, that they should first be made to feel, experimentally, the hollowness of human friendship, the presumptuous emptiness of human hopes. I find more substantial comfort now in pious George Herbert's Temple, which I used to read to amuse myself with his quaintness, in short, only to laugh at, than in all the poetry since the poems of Milton.'[29] This personal response is evident in Coleridge's posthumously published 'Notes on Herbert's *Temple* and Harvey's *Synagogue.*'[30] The notes show a careful reading of the poems, with Coleridge alert to religious meaning as well as to language and rhythm. Aware of his earlier failure at total response, Coleridge attempted to formulate a statement of the indivisibility of Herbert's aesthetic and religious achievement:

> G. Herbert is a true poet, but a poet *sui generis*, the merits of whose poems will never be felt without a sympathy with the mind and character of the man. To appreciate this volume, it is not enough that the reader possesses a cultivated judgment, classical taste, or even poetic sensibility, unless he be likewise a *Christian*, and both a zealous and an orthodox, both a devout and a *devotional* Christian. But even this will not quite suffice. He must be an affectionate and dutiful child of the Church, and from habit, conviction, and a constitutional predisposition to ceremoniousness, in piety as in manners, find her forms and ordinances aids of religion, not sources of formality; for religion is the element in which he lives, and the region in which he moves.[31]

Historically, Coleridge's statement was inaccurate: Herbert's most extravagant admirers during the preceding one hundred years were not Anglicans; they had 'felt sympathy' with something in Herbert's poetry which did not involve a 'constitutional predisposition to ceremoniousness.'

Coleridge's remarks were continually parroted during the nineteenth century. In the editorial prefaces to the countless editions of *The Temple* (after 1799 new editions appeared slightly oftener, on the average, than every four years), potential appreciation of Herbert often seems confined to well-bred members of the Church of England with a taste for the quaint. In 1885, Ernest Rhys could remark with justice, 'Quaintness is the term that has been most usually applied by the critics to Herbert's poetry,'[32] and the word was used with its full aura of affectionate patronization. The attitude of the well-bred Anglican gentleman was expressed by J. Henry Shorthouse: *The Temple*, like the Church of England, was concerned with the 'gospel of refinement'; although he believed John Keble's poetry to be finer, Shorthouse valued that of Herbert and his 'fellows' (Donne, Wotton, George Wither, Quarles, and Vaughan) because 'they showed the English people what a fine gentleman who was also a Christian and a Churchman might be. They set the tone of the Church of England, and they revealed with no inefficient or temporary effect to the uncultured and unlearned the true refinement of worship.'[33]

But before the publication of Coleridge's 'Notes on *The Temple,*' Emerson had read *The Friend* and *Biographia Literaria* and had discovered Herbert with a youthful joy in which Anglicanism had little part. His enthusiasm, manifested continually in his writings, was to last throughout his life and to culminate in his inclusion of fifteen poems from *The Temple* in *Parnassus,* with the remark, 'So much piety was never married to so much wit.'[34] Emerson's liking included but did not depend upon Herbert's 'quaintness': 'Read Herbert. What eggs, ellipses, acrostics, forward, backward and across, could not his liquid genius run into and be genius still and angelic love? And without soul, the freedom of our Unitarianism here becomes cold, barren and odious.'[35] Emerson's immediate response, noted in his journal, was genuine and just; it was in his works intended for publication that Herbert became an Emersonian. In the crucial final chapter of *Nature,* Emerson quoted five stanzas of 'Man,' the same poem which had proved to John Reynolds Herbert's prophetic Newtonianism. To Emerson the poem proved that Herbert was a prophetic transcendentalist. *Nature* probably helped to establish Herbert's influence on the verse of the other New England 'transcendentalists.' Thoreau's debt is obvious in such poems as 'I am a parcel of vain strivings tied' and 'Friendship.'[36] If Channing attributed Emerson's 'Grace' to Herbert,[37] the compliment was returned when eight lines from Herbert's 'Mattens' were published in 1945 as a poem by Emily Dickinson.[38] In both cases the lines concerned were significantly few. In more extended compositions the differences between the poems of Herbert and these nineteenth-century poets would be readily perceived, for the transcendentalists' response to Herbert was fragmentary. The stanzas of 'Man' which Emerson omitted from his quotation of the poem in *Nature* were exactly those which both clearly establish the Christian meaning of the poem and make evident its logical structure. The rejection of Herbert's logical theology, coupled with the conviction that his poetic mastery could somehow be achieved by 'greatness of soul' alone without particular attention to technique,[39] caused Herbert's influence to be felt only in lines or short passages—although, occasionally, passages of a fine intensity.

The two best English poets strongly influenced by Herbert in the nineteenth century accepted *The Temple* with fewer excisions. Christina Rossetti and Gerard Manley Hopkins were attracted both by Herbert's religious content and his poetic technique. As a child Christina Rossetti imitated Herbert's poetry,[40] and Herbert's example contributed to the success of some of her best, mature devotional poems. Nineteenth-century language and her almost fatal facility often obscured her debt, but in a lyric such as 'Good Friday' ('Am I a stone, and not a sheep'), Herbert is creatively present; and 'Up-Hill,' one of her most successful poems, shows Herbert's deceptively simple dialogue put to personal use.[41] We do not have to believe that George Herbert was Hopkins's 'strongest tie to the English Church'[42] to realize Hopkins's affection for and debt to Herbert. Like Emerson, Hopkins preferred Herbert to Vaughan, and he thought of Herrick and Herbert together as the last poets of the Elizabethan tradition.[43] Hopkins was fascinated by Herbert's experiments with rhythms, alliteration, and related sound patterns, as well as by his imagery.[44] Occasionally, phrases which are most characteristic of Hopkins seem to be taken from Herbert. In 'Heaven-Haven,' Hopkins may have remembered the final line of 'The Size,' '*These seas are tears, and heav'n the haven.*' The 'Ah, my dear' of 'The Windhover' had been used for similar effect in Herbert's 'Love (III),' and the 'thousands of thorns, thoughts' of 'Tom's Garland' is a precise echo of 'Love unknown': 'I found that some had stuff'd the bed with thoughts, I would say *thorns*.' Although Hopkins left the English Church, he did not give up his tie to George Herbert. Both Rossetti and Hopkins seem to have understood and responded to Herbert's poems as much as was compatible with their own identities as poets, but neither of them left followers capable of inheriting or increasing their understanding. For Herbert's reputation the twentieth century required a new beginning.

George Herbert Palmer's publication of his edition of

The English Works of George Herbert[45] placed all subsequent readers in his debt. Although the edition was a labour of love, Paul Elmer More justly remarked that Palmer did not altogether avoid 'bowing the knee to the Idol of the Present.'[46] Palmer was embarrassed by Herbert's theology, and despite many acute remarks concerning the poetry, his tone was frequently apologetic: he began his prefatory essay with an apology for a 'gentle and incomplete poet,' and he remarked that 'even restricted times and poets work out necessary elements of human nature.'[47] But the 'present' of 1905 showed its most damaging influence in Palmer's attempt to rearrange the poems in *The Temple* so that they would form a chronological 'spiritual autobiography.' The attempt reflected the tendency (still popular today) to consider the artist's life more interesting than his work. Granted such a biographical interest and faced with the marked fluctuations of mood in *The Temple*, what could one more naturally assume at the turn of the century than that the arrangement of the poems was meaningless, that the 'true' personal development of the poet was from faith to doubt, from joy to despair?

Despite such failings, Palmer's edition was both appealing and informative, but it was hardly calculated to inspire a new generation of readers and writers. The 'rediscovery' of Donne, whether calculated or not, did that. Already the subjects of a good deal of interest in the 1890's,[48] Donne and 'metaphysical poetry' became the chief concerns of modern criticism only after the publication of H. J. C. Grierson's edition of Donne's poems (1912), his *Metaphysical Lyrics & Poems of the Seventeenth Century: Donne to Butler* (1921), and the early essays of T. S. Eliot.[49] What occurred was a poetic and critical revolution, in which the modern version of 'metaphysical poetry' replaced the Romantic and Victorian and Georgian standards. Eliot was the central figure, but Donne became the central symbol. If in the process Donne's poetry and personality suffered distortion,[50] that distorted image was the important element which affected the reputation of Herbert's poetry. The 'bizarre' quality of Donne's poetry was a thing of praise for Grierson, and, at least to the later critics, so was the fact that Donne 'is more aware of disintegration than of comprehensive harmony.'[51] Philosophically, scepticism was considered a positive and almost essential asset. In spite of Eliot's conception of 'unified sensibility,' the divided mind was held at a premium, and the 'tortured individual' was as highly esteemed as ever in English criticism. A major historical assumption was that 'metaphysical poetry' was a specific, distinguishable (or, rather, the only distinguished) body of poetry in seventeenth-century England, and that Donne, in more than one sense, was 'the great master of English poetry in the seventeenth century.'[52] It was occasionally assumed that whatever was of value in poetry after or even contemporary with Donne's must have its origin in the work of the master. 'Like Donne' and 'unlike Donne' became accepted critical terms expressing, respectively, approval and disapproval.

In the nineteenth century Herbert had frequently been viewed as a romantic *manqué*. In 1863, for example, John Nichol, after lamenting Herbert's lack of taste, his 'grotesque vein of allegory,' his 'conceits which seem to approach irreverence,' granted high praise to 'the tender grace of some of his verses, as "Peace" or "Virtue," which Shelley might have written.'[53] The view of Herbert as an inferior John Donne was hardly more illuminating. Exactly those elements which had earlier seemed excessive faults now appeared to be deficient virtues. Although the critics found much to praise, obviously Herbert was not so much 'like Donne' as Donne was like Donne. And the general conclusion seemed to be that Herbert was a poet with a 'smaller character' of mind and sensibility, of 'narrower experience,' lacking in 'intellectual sophistication' and 'complex moods.' As a result of these personal limitations his 'choice of subject matter' was 'limited,' and the 'texture' of his poems 'simplified' (he reduced 'the number of associated ideas' and made 'the sequence of images more homogeneous'). Herbert's formal concerns and achievements were attributed to a personal 'affinity for neat designs and comfortable limits.'[54] In short, in Grierson's phrase, Herbert was 'not a greatly imaginative . . . poet.'[55]

There were (there always are) exceptions. In 1900 Edward Dowden had published a suggestive essay on Herbert,[56] largely independent of the conventional opinion of the time, and he had honourable successors. T. S. Eliot was, characteristically, ahead of his followers. In the Clark Lectures of 1926 Eliot had criticized Donne in a fashion which might have jeopardized the reputation of a lesser critic,[57] and he had also perceived the grave dangers involved in the attempts at a rigid formulation of 'metaphysical poetry.'[58] In the same year in which his *Collected Essays* appeared, Eliot wrote a brief note on Herbert which seems to have been a disavowal of over-anxious followers as well as of nineteenth-century pietists: 'Whatever Herbert was, he was not the prototype of the clergyman of Dickens's Christmas at Dingley Dell. . . . The usual opinion, I believe, is . . . that we go to Donne for poetry and to Crashaw for religious poetry; but that Herbert deserves to be remembered as the representative lyrist of a mild and tepid church.' Eliot discussed the 'spiritual stamina' of Herbert's work and insisted, 'Throughout there is brain work, and a very high level of intensity: his poetry is definitely an *œuvre* to be studied entire.'[59]

It was Austin Warren, however, who published one of the first and still one of the best extended modern essays on Herbert. Warren pictured Herbert as an individual poet whose literary achievement was intimately related to his religious experience, and whose poetry, 'put beside Donne's, is seen to have its own "end"—as coherent and "pure" as Donne's, but other.'[60] Since that time a number of individuals have done excellent work on Herbert, most notably F. E. Hutchinson (whose fine edition established an acceptable text for all of Herbert's writings and also, in its notes and commentary, solved many of the scholarly problems), L. C. Knights, and Rosemond Tuve.[61]

These valuable recent studies of Herbert seem to be part of a still indefinite but generally developing change in the critical climate. While by no means abandoning that 'close analysis' which was the major contribution of English literary criticism between the two wars, the best of recent criticism places a growing emphasis on order rather than

tension or conflict as a literary value, and it recognizes that
the 'wholeness' of a poem does not necessarily demand a
sharply fragmented texture. Whereas the critics have established their contention that critical writing should aim at
exegesis and formulation of relevance to the reader of the
present, the scholars have shown that present interpretation
can be 'relevant' only when based on an understanding of
the work within its cultural context. There seems, today, a
more general willingness on the part of both critics and
scholars to recognize the 'impurity' of language and the
inevitable 'impurity' of the literary work of art: it is difficult
any longer to pretend that the ideas and beliefs of a poet
are of no importance in determining our response to his
'aesthetic structure.' Of wider significance than the developments in literature is the change during the past twenty
years in the 'intellectuals'' attitude toward religion. It is now
possible to treat seriously the thought of a seventeenth-
century Christian without either apologies to the gods of
inevitable progress, an air of bravura, or an attempt at
literary psychoanalysis. An atmosphere is forming more con-
genial to the appreciation of Herbert as well as Milton.
Today, as in the past, it is impossible fully to perceive or
respond to Herbert's aesthetic achievement without an
understanding of the religious thought and experience
which is both its subject and its inspiration.

CHAPTER II

The Life

THE poems represent the life which mattered most to George Herbert and which should matter to his readers; but after centuries of biographical interpretation, the most serious reader may find that those poems begin to read like glosses on a suspect biography. In defence of the text we are forced to re-examine the traditional version of the life and, at least, to question those interpretations which make the poetry more rather than less difficult. The most prevalent and dubious practice of Herbert's biographers has been to accept *The Temple* as a simple and direct autobiographical statement, to construct a 'life' based on such a reading of the poems, and then to use it as the major criterion for criticizing and even dating Herbert's work. In the process Izaak Walton's *Life* has been the prime source.

Based on a good deal of personal research (Walton never knew Herbert), Walton's *Life* is just in certain outlines as well as details. The 'holiness' of the last years at Bemerton is well attested, as is Herbert's 'courtliness' at Cambridge. But when Walton wrote in 1670, the years before the war appeared more golden than they really were; and, with his attempt to present the model of 'primitive piety,' it was only natural that Walton should emphasize Herbert's relations with Laud and Donne and Andrewes, and that he should suppress information which might provide unnecessary complications. It was hardly to Walton's purpose to remind his readers that George Herbert's oldest brother, Edward, Lord Herbert of Cherbury, although 'a man of great learning and reason,' was also notoriously unorthodox; that Sir John Danvers, Herbert's step-father, friend, and overseer of his will, was one of the leading regicides; or that any difference of opinion separated Bishop Williams, Herbert's chief patron within the Church, from Laud and his party.[1] In spite of the names and dates, Walton's image of Herbert seems to move through a pastoral Eden remote from the realities of early seventeenth-century England. There are, it is true, temptations, but the time when the apple was taken seems still in the future, and the final triumph of 'holiness' seems a triumph of innocence over experience rather than of reality over illusion, or the regenerated over the 'old' man. In a sense which Wordsworth hardly intended, Herbert's name becomes one of those

> Satellites burning in a lucid ring
> Around meek Walton's heavenly memory.

For too many readers Walton's *Life* has conveyed the impression that Herbert was a lovable but almost totally naïve man—an impression which a close reading of the poetry contradicts. Even apart from the poetry, however, it would scarcely be safe to conjecture that George Herbert was an innocent. The first half of the seventeenth century in England made both simple ignorance and simple-minded innocence rare among educated men. Herbert's associations with his family, patrons, and friends were such as to make him aware of the various currents and countercurrents in literature, religion, and politics. The fact that *The Temple* shows extraordinarily few borrowings from earlier writers was the result of Herbert's conscious choice rather than of his limited knowledge.[2] Herbert knew most of the groups and factions which made up his complex age, and he did not give fanatical allegiance to any one of them.

The fifth son of Richard and Magdalene Herbert, George Herbert was born on April 3rd, 1593, in Montgomery.[3] The Herberts had been for over two centuries one of the most distinguished families in England and Wales. With the death of Richard Herbert in 1596, the care of his large family (seven sons and three daughters—'*Iob's* number and *Iob's* distribution') was left to the mother, the celebrated friend of John Donne, and she took them to live first with her mother, Lady Newport, at Eyton, then to Oxford and London. Magdalene Herbert's sons were reared in a witty as well as pious household; their training in the two great.

seminal literatures, the Bible and the classics, began at home.[4]
John Donne's famous funeral sermon bears witness to
Magdalene Herbert's grace, intelligence, and literary and
musical taste: 'Her inclination, and conuersation,' were
'naturally, cheerfull, and merry, and louing facetiousnesse,
and sharpnesse of wit.'[5] In a family of the Herberts' position
all seven sons were 'brought up in learning,' but Magdalene
Herbert's influence is probably partly responsible for the
fact that two of her sons became poets and another tried his
hand at verse.[6] Her piety also proved influential, particularly
for her son George. While its various elements were not
uncommon, probably few families practised her precise combination of systematic observances, including Psalm singing
'euery Sabbath' night, prayers from *The Book of Common
Prayers* twice daily, and church attendance every time the
doors were open. Her devotion to the Established Church
was entire: 'For, as the *rule* of all her *ciuill Actions*, was
Religion, so, the *rule* of her *Religion*, was the *Scripture*; And,
her *rule*, for her particular vnderstanding of the *Scripture*,
was the *Church*. She neuer diuerted towards the *Papist*, in
vnderualuing the *Scripture*; nor towards the *Separatist*, in
vnderualuing the *Church*.' Moreover, her refusal to employ
'art' in 'person' or 'attire' seems to have been a matter of
scruple as well as taste.[7]

When George Herbert was about twelve years old he
went to Westminster School (where his brother Charles was
already a student), and he remained there until his election
to Trinity College, Cambridge, in 1608. When Herbert and
his distinguished classmate Henry King entered Westminster, Lancelot Andrewes had probably just vacated the
deanery, but whether Herbert came to know Andrewes then
or afterwards, he later fully expressed his admiration for that
nearly sainted figure.[8] Admiration for the bishop who was
'content with the enjoying without the enjoining' was, however, as Milton showed, limited to no party. Nor did educa-
tion at Westminster characteristically produce 'Arminians.'
Two of Herbert's contemporaries at both Westminster and
Trinity who became most distinguished in religious affairs
were John Hacket, later the bishop biographer and protégé

of Bishop Williams, and Charles Chauncy, second President of Harvard College.[9]

Magdalene Herbert married the youthful Sir John Danvers in the spring before George Herbert matriculated at Trinity on December 18th, 1609. For the following New Year's Day Herbert sent to his mother two sonnets which advocated religious rather than secular love as the subject of poetry, and his accompanying letter contained the first of many references to his ill health. Those two sonnets, extraordinary performances for a seventeen-year-old, already showed a precocious literary sophistication. Both the sophistication and the evident influence of Sidney might almost be assumed from the very name 'Herbert,' for George Herbert's fourth cousins[10] and future patrons were William and Philip Herbert, third and fourth Earls of Pembroke, the sons of Sidney's sister Mary. William, the most wealthy nobleman in England of the time,[11] continued his mother's practice and patronage of English poetry; he was friend or patron to most of the best poets of the age.[12] As an adolescent and an adult, Herbert probably read the poetry of the Sidney-Herbert connection for politic as well as literary reasons.

When Herbert left Westminster to go to Trinity, he must have found the new religious atmosphere a decided contrast to the old. Under Andrewes's direction the services at Westminster had come to be among the highest in England, while since the days of Elizabeth Cambridge had been 'advanced' in its Protestantism, and of all the colleges Trinity was second only to Emmanuel in the number of university men it furnished to New England.[13] At Trinity the communion table remained in its lengthwise position in the middle of the chapel, and the sartorial regulations were generally ignored by George Herbert as well as others.[14]

Herbert's literary career officially began shortly before he received his B.A. with the publication of a Latin poem commemorating the death of Prince Henry. Before he received his master's degree in 1616, he had been elected first minor and then major fellow of Trinity, and he continued his studies in classics and divinity after he took his degree. In 1618 he was appointed Praelector or Reader in Rhetoric. Herbert had already done some work for the University Orator, Sir Francis Nethersole, and on October 21st, 1619, he was appointed deputy during Nethersole's absence. On January 21st, 1620, Herbert was elected the new Public Orator of the University. Those appointments are measures of the general recognition that in an age and university of classicists Herbert's knowledge and practice were among the best. Herbert described the Orator's post in a letter to his step-father, Sir John Danvers: 'The Orators place (that you may understand what it is) is the finest place in the University, though not the gainfullest; yet that will be about 30. *l. per an.* but the commodiousness is beyond the Revenue; for the Orator writes all the University Letters, makes all the Orations, be it to King, Prince, or whatever comes to the University; to requite these pains, he takes place next the Doctors, is at all their Assemblies and Meetings, and sits above the Proctors, is Regent or Non-regent at his pleasure, and such like Gaynesses, which will please a young man well.'[15] In 1620 and 1621 Herbert was busy with official letters, and he delivered three orations in 1623. In the years from 1619 to 1623 he composed five more or less 'official' Latin poems, as well as most of his other Latin verse: *Musae Responsoriae* was probably written in 1620 or shortly thereafter, and *Passio Discerpta* and *Lucus* belong in part at least to 1623.[16] In addition to polishing and displaying his classical learning (in contrast to the careful exclusion of classical allusions from his English poems, the Latin poems, epistles, and orations are heavily sprinkled with references to Greek and Latin literature[17]), Herbert was also acquiring the best possible introduction to the 'new philosophy': during this period he translated parts of Bacon's *The Advancement of Learning* for incorporation in *De Augmentis Scientiae*.

The years at Trinity proved educative in other ways as well. Herbert's official and personal relationships increased his knowledge both of contemporary literature and of the multifarious religious differences of his time. He must have known Giles Fletcher during the nine years (1609-18) when both were at Trinity—particularly since *Christs Victorie, and*

Triumph (1610) had established Fletcher as Trinity's chief religious poet. And he knew Fulke Greville both as a literary figure and Chancellor of the Exchequer.[18] He undoubtedly knew of the exchange of complimentary verses between his brother Edward and Ben Jonson, as well as the work of Edward's other friends, Aurelian Townsend and Thomas Carew.[19] Sir Robert Harley, who became one of the most extreme Presbyterian iconoclasts, married Magdalene Herbert's niece and was on excellent terms with his 'cousin George.'[20] Edward Herbert, by contrast, had no strong objections to the Church of Rome, but his real earnestness was confined to those five points of natural religion which earned his reputation as the first English deist. There seems to have been little sense of strain between the brothers, however, for Edward dedicated the manuscript of *De Veritate* to George Herbert and William Boswell—with the request that they expunge anything which was against 'bonos mores' or the true Catholic faith.[21] Ecclesiastical party had as little to do with George Herbert's college friendships as with his family relations. Sir Francis Nethersole, his 'ancient acquaintance,' was a strict Protestant with Presbyterian leanings. Herbert's deputy Orator, Herbert Thorndike, on the other hand, was thought by John Henry Newman to be the only Anglican of the seventeenth century who possessed the 'true Catholic doctrine' of the eucharist.[22] And Henry Fairfax, one of Herbert's closest friends, was a model moderate: during the Civil War he made his rectory a place of refuge for both royalist and parliamentarian friends and relatives.[23] One is impressed not only by the variety of influences to which George Herbert was exposed, but also by the wide toleration of religious differences which he must have shown.

Herbert's enthusiasm for the Orator's position at Cambridge did not long survive his flurry of activity from 1619 to 1623; he was rarely in Cambridge after the early part of 1624. Almost certainly the influence of his cousins William and Philip accounts for Herbert's election as M.P. for Montgomery to the Parliamentary Session of February 19th to May 29th, 1624.[24] On June 11th of that year he was granted six months' leave of absence from the Oratorship 'on account of many businesses away,' and on December 6th, at the end of his leave, the politic and worldly Bishop John Williams, the future author of *The Holy Table, Name and Thing*, granted Herbert a share of the living at Lladinam, Montgomeryshire. Herbert's duties at Cambridge were taken over by his deputy, and Herbert Thorndike delivered the oration on the death of King James, an occasion, like the marriage of Charles, for which Herbert contributed no official verses. His poem on the death of Bacon (1626) was no part of Herbert's duties.

According to Walton, Herbert was with a 'Friend in Kent' for a while after the death of King James. This was probably after the session of Charles's first Parliament (May 18th to August 12th, 1625), to which Herbert was again elected. On December 21st, 1625, the poet was at Sir John Danvers's house in Chelsea, where John Donne was staying during the plague. We do not know when Herbert was ordained deacon, but he was described as such on July 5th, 1626, when he was instituted by proxy at Lincoln into 'the canonry and prebend of Leighton Ecclesia'—another sinecure secured from Bishop Williams.[25] The ordination did not commit Herbert to parochial life, but it did bar him from civil employment. For about a year, beginning in the summer of 1626, Herbert seems to have been recuperating from ill health at the home of his brother, Sir Henry Herbert, Master of the Revels at Court since 1623.[26] Magdalene Herbert Danvers died in June 1627, and George Herbert's *Memoriae Matris Sacrum* was entered at Stationers' Hall on July 7th—a date which indicates Herbert's phenomenal facility in the composition of the fourteen Latin and five Greek poems which make up that volume. Herbert had already unofficially taken leave of his university post in a letter of advice to his successor, Robert Creighton.[27] He officially gave up his position as Orator on January 28th, 1628.

Herbert's whereabouts from 1627 until 1629, the years in which he probably wrote many of the poems in *The Temple*, are uncertain. He seems to have lived for about a year with the Earl of Danby, Sir John Danvers's brother, at Dauntsey. On March 5th, 1629, he was married to Jane Danvers, Danby's cousin, in the church at Eddington. A year after his marriage he was living at Baynton House, his wife's home, when the offer of the church at Bemerton arrived. Walton's account of Laud's and Charles's 'persuasion' of Herbert to accept the gift of Bemerton seems to be a pious fiction;[28] actually, Herbert's patrons and associates within the Church belonged almost exclusively to the group opposed to Laud. Philip Herbert, fourth Earl of Pembroke, as the candidate of the anti-Laudian faction, had just lost to Laud the bitter election for the Chancellorship of Oxford on April 12th, 1630, when he obtained from King Charles four days later the small favour of the appointment of George Herbert to Bemerton, a living ordinarily within the Earl of Pembroke's gift.[29] Herbert supposedly served as chaplain to that same Philip.[30] And the Bishop of Salisbury who instituted Herbert on April 26th and ordained him priest on September 19th was the Low-Church John Davenant, who had incurred Harsnett's and Laud's wrath for his sermon on predestination and who supported John Durie's schemes for Protestant union.[31]

The final three years of Herbert's life were extraordinarily full. In addition to punctilious attention to his parish duties, he was engaged in repairing and rebuilding the churches and rectory, and he also assumed the care and rearing of his orphaned nieces. He engaged in considerable correspondence and developed friendships with Nicholas Ferrar, Arthur Woodnoth, and others connected with Little Gidding, that unique experiment in familial monasticism which, depending on the knowledge and prejudices of the observer, has been called papist and Puritan, Anglo-Catholic and platonic. This, too, was the period of Herbert's greatest literary activity. He translated Luigi Cornaro's *Treatise on Temperance*, annotated Valdesso's *Considerations*, and wrote *A Priest to the Temple*. Most important of all, he revised many of his earlier poems and composed over half the poems in *The Temple*. He was ill during much of the time, and he maintained Nathaniel Bostock as curate during.

the three years and secured a second curate when his illness grew worse. His will, drawn up a short time before his death, named Arthur Woodnoth as executor and Sir John Danvers as overseer. He died on March 1st, 1633, and was buried on March 3rd at Bemerton. So far as we know, neither institutions, friendships, nor family relations ever placed an excessive strain on Herbert's 'bonds of charity.'

Whatever the nature of the change from the Cambridge orator to the parson-poet of Bemerton, it was a change made with an intimate knowledge of all the literary and religious complexities of early seventeenth-century England. Perhaps that transformation was not quite so great as it seemed to Walton and even to Herbert in retrospect. Although we can never know with any finality the crucial movements of the heart, inscrutable to the man who experiences them as well as to the would-be observer, we can determine the sequence of some of the external manifestations, as well as the material setting in which the change took place; and even the condition of the heart, like the 'songs the Sirens sang,' is a matter not beyond all conjecture.

Walton's account leaves the reader with certain crucial questions. Why did Herbert postpone taking even deacon's orders until 1626? Why did 'all Mr *Herbert*'s Court-hopes' die in 1624 and 1625 with the deaths of Lodovic Stuart, second Duke of Lennox and Duke of Richmond; James, Marquis of Hamilton; and King James? After Herbert had declared his intention of giving up hope for civil preferment by taking deacon's orders, why was there no offer of ecclesiastical preferment until the extremely modest gift of Bemerton in 1630? And why, finally, did Herbert accept that offer? Walton is not concerned with the external events. His outline of Herbert's psychological development follows a simple pattern: after a pious rearing, Herbert was dazzled by worldly ambition; after sickness and the frustration of that ambition, he decided to enter the priesthood. The sickness was important, but considered alone it provides an adequate answer to none of the questions. There is also a central core of truth in Walton's remarks about the ambition and the frustration, but Walton's dramatization can lead to radical misunderstanding—particularly today.

For Herbert's change was no sudden conversion: from his seventeenth year he showed continued devotion to religion. In 1618 he was 'setting foot into Divinity, to lay the platform of [his] future life.'[32] In the same year, with no apparent sense of incongruity, he was also writing of Court gossip to Sir Robert Harley, of French wit and fashion to Henry Herbert, and he was composing the religious poem, 'In Natales et Pascha Concurrentes.'[33] 1623, the year of the three extant orations, and 1624, when, according to Walton, Herbert 'enjoyed his gentile humor for cloaths, and Court-like company, and seldom look'd towards *Cambridge*, unless the King were there, but then he never fail'd,'[34] seem to have been the same years in which Herbert was writing his finest and most devout Latin poetry. Before Herbert was ordained priest in 1630, he was already one of England's greatest religious poets.[35] Whatever Herbert's 'worldly ambition' during those years, it did not involve 'giving up' religion.

When he was trying to secure the post of University Orator, Herbert made a statement about that position which should be taken seriously. Sir Francis Nethersole had expressed doubts as to whether he should accept it: 'he fears I have not fully resolved of the matter, since this place being civil may divert me too much from Divinity, at which, not without cause, he thinks, I aim; but, I have wrote him back, that this dignity, hath no such earthiness in it, but it may very well be joined with Heaven; or if it had to others, yet to me it should not, for ought I yet knew . . .'[36] There is no evidence that at any time during his life Herbert abandoned his early plan to base his career on 'Divinity,' to further the cause of religion; there is also no evidence that before 1626 he abandoned his hope for great place in civil affairs. Theoretically at least, there was no necessary contradiction. History, particularly since the Reformation, was filled with examples of religious men who had done great things for the Christian state. Even among those whom Herbert knew in England, one does not have to search for examples. The scope of Andrewes's 'sanctity' was merely increased by his position as bishop and member of His Majesty's Privy Council, and Sir Francis Nethersole himself had shown how a man in civil employment could use all the power in his possession for the cause of a Protestant Europe.

After the hope had been abandoned, it was easy to see the element of worldly pride involved in the desire. After disillusionment Herbert could denounce what he had once desired:

> I now look back upon my aspiring thoughts, and think my self more happy than if I had attain'd what then I so ambitiously thirsted for: And, I can now behold the Court with an impartial Eye, and see plainly, that it is made up of *Fraud*, and *Titles*, and *Flattery*, and many other such empty, imaginary painted Pleasures: Pleasures, that are so empty, as not to satisfy when they are enjoy'd; but in God and his service, is a fulness of all *joy* and *pleasure*, and no satiety . . . and I will always contemn my birth, or any title or dignity that can be conferr'd upon me, when I shall compare them with my title of being a *Priest*, and serving at the *Altar* of *Jesus my Master*.[37]

We should, however, beware of agreeing too easily in that condemnation. In his enormous disappointment Herbert may have detected that, in his earlier hopes, he had desired 'the right things for the wrong reasons.' There was, however, nothing sinful in the desire for important 'Employment' expressed in the two poems so entitled—employment in which

> The sweetnesse and the praise were thine;
> But the extension and the room,
> Which in thy garland I should fill, were mine
> At thy great doom.

Activity *was* to a large extent Herbert's measure of religious achievement, and he really believed, at least at one time, that

God's will had 'Ordain'd the highest to be best.' It was particularly bitter for a man who believed that to reach his thirty-seventh year with no active 'Employment':

> But we are still too young or old;
> The Man is gone,
> Before we do our wares unfold:
> So we freeze on,
> Untill the grave increase our cold.

Whatever Herbert's attitude, his unemployment was a material fact: from 1619 until 1630 there was no offer of employment from that Court to which he looked.

The relations of Herbert and his family to the Court and the political issues of the time throw some light on why Herbert's early ambitions were never fulfilled and on the nature of his final renunciation. Although there were many younger sons of good family who could find no place for their abilities in the Courts of James and Charles, before 1619 the prospects of George Herbert were particularly good. Neither 'the passion and choler to which all . . . [the Herberts were] subject'[38] nor the pride which caused George Herbert to keep 'himself too much retir'd, and at too great a distance with all his inferiours'[39] seemed disadvantages: an exaggerated sense of honour, whether Welsh or Scots, was no handicap in the reign of James. Although George Herbert did feel handicapped by his lack of money (the annuities which the younger sons received from their elder brother's estate came to only thirty pounds and were not always paid on time[40]), Sir John Danvers was consistently generous.[41] Both Lodovic Stuart, then Steward of the King's Household, and the Earl of Pembroke had already shown their willingness to receive favours from Edward Herbert and to return them,[42] before he sailed for France as the new Ambassador on May 3rd, 1619. Without any dependence on his brother's new position, George Herbert was practically assured of his election as University Orator,[43] the post which had served as a prelude to careers as Secretaries of State for the two former Orators, Sir Robert Naunton and Nethersole. Herbert's public university lectures, in which he analysed King James's orations as models far surpassing those of the ancients,[44] had not injured his chances for advancement by that monarch.

The year 1620, which began with Herbert's election to the Orator's post, promised even more. King James was pleased with Herbert's letter of thanks for the royal *Opera Latina*,[45] and *Musae Responsoriae*, with its three complimentary poems for James (plus one each for Prince Charles and Bishop Andrewes), boded well for the future. Herbert's friendship with Andrewes was probably growing, but Francis Bacon, the Lord Chancellor, was the most powerful and the most assiduously cultivated acquaintance. Between June 1620 and May 1621 Herbert wrote three letters and three Latin poems to Bacon. Herbert's longest and best poem to Bacon, 'In Honorem Illustr. D. D. Verulamij,' far surpassed in scope and intensity anything required of the Latin Orator in his official capacity, but if the poet hoped for advancement through Bacon's influence, he was disappointed. The poem in which he had called Bacon 'veritatis Pontifex' was written embarrassingly near to the time when Bacon was charged, convicted, and sentenced for bribery.[46] His immediate prospects may have been further dimmed by Sir Edward Herbert's sudden recall from France in the following July.

Despite a few ominous developments, by 1623 there were grounds for renewed hope. Edward Herbert had returned as Ambassador to Paris in 1622, and George Herbert again pleased King James with an oration and epigram on March 12th, 1623.[47] Henry, knighted in August with the Marquis of Hamilton's sword, became Master of the Revels, and Thomas Herbert commanded one of the ships which brought Prince Charles back from Spain on October 5th. The return of Charles was an occasion for public celebration. The proposed Spanish marriage had been immensely unpopular in England, and there had been fear for the Prince's safety during the almost eight months of his absence. Nothing could have pleased the general populace more than Charles's safe return—without the Infanta.[48]

The Cambridge celebration provided an ideal opportunity

for the Latin Orator to bid for Charles's favour. On October 8th, George Herbert gave his most important oration, 'Oratio Caroli Reditum ex Hispanijs celebrans'; so far as we know, it was the last occasion on which he had personal contact with any member of the royal family. Samuel R. Gardiner's account of the occasion deserves serious consideration:

> The oration with which he welcomed Charles on his return from Spain was an evidence of the sincerity with which he could not help accompanying flatteries neither more nor less absurd than those which flowed unmitigated from the pens of so many of his contemporaries. It was no secret that the Prince had come back bent upon war. Herbert disliked war, and he could not refrain from the maladroit compliment of commending Charles for going to Madrid in search of peace. All that he could bring himself to say was that, as war was sometimes necessary, he would be content to believe any war to be necessary to which James should give his consent. . . . From Charles, rushing headlong into war, the lover of peace had no favour to expect.[49]

James's opposition to a Spanish war was as well known as Charles's determination to have war. The long poem 'Triumphus Mortis' or 'Inventa Bellica,'[50] written at about this time, supports the conjecture that Herbert devoted one-fifth of his oration to a denunciation of war because of his convictions rather than because of his political ignorance. The burden of the poem is that the discoveries for waging war, culminating in the monk's discovery of gunpowder—'worse than the torments of the Jesuits'—have resulted in the triumph of death. Herbert had stronger reasons for the intensity of his attitude than his conviction that war was hostile to the Muses. His brother William had fought in Denmark and the Low Countries, where he died. Richard Herbert, after years of military service, had been killed when fighting with the notorious Mansfeldt at the relief of Bergen-op-Zoom in 1622. Thomas had been with the ill-equipped and ill-destined expedition of Robert Mansell to Algiers in 1620-21. Do we have one life only to kill six hundred?[51] Is the one who suffers or who wages war more wretched?[52] The meaning of a fateful history is that 'The race shall pay in full for Abel's blood.'[53]

George Herbert's 'Court-hopes' may have died on October 8th, 1623. If they did not, his membership in the Parliament of 1624,[54] where he undoubtedly renewed the acquaintance with Nicholas Ferrar begun at Cambridge,[55] would not have lengthened their expiring life. For both Herbert and Ferrar, who later styled each other most 'intire Friend & Brother,' the Parliament session of 1624 may have made high office at Court seem undesirable. The issues before the Parliament were complex and alliances often uncertain. In the important area of foreign policy (inextricably involved with the religious question), Parliament, King James, and Charles and Buckingham all wanted war— but different wars. The Privy Council steered an uneasy course among the projected policies, and Herbert's potential patrons, Pembroke, Williams, and Hamilton, found themselves continually at odds with Buckingham.[56] His expressions of the previous year indicate that Herbert could hardly have liked any of the war-like alternatives. But Herbert was more personally involved in the threatened dissolution of the Virginia Company.[57] Although the Company had been in difficulties for a number of years, the attacks on it from within and without began in earnest in 1623 and reached their height in 1624. Herbert's closest friends and relatives were among the leading administrators; with their moral and financial interests threatened, they openly took the offensive in the session of 1624 against the will of King James. Nicholas Ferrar both helped to draw up the charges of impeachment and spoke against Middlesex, partially because of Middlesex's 'activity to take the Patent from the Company, under the pretence, that it should be, & yeild to the King a greater Revenew than it did.'[58] With the rumour that the Crown intended to seize the records of the Company, Herbert's step-father, Sir John Danvers, had them copied and sent to the Earl of Southampton for safekeeping.[59] On April 28th, 1624, Danvers and Nicholas Ferrar joined Sandys and Cavendish in presenting their complaints to a committee of the whole House of Commons.[60] On the following morning, however, a message from James forbade the Parliament to concern itself with the matter. The session ended, disastrously, on May 29th.[61] On July 24th the Court of the King's Bench rendered its expected decision that the charter of the Virginia Company was null and void.

The year 1624 seems to mark the beginning of Sir John Danvers's hostility to the Crown. In the following year, on the occasion of the great plague, Nicholas Ferrar retired from the world to Little Gidding. Like Herbert, he signalized his abandonment of civil affairs by his ordination as deacon in 1626. Again like Herbert, he was thought to have 'lost himself in an humble way.'[62] But for a religious man who had given so much hope and effort to the success of the Virginia Company (that enterprise which promised to combine so ideally the advancement of England's glory, religion, and trade), the events of the preceding years must have proved almost totally disillusioning about the satisfactions to be gained from following the non-humble 'ways' of the Court. At Little Gidding, Ferrar devoted himself to the familial and communal practice of piety. That he rejected employment within the Church as well as within the secular government was indicated by his steadfast refusal to be ordained priest.

Ferrar, however, had an income and land to which he could retire; George Herbert had neither. He could hardly have looked forward to attendance at Charles's first Parliament (June 18th to August 12th, 1625), particularly after Sir Edward Herbert's recall from France in disgrace.[63] When Parliament met it faced an unbroken record of military and diplomatic failures. Although there was hope that the new King might attempt to heal the breach with Parliament, the session was doomed from the beginning by the divergence of interests and by Charles's and Buckingham's disastrous lack of political acumen.[64] At the end of the session one of the angry Parliament's charges was particularly likely to discourage honest men who looked to the Court for employment: Buckingham was accused of selling to the highest bidder such offices as he had not filled with his obsequious followers.

It was probably after this session that Herbert 'betook himself to a Retreat from *London*, to a friend in *Kent*,' and on his return to London did 'acquaint a Court-friend with his resolution to enter into *Sacred Orders*.'[65] The resolution was put into effect before July 5th of the next year. Herbert's action might be interpreted as an expression of despair at his prospects for advancement: seven years of waiting on the Court had produced no fruit. It seems more likely, however, that the action implied an abandonment of his hope that, for a person of his connections and convictions, a 'life based on divinity' and 'great place' in civil affairs were then compatible. Andrewes as well as Bacon died in 1626; and for those few Elizabethans remaining, whatever their ages and however strongly they clung to the older theories, it was becoming increasingly difficult to put into practice that ideal of a government in which a Sovereign ruled (according to the law and with the advice of Parliament) a peaceful and prosperous state, of a Church which was at once rational and 'catholic,' firmly Protestant yet orderly, a representative of the reasonableness as well as the beauty of holiness.

To Herbert's announcement, only Bishop Williams, now totally in disfavour, responded immediately. On July 21st, 1627, however, Sir Edward Herbert, George Herbert, and their first cousin, Thomas Lawley, received the joint grant of the manor of Ribbesford.[66] From a financial point of view it was a considerable recognition, for Sir Henry Herbert paid £3000 for the manor before the end of that year; it was not, however, a living; it solved none of the problems of 'employment.' Since Herbert's potential patrons were fewer after 1626, an offer of importance from the powers at Court was then even less likely than it had been before. Moreover, an examination of Herbert's religious position shows that, however attractive Laud and Charles may later have found the aesthetic record of the 'Bemerton piety,' they would hardly have considered Herbert a promising candidate for a major role in the party of 'thorough.'

The years from 1626 to 1629 seem to have been the blackest of all for Herbert. Suffering almost constantly from ill health, he was at the same time tortured by his sense of the lack of purpose and meaning in his life. All the years of preparation and study were apparently to go for nothing. How was he to account for those God-given gifts of ability and training if all the channels through which he might fully use them were closed? But with such questioning came also the suspicion that in his desire for great place he had confused God's glory with his own vanity. If that had been and was perhaps still to some extent true, was he actually worthy even of taking priest's orders? Unable to distinguish honestly his own motivations in the past, might he still be deluded? Was he now considering ordination as priest as a means of serving God or as a solution to his own worldly problems? For a man of Herbert's conscientiousness the examination of the heart revealed infinite possibilities for self-deception.

The problem could only be resolved through an attempt at total submission to the will of God. The self-centred pride which wished to take 'the way that takes the town'[67] must be firmly rejected; but equally firm must be the rejection of a sense of unworthiness so strong that it prevented all action. The latter stemmed from a continuing preoccupation with 'self' which, carried to its logical conclusion, implied a distrust of God's grace—that grace which could create of 'earth and clay' a sacred vessel.[68] Herbert's acceptance of Bemerton and his ordination as priest were marks of the submission of self in both those senses. After thirty-seven years of preparation the final three years of his life were spent in total devotion to employment. Herbert's life at Bemerton was not at all an 'escape' from the world—unless we wish to limit the participants in the world, either in the seventeenth century or today, to the rulers, the politicians, the bishops, and the courtiers, those who function in the important and abstracted realm of national policy. The role of country parson, seriously undertaken, required that Herbert come to terms with the lives of ordinary Englishmen in a manner not required for University Orators, Foreign Secretaries, or, even, Bishops. The writings of the last three years show that the process enriched both his poetry and his religion.

D

Of Herbert's final attitude toward life in England, 'The Parson's Surveys,' chapter xxxii. of *A Priest to the Temple*, provides one of the most condensed and illuminating statements. A general survey of the proper state and calling of the sons of the gentry, the chapter proceeds from the premise that 'The great and nationall sin of this Land he esteems to be Idlenesse; great in it selfe, and great in Consequence,' and Herbert emphasized the crucial necessity that each individual should have a calling, both because of God's laws and the good of the 'Common-wealth.' He then outlined the proper callings for men in various situations.

The marryed and house-keeper hath his hands full, if he do what he ought to do. For there are two branches of his affaires; first, the improvement of his family, by bringing them up in the fear and nurture of the Lord; and secondly, the improvement of his grounds . . . and ordering his land to the best advantage both of himself, and his neighbours. . . . But if after all this care well dispatched, the house-keepers Family be so small, and his dexterity so great, that he have leisure to look out, the Village or Parish which either he lives in, or is neer unto it, is his imployment. Hee considers every one there, and either helps them in particular, or hath generall Propositions to the whole Towne or Hamlet. . . . But if hee may bee of the Commission of Peace, there is nothing to that: No Commonwealth in the world hath a braver Institution then that of Justices of the Peace.

When still single, the heirs are 'to mark their Fathers discretion in ordering his House and Affairs' and to look for improvements. They 'are to read Books of Law, and Justice; especially, the Statutes at large.'

As for better Books of Divinity, they are not in this Consideration, because we are about a Calling, and a preparation thereunto. But chiefly, and above all things, they are to frequent Sessions and Sizes; for it is both an honor which they owe to the Reverend Judges and Magistrates, to attend them, at least in their Shire; and it is great advantage to know the practice of the Land; for our Law is Practice. Sometimes he may go to Court, as the eminent place both of good and ill. At other times he is to travell over the King's Dominions, cutting out the Kingdome into Portions, which every year he surveys peece-meal. When there is a Parliament, he is to endeavour by all means to be a Knight or Burgess there; for there is no School to a Parliament. And when he is there, he must not only be a morning man, but at Committees also; for there the particulars are exactly discussed, which are brought from thence to the House but in generall.

There seems to be an element of personal heat in Herbert's description of 'younger Brothers, those whom the Parson finds loose, and not ingaged into some Profession by their Parents, whose neglect in this point is intolerable, and a shamefull wrong both to the Common-wealth, and their own House.' After condemning the life of the young gallant, Herbert recommended first the study of Civil Law and then the 'Mathematicks, as the only wonder-working knowledg,' particularly 'the two noble branches thereof, of Fortification, and Navigation. . . . But if the young Gallant think these Courses dull, and phlegmatick, where can he busie himself better, then in those new Plantations, and discoveryes, which are not only a noble, but also as they may be handled, a religious imployment? Or let him travel into *Germany*, and *France*, and observing the Artifices, and Manufactures there, transplant them hither, as divers have done lately, to our Countrey's advantage.'

Much of this is familiar. In its emphasis on national welfare, both moral and economic, and on the necessity of the gentry's living on their land, the survey might have been written by an Elizabethan. In the tremendous emphasis on the importance of a calling and of industry, it is close to what we have come to know as 'the spirit of Protestantism,' common to English religious writings for the better part of three centuries.[69] Yet there is some strangeness. The married 'house-keeper' is allowed no activities outside his family, estate, and parish. Only before marriage is the heir allowed to travel or to go to Court, almost ominously described as 'the eminent place both of good and ill.' The younger son who is unsure of his calling is to prepare only for law, the army or navy, or to engage in colonization or manufacturing. Herbert retains in large measure the traditional political ideal of Elizabethan times: the King is important both as fact and symbol throughout *A Priest to the Temple*, and Parliament, although it had not met for four years (and was not to meet for eight more), seems of almost equal importance—'there is no School to a Parliament.' But the Court, that symbol of the nerve-centre of national life, is conspicuous by its absence. Neither the heir nor the younger sons are, we gather, ever to seek employment there. It was, perhaps, by forgetting the Court and returning to the realities of English rural life that one could retain a belief in the good old ways.

Herbert's conclusion that 'Perhaps great places and thy praise Do not so well agree'[70] was, from his experience and that of Nicholas Ferrar and others, inevitable. Although his formulation would have been accepted by many individual Christians throughout the ages, it was 'a departure from the idea of a continuous Christian Commonwealth which is at once worldly and other-worldly.'[71] 'The idea of a continuous Christian Commonwealth' was taken up by Laud in his individual manner and developed, in different terms and with few doubts, by the 'Saints' of a later day in both Old and New England. If Herbert abandoned the attempt to reconcile earthly and heavenly greatness, if he seems to have seen as doomed the attempt to establish the Kingdom of Heaven by an earthly government, he turned with continued devotion to the other chief problem for the Anglican of his day: 'how to reconcile in his life the religious and moral teaching of the Reformation with the aesthetic doctrines of the Renaissance.'[72] To that problem Herbert worked out a fully satisfactory solution.

CHAPTER III

Religion

IT is difficult to make our fairly rigid modern conceptions of Puritan and Anglican, or of high, broad, and low, apply to a man who was engaged in no major theological or ceremonial controversies after his university days and who died before 1640. The religious differences in Herbert's lifetime, moreover, were much more complicated than the modern labels indicate. Herbert's great friend Nicholas Ferrar, for example, was by no means generally considered an Anglo-Catholic in his own day, as he is in ours. With the Bible, Foxe's *Book of Martyrs*, and the Prayer Book as his guides, Ferrar attempted to follow scrupulously the doctrines and practices of the Church of England. He was, however, 'torn asunder as with mad horses, or crushed betwixt the upper and under milstone of contrary reports; that he was a Papist, and that he was a Puritan,' and he remarked that '*to fry a Faggot, was not more martyrdome then continuall obloquy.*'[1] At Little Gidding he strictly celebrated the fasts and held 'Vigils or Night-Watches'; his chapel was elaborately decorated and provided with candles and an organ, and two of his nieces took vows of perpetual virginity. It was little wonder, then, that a hostile pamphlet was addressed to Parliament in 1641 entitled, *The Arminian Nunnery: or, A Brief Description & Relation of the late erected Monasticall Place, called the Arminian Nunnery at Little Gidding in Huntingdon-shire.* Yet Ferrar was a friend to Bishop Williams as well as Laud, the communion table in his chapel was placed in the 'low' east-west position, and he said, 'I as verily believe the Pope to be Antichrist as any article of my faith.' At least one visitor to Little Gidding described the family as 'orthodox, regular, puritan protestants'; and for the attitude it expresses toward profane literature, Nicholas Ferrar's death-bed statement might have been written by an Anabaptist:

49

In as much as all the Comedyes, Tragedyes, Pastoralls &c: & all those they call Heroicall Poems, none excepted; & like wise all the Bookes of Tales, wch they call Novells, & all feigned Historyes written in Prose, all Love Hymns, & all the like Bookes are full of Idolatry, & especially tend to the Overthrow of Christian Religion, undermining the very Foundations thereof, & corrupt & pollute the minds of the Readers, with filthy lusts, as, woe is me, I have proved in my self. In this regard, therefore, to show my detestation of them to the World, & that all others may take warning, I have burned all of them, & most humbly have, & doe beseech God, to forgive me all my mispent time in them, & all the sinns that they have caused in me, wch surely, but for his infinite Grace, had carryed my soule down into Hell long ere this. And I profess to be of Mr Galliatius his opinion, that the having an Orlando in the House, is sufficient ground to have it burnt down over y^r heads, that truly feare God. I beseech all that truly feare God, that love Jesus Christ, to consider these things well. Amen, Amen, Amen.[2]

To simplify the religion of Nicholas Ferrar or most other seventeenth-century religionists is to falsify; to understand, one must see individual religious experience within the light of the various movements of the time.

During the years of George Herbert's maturity, the members of the Church of England were troubled chiefly by questions concerning church government, ritual, theology, and the proper conduct of the personal life. On none of these issues was there simply one Puritan and one Anglican position. Hooker had, in a measure, rationally established the fact that episcopacy was the 'fit' form of government for the English Church, but one cannot guess how many members of the Church were convinced by his reasons. Even among those who accepted episcopacy, attitudes varied from the extreme Anglo-Catholic belief in its divine and irrevocable ordination to Archbishop Ussher's scheme for a modified episcopacy approaching presbyterianism, and included in the spectrum the acceptance of that form of church government as a suitable *modus vivendi* (approved by Calvin for certain situations) and the fairly bald Erastianism of James I.

As for the ritual, the more radical Puritans expressly desired to 'complete the work of Reformation,' and to purge the Prayer Book of 'papist' legacies. The specific objections, catalogued in the 'Millenary Petition' of 1603 and repeated until the Civil War, included the use of the cross in baptism, 'interrogatories ministered to infants,' confirmation, the surplice, bowing 'at the name of Jesus,' 'divers terms of priests, and absolution, and some other used, with the ring in marriage, and other such like in the book.'³ Such 'Anglicans' as Richard Montague and John Cosin, on the other hand, wished to change the Prayer Book in a Catholic direction. Some were satisfied with the decisions of 1562, but even among them a distinction can be drawn between those who accepted that settlement as divinely inspired and those who considered it a useful compromise.

The complexities of Anglican theology before 1640 have been accurately described by Helen C. White: 'The English Church still officially accepted the main tenets of continental Protestantism, Justification by Faith, Predestination and Election, and the reliance on Scripture as the final authority. In actual practice, of course, no one of these theories was applied with the rigor and literal consistency which a Calvin or John Knox had contemplated . . . on the one hand an even violent adhesion to the watchwords of the Reformation, and on the other, when theory came to be put into practice, a hundred modifications and attenuations of the principles so passionately accepted.'⁴ Officially and theoretically, however, the issues were fairly clear before 1625: 'During the lifetime of James I . . . Calvinism was still the prevailing theology favoured by the Court, and, to a large extent, by the Universities.'⁵ After his experiences with the Presbyterians in Scotland, James supported episcopacy and the Prayer Book: 'While I am in England I will have bishops, for I had not been so quietly settled in my seat but for them.'⁶ But that did not mean that he had abandoned Calvinist theological orthodoxy. The selection of Abbot as Archbishop in 1611 was second only to the dispatch of the English representatives to the Synod of Dort in 1619, as evidence of James's continued opposition to Arminianism.

The influence of the Arminians increased toward the end of James's reign, but official favour came only with the accession of Charles.[7] Herbert, however, retired from the University and from Court shortly after Charles's accession.

The question of the proper conduct of personal life is more difficult to define. In the larger sense it went beyond specific rules and prohibitions to involve the entire 'practice of piety,' the meaning and direction of the earthly life. For everyday purposes, however, Puritans were recognized both on the stage and in official decrees as 'precisians' who 'discouraged any lawful recreation' on Sundays (and eventually on any other days)—'such as dancing, either men or women; archery for men, leaping, vaulting, or any other such harmless recreation . . . having of May-games, Whitsun-ales, and Morris-dances; and the setting up of May-poles and other sports therewith used.'[8] It is perhaps true that the stricter Calvinists tended to emphasize these particulars more than the not so strict, as it is likely that the rank and file of the Parliamentary army were more devout than the majority of Charles's: political considerations aside, those seeking ethical and religious change are usually more seriously 'concerned' than those defending the *status quo*. But no theological group, no group with a particular attitude toward church government or ritual, had a monopoly on precisianism. The word 'Puritan' could be applied to any man who lived according to a strict rule and who might or might not be critical of his neighbours for their failures.

One can, therefore, construct an abstract picture of the 'true-blue Puritan' and the 'Anglo-Catholic'—both members of the Church of England. The Puritan would believe that the Church of England had not finished the work of Reformation, that the Presbyterian or Congregational form of church government was divinely authorized in the New Testament, that set prayers and any rites used by the Church of Rome were anathema and inventions of the Antichrist. He would believe that Justification by Faith, Predestination, and Election should be interpreted in the strictest fashion. Rome was 'the whore of Babylon' and no part of the 'true

Church,' while the Church of England *was* part of the 'true Church' only in so far as it partook of the doctrines of Geneva. In his personal life he would be a precisian, believing that all idleness, levity, and 'foolish jesting' should be suppressed by the Church. The Anglo-Catholic, on the other hand, would believe that the settlement of 1562 was contaminated by the heresies of Luther and Calvin; that episcopacy was the only divinely authorized form of church government; that as much of the ancient ritual should be revived as had not been the subject of unsound innovations by Rome. Doctrinally, he would place a larger than usual emphasis on free will, the power of man's reason, and the efficacy of works. He would therefore emphasize the continuity of the Catholic tradition rather than the purification of the Reformation, and he would consider the Church of Rome a true though misguided member of the Church, while he might deny that Geneva was a true Church at all. He would believe that lawful recreations were many, that those hallowed by custom were even laudable, and in general, that aristocratic pleasures were no bar to the Christian life.

In the England of 1609 to 1633 there were individuals who conformed to these patterns; they were far fewer than most of the discussions of the period's churchly affairs lead the modern reader to believe. The great majority, not only of the members of the Church of England but even of the theological disputants and the bishops of the Church, cannot be so easily categorized. Those who sought the much-praised *via media* between the two extremes found that it was no marked highway but a vaguely defined area; the paths which conscientious searchers for the truth found through it were rarely identical. Such a situation did not at all mean, however, that life in the Church of England was a pattern for Hobbes's view of the state of nature. The Anglican Church before 1633 was in one sense more truly 'catholic' than the Anglo-Catholics of the nineteenth century wished to believe. So long as an individual subscribed to the Articles, attended services a few times a year, and was not too singular in his actions, a wide latitude of belief and practice was

allowed. Nor did differences on few or many matters necessarily prevent individuals from living within the 'bonds of
Christian charity.' Laud himself insisted that the Church
did not require agreement in 'particulars,' and his patronage
of William Chillingworth and John Hales showed that the
Archbishop could tolerate speculative diversity.[9] 'Debates
and fretting jealousies,' according to Herbert, were the
source of those 'Church-rents and schismes' which blasted
the 'Brave rose.' Many Englishmen desired to avoid the
controversial issues and to emphasize that 'practical
Christianity' upon which there was fair agreement.

The area of potential agreement included the devotional
life and everyday activity. The 'Imitation of Christ,' whether
as a volume or a practice, was common to most of the religious
readers and writers of the time. Although Catholic influence
was feared in England, it was often not recognized: Quarles's
translation of the Jesuit Herman Hugo's *Pia Desideria* (with
the Counter-Reformation plates intact) became a favourite
volume, particularly among the Puritans.[10] A remarkable
quantity of religious reading was shared by all parties, both
within and without the Church of England.[11] St Augustine
and other early Church fathers were considered generally
authoritative, and St Bernard of Clairvaux, having received
the approval of Aquinas, Calvin, and Luther, was widely
read. Calvin, Beza, and the other leading continental writers
were the property of most English Protestants. Immensely
popular contemporary books of devotion often failed to dis-
close the ecclesiastical and theological positions of their
authors.

We cannot identify George Herbert with a specific ecclesiastical party, for Herbert died just five months before Laud
succeeded to the episcopal throne, and we have no information as to how he would have reacted to Laud's attempt at
enforced conformity.[12] For a religious man of the early
seventeenth century who was neither at Great Tew nor
fought in the wars, and who was at Cambridge too early to
be a professional Platonist, it is particularly necessary to go
to his writings. In *Musae Responsoriae*, *The Temple*, *A Priest
to the Temple*, and his 'Briefe Notes' on Valdesso, Herbert

left a consistent account of his most important religious beliefs.

Herbert's *Musae Responsoriae* was occasioned by the belated publication in 1620 of a two-hundred-line Latin poem by Andrew Melville,[13] the reformer of the Scottish universities and the former pupil of the famous Peter Ramus. Melville had written *Pro Svpplici | Evangelicorum Ministrorum in Anglia | Ad Serenissimum Regem | contra Larvatam geminae Academiae Gorgonem Apologia, sive Anti-tami-cami-categoria* as a violent reply to Oxford and Cambridge's resolutions against the Millenary Petition of 1603. Melville did not confine himself to a defence of the Petition's paragraph on ritual which the universities had particularly attacked; he took the offensive with a denunciation of proud and ambitious prelates and the English ritual, 'comparing a set liturgy to the magic wheel of incantation, the priest's words at infant baptism to the noises of a screech-owl, and church music to the clash of Phrygian cymbals.'[14] George Herbert, the young Latin Orator, may have felt it his duty to defend his University as well as his Church against Melville's printed charges; the defence, moreover, was sure to please King James. In the epigrams of *Musae Responsoriae* Herbert gave the only full expression of his attitude toward the Puritanism of the Millenary Petition. Despite the playfulness, the wit, and the politic timing, the poems indicate the nature of Herbert's early defence of the English Church.

In his fourth epigram Herbert outlined the three-part division of Melville's poem and the grounds of disagreement: 'the first is opposed to sacred rites; the second preaches holy authors; the third is full of God. We agree on the last two: I too praise pious men, and I reverence the divine attributes. Only the first gives us a battlefield for our quarrel.'[15] Herbert made it quite clear that the quarrel was confined to the first sixty-four lines of Melville's poem. He approved of Melville's remarks concerning the nature of God and of his praise of continental divines; and he insisted that the 'great names,' 'Martyr, Calvin, Beza, and the learned Bucer,' whom Melville summoned as his allies, 'steadfastly refuse to oppose us.'[16] Except when he digressed to make fun of Melville's Latin[17] or of Puritan taste and nasal accents, Herbert confined himself to the defence of 'rites,' in the general sense of the 'discipline' of the English Church.

On first reading, one is tempted to dismiss the 'defence' as only facetious, for Herbert overlooked no opportunity for a pun or a display of verbal fireworks.[18] Yet Herbert could afford to be witty about almost any specific rite exactly because of the nature of his belief in the ritual. He valued symbols and order for the sake of the thing symbolized and for the reasonableness of order in an ordered universe. He never defended any specific rite primarily as divinely inspired or essential to salvation, but as 'just' or beautiful or reasonable. The epigram 'De Episcopis,' for example, begins as if it were to defend the necessity of the Apostolic succession; but, after the charge that those who seek the destruction of the bishops act out of frustrated ambition, the point of the poem comes with the conclusion: 'O blind people! if it is good to have an overseer, why do you refuse? if it is evil, how much better it is to have a few instead of all be bishops.'[19] The question of church government resolved itself into a matter of the unreasonableness of dissent.

The rites which to Melville were only vestiges of superstition and popery were to Herbert valuable symbols, similar to those very types of Christ which the Puritans cherished. The conceits in Herbert's poems are not incongruous because he conceived any objection to God's own symbolic method as so obviously ridiculous. Puritans seem to be as much afraid of the sign of the cross as are demons; the Apostles thought it a crime to be ashamed of the cross of Christ; the cross is a natural symbol for everyone makes it when he swims; for everyone, willing or not, there is a cross.[20] 'Churching' is reasonable because it is proper that parents should praise God when children are too young to do so; if we give thanks for daily bread, we should do so for our own flesh; pious souls are thankful for all occasions for prayer, and certainly do not object to this one; it is particularly proper that as once woman, conscious of the plucked apple, groaned because of childbirth and fled as one cursed from an angered God, so now she should return as one blessed to a gentle God.[21]

These early Latin poems do not necessarily define Herbert's beliefs and attitudes ten years later; yet on the only occasion when he publicly assumed the role of opponent of the Puritans Herbert did not, significantly, attack either Calvinist theology or Calvinist leaders. He may have truly believed that, 'When Christ looks down from heaven, he says, "Only England shows me my full worship,"'[22] although that statement seems to be chiefly important as part of his address to 'His Serene Highness,' James. Certainly he did not believe that any of the Anglican rites were hostile to the will of God. But the fact that the worship of the Church of England was most 'full' did not at all mean that the Presbyterian was not a true Church. It was possible to be snobbish about its unlearned followers and to ridicule its perfectionism,[23] but finally the differences for Herbert were reasonable and aesthetic; and as a reasonable man he asked Melville not to think too harshly of his 'toothless Muse,' and he called him 'bene doctus, et poeta.'[24] It was also reasonable that James should 'lead his own lambs, safest in the middle way.'[25]

Walton tells us that Herbert took part in another 'modest debate' during his years at Cambridge. This time it was with Bishop Andrewes, and the issues concerned '*Predestination*, and *Sanctity of life*.' Since both Herbert and Andrewes were charitable souls, it was a friendly debate, which ended when Herbert 'did not long after send the Bishop some safe and useful *Aphorisms*, in a long Letter written in Greek; which Letter was so remarkable for the language, and reason of it, that after the reading it, the Bishop put it into his bosom, and did often shew it to many Scholars, both of this, and forreign Nations; but did alwaies return it back to the place where he first lodg'd it, and continu'd it so near his heart, till the last day of his life.'[26] The problem of predestination and sanctity of life (it could hardly be separated into two problems) was crucial for anyone seriously concerned with Christianity. Did the individual's 'free will' play any part in salvation? Was 'sanctity of life' a method for achieving salvation, or was it a gift from God which gave assurance that salvation was already achieved? Or, could it even be on occasion the response to Satan's most dangerous temptation, the temptation to believe that one can 'deserve' God's grace? In view of Andrewes's position as the intellectual leader of the Arminians, one knows what side he took in that debate. The loss of the 'Letter written in Greek' with the 'safe and useful *Aphorisms*' which Andrewes so much valued is particularly unfortunate, since it must have shown how much agreement was possible in a controversial age between individuals who, with no social, political, or ecclesiastical barriers, charitably sought to resolve the apparently irreconcilable issues of predestination and free will. For *The Temple* shows that Herbert believed as strongly in predestination and the doctrine of the Covenant of Grace as he believed in the significance and beauty of the ritual.

In the final line of 'The Water-course' Herbert expressed his belief in predestination in a manner which should have satisfied any Calvinist: God is described as he

$$\text{Who gives to man, as he sees fit,} \begin{cases} \text{Salvation.} \\ \text{Damnation.} \end{cases}$$

Herbert also once summarized another author's fairly complex discussion of God's 'Mediate' and 'Immediate' wills with the remark, 'He meanes a mans fre-will is only in outward, not in spirituall things.'[27] Herbert's fascination with the manner in which God rules and knows 'to each minute of an houre' everything from 'The smallest ant or atome' to civilizations, led him to write his one 'prophetic' poem, 'The Church Militant,' in which he traced the course of a predestined history until the Day of Judgment: the Church follows the Sun in a westward course, always preceded by 'Empire and Arts' and always followed by a triumphant Sin and degeneration; when it reaches its point of origin, the cycle will be complete, and 'judgement shall appeare.'[28]

The poems in *The Temple* show what the important theological issues were for one believer in predestination; they are also the primary evidence by which the significance of the 'holy life' at Bemerton can be determined. 'Mr Herbert's Temple & Church Militant explained and improved by a discourse upon each poem critical and practical,'[29] a neglected manuscript by an otherwise unidentified George Ryley, dated March 24th, 1714/15, offers more insight into the theological significance of the poems than does any other volume. Ryley's individual analyses of all the poems provide the fullest exegesis of *The Temple* yet made; they also point out the elements in the poems which the Puritans and later nonconformists found so attractive. To Ryley the chief significance of the poems in 'The Church' was obvious: 'In the generall we have in these poems a description of the disposition of a sound Member of the Church, which is the Body of Christ.'[30] The 'many spiritual Conflicts' 'pictured'[31] in the poems were for an experienced reader proofs of that soundness. Anyone who knew the biographies of Christian saints would recognize that the 'most gracious and devout' are always the 'most conscious of lack of grace and dulness': '*Ignoti nulla cupido* . . . those (few, alas) happy souls that are acquainted with him and have tasted that he is gracious, are so ravished with his beauty that they are never satisfied with any, the best, glympses they can have of him here, nor ever will be, till they awake in the morning of the Resurrection with his likeness.'[32] No Christian could achieve that ideal of the perfect conformity of his will to God's; the nearer he came to it the more conscious he would be of his imperfections and of the inexorable need for daily repentance. There was, moreover, as Ryley pointed out in his commentary on 'The Crosse,' a particular source of affliction in the Christian's consciousness both of his own responsibility and of God's predetermining will: 'It is commonly very cross the grain to learn that we *must work out our salvation*; and yet that 'tis *God alone that worketh in us to will and to do, Phillip.* 2. 12, 13; that we must labour as those that would take the Kingdom of Heaven by violence; and yet, after we have done all, we are *unprofitable servants. Luk.* 17. 10.'[32] Ryley's great admiration for *The Temple* is largely based on the fact that Herbert had shown in the poems how it was possible, in the middle of those afflictions and conflicts, to achieve joy and assurance of salvation through an understanding of the Covenant of Grace: 'Assurance is the naturall conclusion drawn from our integrity; which is measured by the conditions in the Covenant of Grace. Such is our present state, that the very exercise of some special graces (as of humility, watchfullness, self-examination, and self-diffidence) is often improved by our subtil enemy, to the exclusion of Assurance. It is rather a mercy that we may, than a duty incumbent on us to, attain to it. I am apt to think, were *Jehovah & his covenant* with us better known, Assurance would not be such a stranger to many sincere Christians as now it is.'[34] Occasionally Ryley's own conviction caused him to bring that doctrine into his exegesis when Herbert was not particularly concerned with it in the text; usually, however, Ryley's knowledge of the doctrines and symbols of the Covenant of Grace enabled him to achieve a clear and convincing analysis.

Herbert's 'Redemption' describes the origin of the Covenant, and Ryley's prefatory comments are to the point:

> The first lease this great landlord gave to man, his tenant, was the covenant of works, by which man was bound to yeild all the profitts of the land to his landlord's use; the condition being, *he that doth them shall live in them, and the soul that sinneth shall dye.* Man breaking the articles of this once, rendered himself for ever incapable of retrieving that loss, or of keeping them for the future; so by these articles he could never *thrive,* that is, never be *justified. But what the law* (that is, this law of works) could not do, God, sending his own Son, &c. hath wrought for us, that is, our Redemption: making us free from the law of sin and death, and granting

us a new *small-rented lease*. This was purchased for us by, and
granted to us att, the death of Christ. These premises will lead us
into the plain sence of this poem.[35]

'These premises' also lead us into one significance of Herbert's characteristic use of legal metaphor. The poem
'Obedience' is a description of the individual's covenanting
with God, with the 'conveyance' of the heart and the whole
man, the grounds for the 'resignation,' and an invitation to
others to join in the 'Deed.'[36] That covenant is made possible
by the Grace of God (it is specifically a 'purchase' of Christ's
rather than a 'gift or donation' of the sinner's), and Herbert's desire is that others will assent to the 'Deed':

> He that will passe his land,
>   As I have mine, may set his hand
> And heart unto this Deed, when he hath read;
>   And make the purchase spread
> To both our goods, if he to it will stand.

Yet the will to 'passe one's land' cannot be achieved without
divine Grace. 'The Holdfast' shows the sinful pride of the
individual who believes mistakenly that he can 'observe the
strict decree Of my deare God with all my power & might,'
or who thinks that he possesses the ability to 'trust . . . in
him alone,' or who even believes that he, of himself, can
admit that all is the gift of God. Every grace is the gift of
God, even the grace to acknowledge our gracelessness; we
are indeed 'darknesse, and weaknesse, and filthinesse, and
shame.'[37] The essential 'act' is that the individual should
abandon the pretence that he *can* act in any way pertaining
to salvation: he must experience the full realization that
salvation belongs to God, that nothing he can do either by
faith or works can help. The doctrine is, moreover, 'com-
forting,' for 'all things' are 'more ours by being his':

> What Adam had, and forfeited for all,
> Christ keepeth now, who cannot fail or fall.

Once the grace of God had led the individual to that
experience and had accompanied it with an understanding.

of Christ's sacrifice and an overwhelming sense of love, the individual could be assured that God had predestined him for salvation; it was exactly that experience which the damned could never enjoy. The way of salvation is foolishness to the world, and God's 'reasons' are part of the mystery:

> But as I can see no merit,
>   Leading to this favour:
> So the way to fit me for it
>   Is beyond my savour.
> As the reason then is thine;
> So the way is none of mine:
> I disclaim the whole designe:
> Sinne disclaims and I resigne.
>
> *That is all, if that I could*
>   *Get without repining;*
> *And my clay, my creature, would*
>   *Follow my resigning:*
> *That as I did freely part*
> *With my glorie and desert,*
> *Left all joyes to feel all smart—*
>   Ah! no more: thou break'st
>   my heart.   ('Dialogue.')

There were moments of paralysing doubt, moments when the elect feared that their experience had been a devilish illusion and that they were eternally damned. 'Perseverance,' the one poem in which Herbert nakedly expressed such a fear, was not included in *The Temple*, doubtless because Herbert did not believe that it would 'turn to the advantage of any dejected poor Soul.'[38] It is one of his most moving poems.

> My God, the poore expressions of my Love
> Which warme these lines & serve them vp to thee
> Are so, as for the present I did moue,
>   Or rather as thou mouedst mee.

But what shall issue, whither these my words
Shal help another, but my iudgment bee,
As a burst fouling-peece doth saue the birds
    But kill the man, is seald with thee.

ffor who can tell, though thou has dyde to winn
And wedd my soule in glorious paradise,
Whither my many crymes and vse of sinn
    May yet forbid the banes and bliss?

Onely my soule hangs on thy promisses
With face and hands clinging vnto thy brest,
Clinging and crying, crying without cease,
    Thou art my rock, thou art my rest.[39]

But such moments seem to have been rare for Herbert. The only expression in *The Temple* of the idea that 'Either the league was broke, or neare it; And, that I had great cause to fear it' is emphatically denied, for the new Covenant cannot fail:

But I will to my Father,
Who heard thee say it. O most gracious Lord,
If all the hope and comfort that I gather,
Were from my self, I had not half a word,
    Not half a letter to oppose
    What is objected by my foes.

But thou art my desert:
And in this league, which now my foes invade,
Thou art not onely to perform thy part,
But also mine; as when the league was made
    Thou didst at once thy self indite,
    And hold my hand, while I did write.

Wherefore, if thou canst fail,
Then can thy truth and I: but while rocks stand,
And rivers stirre, thou canst not shrink or quail:
Yea, when both rocks and all things shall disband,
    Then shalt thou be my rock and tower,
    And make their ruine praise thy power.

                ('Assurance.')

Such an assurance (which John Donne was rarely able to communicate in his poems) left the religious man and the poet free to pass beyond the 'milk' of salvation to the 'meat' of the problems of the Christian life.

The business of the Christian life was the glorification of God, and that required not only devotion and worship but also extremely practical activity in society. The commandments were simple and clear:

> Love. God, and love your neighbour. Watch and pray.
> Do as ye would be done unto.
> O dark instructions; ev'n as dark as day!
> Who can these Gordian knots undo?   ('Divinitie.')

An intense conviction that Mary's 'flowers' of contemplation could not be divorced from Martha's 'fruits' of the active life made sickness more fearful than death.[40] The necessity of activity was particularly urgent for a Country Parson, because 'The Countrey Parson is in Gods stead to his Parish, and dischargeth God what he can of his promises.'[41]

A Priest to the Temple, or, The Countrey Parson His Character, and Rule of Holy Life is the sincere, pious, and extraordinarily practical record of what Herbert conceived the Parson's duties to be—'Not that I think, if a man do not all which is here expressed, hee presently sinns, and displeases God, but that it is a good strife to go as farre as wee can in pleasing of him, who hath done so much for us.'[42] In his station as 'the Deputy of Christ for the reducing of Man to the Obedience of God,' the Parson acted as legal adviser and herbalist as well as the shepherd who attempted to 'reduce' 'to the common Faith' 'any of his parish that hold strange Doctrins' through prayer, 'a very loving, and sweet usage of them,' and certain outlined arguments.[43] In his 'character' of the Parson, Herbert showed himself a devoted son of the Church of England who followed the Prayer Book faithfully if liberally.[44] One of his most significant statements in the volume is his formulation, after a precise description of the furnishings and condition of 'The Parson's Church,' of the 'rules' which gave meaning to all the rubrics:

> And all this he doth, not as out of necessity, or as putting a holiness in the things, but as desiring to keep the middle way between superstition, and slovenlinesse, and as following the Apostles two great and admirable Rules in things of this nature: The first whereof is, *Let all things be done decently, and in order*: The second, *Let all things be done to edification*, I *Cor.* 14. For these two rules comprize and include the double object of our duty, God, and our neighbour; the first being for the honour of God; the second for the benefit of our neighbor. So that they excellently score out the way, and fully, and exactly contain, even in externall and indifferent things, what course is to be taken; and put them to great shame, who deny the Scripture to be perfect.[45]

In the Christian's life, as well as in the Church, all things must be done both 'decently' and 'to edification.' Whether it was in administering the sacraments, sweeping a floor, serving as a Justice of the Peace, or writing poetry, the dual 'object of our duty,' God and man, must always be perceived; and order and rational 'edification' were inevitably the proper expressions of love.

It was this emphasis on the value and the significant inseparability of contemplation and action, of faith and reason, of God's creation on this earth and in heaven, which enabled Herbert to avoid the 'superstitious' rejection of the material and the 'slovenly' rejection of form. Herbert was never tempted to worship the 'idea' in its abstraction: the Incarnation had proved to him that Christ was the only '*anima mundi*,'[46] and he repeated more than once the idea that 'Creatures are good, & have their place.'[47] The proper service of God required the fullness of God's creation; the rejection of any part of it implied the Manichean heresy that evil had the power of creation.

The rejection of the goodness of the material world was sometimes joined in Herbert's day with the dependence of the individual upon private 'motions' of the spirit. In an extreme form such a principle led to the conclusion that an individual could, through the infusion of the spirit, achieve perfection on this earth; and the antinomian conclusion was that individual inspiration was more to be trusted than the 'fleshly' laws set forth in the Bible. In his 'Briefe Notes' to Valdesso's *The Hundred and Ten Considerations*, Herbert showed most clearly his attitude toward perfectionist tendencies, whether Catholic or Protestant. Juán de Valdés, a correspondent of Erasmus's, was an associate of the Illuminés in Spain.[48] Herbert approved of his devotion to Christ and his 'many pious rules of ordering our life,'[49] but he unerringly detected and condemned his exaltation of inspiration above the Scriptures, his quietism, and his implicit anarchism.

To Herbert, Valdesso's 'opinion of the scripture is unsufferable,' for 'the Word hath the precedence even of Revelations and Visions.'[50] The Scriptures are God's Word and the individual sacrifices none of his own light by giving them complete trust: 'by trusting in the word of God they trust in God. Hee that trusts in the Kings word for any thing trusts in the King.'[51] The assumption from which Valdesso's opinion derived, that the Spirit actually perfects men in this world, is equally reprehensible. Man cannot free himself from sin: 'I can no more free my selfe from actuall sinnes after Baptisme, then I could of Originall before, and without Baptisme. The *exemption* from both, is by the Grace of God.'[52] Some of the heathen, such 'as *Socrates* and *Aristides*, &c.,' were able to free themselves from the opposites of the Moral (not the Theological) Virtues 'only by the generall Providence of God'; in that process, however, 'the naturall concupiscence is not quite extinguished, but the heate of it asswaged.'[53] Herbert agreed that belief by 'revelation' rather than by 'relation' was characteristic of the Christian experience, but he had his own definition of 'revelation': 'A generall apprehension, or assent to the promises of the Gospell by heare-say, or relation from others, is not that which filleth the heart with joy and peace in believing; but the spirits bearing witnesse with our spirit, revealing and applying the generall promises to every one in particular with such syncerity and efficacy, that it makes him godly, righteous, and sober all his life long; this I call *beleeving by Revelation, and not by Relation.*'[54] This did not at all mean that anyone other than Christ could achieve perfection; Valdesso's attempt to 'justify' all the actions of the biblical 'Saints' was mistaken: ' . . . concerning *Abraham* and *Sara*, I ever tooke that for a weaknesse in the great Patriark: And that the best of Gods Servants should have weaknesses is no way repugnant to the way of Gods Spirit in them, or to the Scriptures, or to themselves being still men, though godly men.'[55]

Throughout his 'Briefe Notes' Herbert attempted to read Valdesso charitably, with the result that his 'explanations' often depart considerably from Valdesso's obvious meaning. But Herbert could no more attempt agreement with the social and moral implications of Valdesso's opinion concerning the 'sonnes of God' than he could with his opinion of the Scriptures. The sixty-second 'Consideration' stated 'That humane wisdome hath no more iurisdiction in the judgement of their workes, who are the sonnes of God, then in the iudgement of the proper works of God,' and Valdesso had gone on to remark that 'Men should not haue had more reason to haue chastised *Abraham*, if he had killed his sonne *Isaac*, then to condemne God, because he slaies many men by suddain death.'[56] The obvious implication was that society had no 'just iurisdiction' over the Saints. Herbert's answer is concise and exact: 'The godly are punishable as others, when they doe amisse, and they are to be judged according to the outward fact, unlesse it be evident to others, as well as to themselves, that God moved them. For otherwise any Malefactor may pretend motions, which is unsufferable in a Common-wealth.' Had Abraham killed Isaac in England, he would probably have been 'justly put to death for it by the Magistrate.' In as much as he had done it at God's command, 'He had done justly, and yet he had been punished justly.'[57] The moral corollary of such consistent exaltation of the inward 'voice of God,' that the individual should wait for 'motions' or specific inspiration before he engaged in any action, was even more dangerous: 'In indifferent things there is roome for motions and expecting of them; but in things good, as to relieve my Neighbour, God hath already revealed his Will about it. Therefore wee ought to proceed, except there be a restraining motion (as *S. Paul* had when hee would have preached in Asia), and I conceive that restraining motions are much more frequent to the godly, then inviting motions; because the Scripture invites enough, for it invites us to all good, according to that singular place, *Phil.* 4. 8.'[58]

In Herbert's profoundly active religious belief there was room neither for 'waiting for motions' nor for the 'banishing of images' of the traditional mysticism of the *via negativa*. Valdesso had admitted images as a useful preparatory step for the 'unlearned': 'The unlearned man, that hath the spirit, serveth himselfe of *Images* as of an Alphabet of Christian Pietie; forasmuch as hee so much serves himselfe of the *Picture* of Christ Crucified, as much as serves to imprint in his mind that which Christ suffered.'[59] Valdesso went on to compare such 'Images' with the 'Holy Scriptures,' and Herbert's attention was chiefly attracted by that blasphemy. But his remark that 'Pictures' may be 'exhausted' 'by a plenarie circumspection' implies in its very casualness that there will always be other 'Pictures.' There is no indication that Herbert ever conceived of the possibility that verbal or mental 'pictures' might be regarded as materials of an inferior order for human religious experience, or that, directed toward God, they interfered in any way with His presence. Herbert could conceive of a divine method of immediate apprehension apart from the senses, but he believed that path to knowledge barred to man:

> The mature intelligence of the angels
> Is not at all like ours. We must
> Call in sense to give us the forms of things;
> And unless the eyes release the outer door
> And bring in grain for our mill,
> Our idle minds often thresh nothing from themselves.
> The rivers of knowledge flow
> Very far away from us;

We cannot grasp even what we are
Except through appearances.
The angels' journey to those waters is not so far;
In no roundabout way they penetrate to knowledge.
For them perpetual windows stand open.
They know themselves through themselves in an easy
    fashion,
And they are also their own mill and grain.[60]

However desirable the knowledge of the angels might be, man was so created that, without a miraculous dispensation of God's grace, he could never achieve it.

Herbert was in no sense a 'mystic,' then, if we limit that word in the current fashion to a contemplative who practises the 'negative way' to union with God. If we extend the definition of the word, however, to include those who are 'initiated into the mystery' of Christ and who believe 'in the possibility of attaining insight into mysteries transcending ordinary human knowledge'[61] while engaged in the active life, then Herbert might be considered a 'mystic' of the *via positiva*, in something of the sense that most devout Christians are at times 'mystics': valuing union with God, but expecting it fully only with death; expressing joy for the moments of the presence of God and lamentations for the days of His absence; believing that the proper service of God consists in works as well as acts of devotion; conscious of sin but striving to conform to the will of God; seeing in the world and human life images which show God's creation and His love. It is this 'catholic' aspect of Herbert's religious experience, conveyed with the utmost skill in *The Temple*, which caused Herbert's poetry to be valued by the devout of nearly all sects. Herbert's 'picture of the many spiritual Conflicts that have past betwixt God and my Soul,' like the devotions of St Bernard and the *Confessions* of St Augustine, represented experiences confined to no one part of the Church universal.

II

CHAPTER IV

The Conception of Form

THERE is a certain irony in the fact that the most formal of seventeenth-century Anglican poems have been so much enjoyed by the anti-formalists in religion and art. The appeal of George Herbert's poetry to the opponents of ritual was a justifying triumph for Herbert's conception of form: in poetry as well as religion Herbert tried to work out a middle way between 'slovenliness' and 'superstition.' It was by means of form that the material could be used in the service of the spiritual, that the senses could be properly employed for the glorification of God.

The problem of the relationship between objects of the senses and Christian worship had been introduced with the beginning of the ritual in the ancient church. In Herbert's England the Puritans and the Catholics marked the limits of theory and practice.[1] For the extreme Puritan, the ritual and 'adornments' in the church were only sensuous barriers (similar to the priest's office) between the naked individual soul and God: the serious business of salvation left no room for them. It was, moreover, presumptuous for sinful man to attempt to honour God through the creation of formal beauty within God's house; the proper method of honouring God, the essence of worship, was to confess one's unworthiness, to pray for forgiveness and God's grace, and to preach the gospel. Christian poetry had its practitioners and its appreciative audience outside the services, and certainly most Puritan preachers believed that the art of logic and rhetoric (so long as they were not separated) were useful handmaidens for the instruction and moving of their audiences. But the idea that ritual or 'ornaments' within the church could either aid the individual worshipper or honour God was alien to the largest segment of Puritan thought. The light of the Spirit should reach the individual directly, like sunlight through pure glass; it should not be contaminated by 'externals,' as sunlight was coloured by the pictured windows of the Papists.

Certain Catholics embraced an opposite attitude which might seem equally 'enthusiastic' to a person who followed Hooker's tradition. In his *Spiritual Exercises* St Ignatius Loyola had stated that 'every meditation or contemplation about a bodily thing or a person, as for example, about Christ, demands the formation of a bodily place in vision,'[2] and his widely practised 'application of the senses' was influential in increasing exactly those sensuous details of Catholic worship to which the Protestants objected. The rich liturgy, rather than obscuring the way to God, came to provide the chief light. The Protestants insisted that the Catholics' engrossment in the sensuous details of worship was divorced from reason, from an understanding of the symbolism: it was idolatry.

Many members of the Church of England tried to find a way between the extremes. George Herbert took a firm and consistent position. As a believer in the Covenant of Grace, he could never allow the ritual to become a substitute for incorporeal experience. Yet Herbert also believed that the individual should not present himself, publicly at least, in disorder before God. God should be worshipped in 'the beauty of holiness,' and He had shown in the 'two Books of His Revelation' that the arrangement of 'objects of the senses' (whether things or words) into a pattern symbolic of divine order was the method of worship which pleased Him. It was also one of the most persuasive means by which men could be led to worship.

The ordering process was important in itself, and the Christian could create 'significant form' in the church even where traditionally none had been intended. Izaak Walton tells that in Herbert's reconstruction of the church at Leighton Bromswold, 'by his order, the Reading Pew, and Pulpit, were a little distant from each other, and both of an equal height; for he would often say, "They should neither have a precedency or priority of the other: but that *Prayer* and *Preaching* being equally useful, might agree like

Brethren, and have an equal honour and estimation.'' '³
Reason and taste substantiated formal construction at every
step. Nicholas Ferrar agreed with Herbert about the proper
design for a church, and Herbert undoubtedly agreed with
Ferrar's opinion of extemporaneous prayers: '*As for extem-
porary prayers*, he used to say, *there needed little other confutation
of them, than to take them in short-hand, & shew them sometime
after to those very men, that had been so audacious to vent them.
Ask*, saith he, *their own judgements of them (for I think they
will hardly know them again), & see if they do not blame
them.*'⁴

The use of reason as confutation of the extemporaneous
implied that the ritual itself must be rational. The individual
who participated in the services must understand the significance of each detail. According to Walton, Herbert's sermons at Bemerton were often devoted to a meticulous
explanation of Anglican formal practice. The individual
should understand the rational 'fitness' of every phrase of
the service, and he should apply that understanding to his
own life. He should even know why particular passages of
Scripture were read on particular days. He must understand
the 'reasons' for all the Holy Days and the symbolic significance of every physical movement of the priest and the
congregation.

Walton described the times when Herbert was 'too
zealous': 'And to this I must add, That if he were at any
time too zealous in his Sermons, it was in reproving the
indecencies of the peoples behaviour, in the time of Divine
Service; and of those Ministers that hudled up the Church-
prayers, without a visible reverence and affection; namely,
such as seem'd to say the Lords prayer, or a Collect in a Breath;
but for himself, his custom was, to stop betwixt every
Collect, and give the people time to consider what they had
pray'd, and to force their desires affectionately to God, before
he engag'd them into new Petitions.'⁵ In the years at
Bemerton Herbert appropriately reserved his outbursts of
'passion and choler' for those who obscured the meaning of
form. Such men offended both God and God's little ones.
For the ritual could become a means of Grace. If every aspect

of it was understood, it could teach the way of salvation and the beautiful pattern of God's creation. Proper worship resulted in an ethical and spiritual ordering of the worshipper's life. That was the ultimate method of honouring God.

Herbert's ideas were by no means original; it is difficult to ascribe to any one man—or civilization—the origins of the analogical habit of mind and the belief that order, measure, proportion, and harmony are both divine and beautiful. He could have found most of the concepts in St Augustine, the only early Church father whose works he mentioned in his will. Karl Svoboda has insisted that Augustine's 'aesthetic system' is the 'most complete' that antiquity has handed down to us: it is 'the crowning synthesis of the ancient aesthetic.'[6] But the most important factor for the Christians who followed was that Augustine's 'synthesis' was built around the central conception of the Christian God. Rightly understood, both ethics and aesthetics were only reflections (and not necessarily differing reflections) of the divine, creating Beauty:

> What innun.erable toys, made by divers arts and manufactures in our apparel, shoes, utensils and all sorts of works, in pictures also in divers images, and these far exceeding all necessary and moderate use and all pious meaning, have men added to tempt their own eyes withal; outwardly following what themselves make, inwardly forsaking Him by whom themselves were made, and destroying that which themselves have been made! But I, my God and my Glory, do hence also sing a hymn to Thee, and do consecrate praise to Him who consecrateth me, because beautiful patterns which through men's souls are conveyed into their cunning hands, come from that Beauty, which is above our souls, which my soul day and night sigheth after.[7]

The ideas of God as the Great Artificer and as Absolute Beauty were theological conceptions with inevitable aesthetic

corollaries, and the work of art could be valued exactly
because it reflected the divine pattern. The ethical life was
beautiful, and an unethical life or poem by definition represented that lack of order called 'ugly' or 'evil'—not a
positive quality, but an absence of the good and the beautiful.
In so far as an object lacked those qualities or had them
imperfectly, it lacked existence; for everything that truly
existed, in the sense that it fulfilled its proper nature, was
good.[8] Any object or fact could therefore become a first
term for almost any number of 'true' metaphorical com-
parisons, since every 'existing' thing derived from and
reflected the divine creation. Long before Donne's playful
poem, Augustine contemplated the flea seriously as an
'aesthetic object.'

There was, of course, an ambiguity in Augustine's thought
(as in that of the Greeks before him and the Christians after)
concerning both the value and the role of beautiful objects
of the senses. They could be mortally dangerous. In the
same paragraph of *The Confessions* in which he had stated the
divine origin of those 'beautiful patterns which through
men's souls are conveyed into their cunning hands,' Augustine had added, 'And I, though I speak and see this,
entangle my steps with these outward beauties; but Thou
pluckest me out, O Lord, Thou pluckest me out; *because
Thy loving-kindness is before my eyes*. For I am taken miserably,
and Thou pluckest me out mercifully; sometimes not per-
ceiving it, when I had but lightly lighted upon them; other-
whiles with pain, because I had stuck fast in them.' Man
fulfilled his proper nature only through the glorification of
God. The fact that material objects of beauty had such
power to intoxicate the senses could lead even a man who
recognized the divine pattern in them to feel the danger of
a sensuous engrossment without meaning and without God.
It could also lead him to attempt to suppress sensuous response. A number of men in seventeenth-century England
were not convinced, as Augustine was, that it was an error
'to wish the whole melody of sweet music which is used to
David's Psalter, banished from my ears, and the Church's
too';[9] and there were Puritans who took more seriously than

Robert Burton the attitude implied by his formulation, 'And what is poetry itself, but, as Austin holds, the wine of error administered by drunken teachers?'[10] God was a spirit even though the Son had been incarnate, and one tradition of Christianity indicated that the mature soul anticipated the joys of heaven by rising above response to the matter of earth.

The more common emphasis, echoed throughout the seventeenth century, was that God's creation was second only to His Word as a source of truth and enlightenment. The danger that the individual might be blind to the truth of the created world, that he might 'rest in Nature, not the God of Nature,'[11] was real, but it could be met. God had provided 'repining restlessnesse' for the man who did not find Him:

> Not that he may not here
> Taste of the cheer,
> But as birds drink, and straight lift up their head,
> So he must sip and think
> Of better drink
> He may attain to, after he is dead.   ('Mans medley.')

God could, moreover, grant the grace for man to perceive the essential relationships:

> Indeed mans whole estate
> Amounts (and richly) to serve thee:
> He did not heav'n and earth create,
> Yet studies them, not him by whom they be.

> Teach me thy love to know;
> That this new light, which now I see,
> May both the work and workman show:
> Then by a sunne-beam I will climbe to thee.
>
> ('Mattens.')

One of poetry's greatest potential values was that God could employ it as a means through which man might perceive those relationships.

If poetry was an imitation of God's creation and possessed the divine power of moving the affections, the use of it for secular ends might come near to blasphemy. Although many Christians enjoyed secular or pagan poetry in a moral manner, there was little doubt that poetry with a Christian subject could be infinitely more pleasant and profitable. Not many men of the seventeenth century were buffeted black and blue by angels of God for their too great love of some profane writer as was St Jerome, but a precisian or parson with a vivid sense of his Christian calling might either abandon the arts of rhetoric and poetry entirely or consecrate their practice to the service of God.

To learn how poetry could be consecrated, Herbert had neither to engage in historical research nor to follow painfully those medieval writings which were read in his day. The religion, the poetry, and 'the arts' of his own day were filled with manifestations of the hieroglyphic view of the universe and of experience, a view which could be basic to the practice of the Christian poet and which contained within itself a formal principle. More important for Herbert than the general notion of the microcosm-macrocosm or even the continual example of the ritual was the Bible.

The ancient four-fold interpretation of the Scriptures, which had inspired so much of medieval allegory and symbolism and had served Dante well, was attacked during the seventeenth century as a barrier to the clear perception of those 'few things needful' to salvation and Christian charity. After all, some schoolmen had acknowledged seven and eight meanings, and such ingenuity obscured the simple 'real' meaning of God's Word. But the older habit of mind was too deeply ingrained to be easily erased. As hermeneutics became a weapon in ecclesiastical controversies, the men who attacked the earlier 'superstitious' interpretations sometimes derived the most metaphorical truths from their 'plain' reading of the Bible. Such an outcome was almost inevitable, for the Bible was filled with metaphors and parables and types, and it declared the cosmological significance of almost everything from the heavens to the ant. In 'Discipline' Herbert echoed the Protestant insistence that the

Bible contained all knowledge and was a complete guide for every action in man's life:

> Not a word or look
> I affect to own,
>   But by book,
> And thy book alone.

The devout Christian attempted to 'apply' almost every passage in the Old and New Testaments to his own moral and spiritual condition:

> Oh that I knew how all thy lights combine,
>   And the configurations of their glorie!
>   Seeing not onely how each verse doth shine,
> But all the constellations of the storie.
> This verse marks that, and both do make a motion
>   Unto a third, that ten leaves off doth lie:
>   Then as dispersed herbs do watch a potion,
> These three make up some Christians destinie:
> Such are thy secrets, which my life makes good,
>   And comments on thee: for in ev'ry thing
>   Thy words do finde me out, & parallels bring,
> And in another make me understood.
>   Starres are poore bookes, & oftentimes do misse:
>   This book of starres lights to eternall blisse.
>
> ('The H. Scripture [II].')

Such an attitude made inevitable a symbolic exegesis of the text. The pattern for exegesis could be found in the Gospels, the Epistles of Paul, and the book of Hebrews, where it was shown how persons and events in the Old Testament had divinely prefigured the life of Christ and Christian doctrine and practice. There are references to almost every one of the specifically biblical types in Herbert's poetry. But once the method had been shown, neither the early Fathers nor the men of the seventeenth century were satisfied with the few types mentioned in the New Testament. Many discoveries of types were individual and eccentric; but there was general agreement, for example, that the twelve tribes of Israel had mystically prophesied the twelve Disciples, that Aaron's chief importance lay not in his historical role but in his embodiment of the type of God's priest, that the bride of The Song of Solomon was a type of the Church, the Bride of Christ. It is important to realize that the types were considered purposeful anticipations by God of the future unfolding of His Will, not merely imaginative analogies drawn by the reader:

> For as the Jews of old by Gods command
> Travell'd, and saw no town;
> So now each Christian hath his journeys spann'd:
> Their storie pennes and sets us down.
> A single deed is small renown.
> Gods works are wide, and let in future times;
> His ancient justice overflows our crimes.
>
> ('The Bunch of Grapes.')

The idea of the types could be extended to profane literature and could partially sanctify it. The structure of the universe and the nature of God's plan were so evident that even pagans had occasionally understood, however gropingly, many religious truths. Sure of the truth (like the Freudians of a later day), the Christian readers welcomed the perceptions of it which they found in classic mythology. Just as Paul had been able to tell the Athenians the identity of their Unknown God, so any educated reader could join Giles Fletcher in telling them the true identity of Orpheus or Zeus or Hercules:

> Who doth not see drown'd in Deucalions name,
> (When earth his men, and sea had lost his shore)
> Old Noah; and in Nisus Lock, the fame
> Of Sampson yet alive; and long before
> In Phaethons, mine owne fall I deplore:
> But he that conquer'd hell, to fetch againe
> His virgin widowe, by a serpent slaine,
> Another Orpheus was then dreaming poets feigne.
>
> ('Christs Triumph over Death,' st. 7.)

The general assumption that 'sensible images' 'shadowed' intellectual or divine conceptions, in the present as well as in the past, made for extraordinary formal parallels between religious and secular 'images,' between, for example, the sacraments and the emblem books. Richard Hooker noted 'that many times there are three things said to make up the substance of a sacrament, namely, the grace which is thereby offered, the element which shadoweth or signifieth grace, and the word which expresseth what is done by the element,'[12] and Rosemary Freeman has recently defined the tripartite formal structure of the emblem.[13] As a good Anglican of his time Herbert believed that 'The H. Communion' and 'H. Baptisme' were the only two sacraments which Christ had ordained for His Church; but that ordination had put the stamp of divine approval on that hieroglyphic practice which the Egyptians were believed to have known and taught to the Greeks, a practice which the emblem books, those best-sellers of their day, typified. Although most men of the seventeenth century would have been shocked by the comparison, the Protestants at least considered both the picture of the emblem and the element of the sacrament 'visible signs and symbols of internal and invisible things.' The elements or signs of the sacrament of communion were the bread and wine; the sign of the emblem was a literal picture, a representation of some symbolic figure or situation which could not be understood without the 'word' and the explanation. The 'word' of consecration of the communion service 'which expresseth what is done by the element' was paralleled by the 'mot' of the emblem, which summarized the bit of moral wisdom which the emblem was to inculcate. That wisdom as it acted on the reader, like the actual grace of the sacrament, had no precise material counterpart. But the emblem's poem, which explained the exact relationship between the motto and the picture and rationally applied the moral to daily life, paralleled the sermon of explanation which usually preceded the celebration of the communion. The emblem book in England, like the Protestant theory of the two sacraments, insisted that the symbol be rationally explained and 'applied.'

The insistence on the interrelations of spiritual reality, the symbol, the word, and the explanation was not confined to the sacraments and the emblem books. The painters, the musicians, and the poets expressed those relationships, sometimes lightly and sometimes seriously, even when by modern canons those expressions seemed to involve violations of the rules of their crafts. Each developed varieties of what may be called hieroglyphic form. Yet the composer no more attempted to convey the exact 'curve of the feeling' of God's 'exalting the humble and meek,' the experience of falling, or the voice crying out of the deep,[14] than the poet tried to 'recreate the experience' of 'Trinitie Sunday,' 'Easter-wings,' or 'The Altar.' Various artists and artisans did believe that symbolic representations which involved more than one sense in apprehension increased the pleasure and therefore the effectiveness of their works. That pleasure derived less from a delight in man's artfulness than from a recognition of the hieroglyphic nature of the universe.

Herbert had taken seriously the Lawyer's summary of the Law and the Prophets: 'Thou shalt loue the Lord thy God with all thy heart, and with all thy soule, and with all thy strength, and with all thy minde, and thy neighbour as thy selfe' (Luke x. 27). His conclusion he phrased in the terms of St Paul: 'Let all things be done decently, and in order,' and 'Let all things be done vnto edifying' (1 Cor. xiv. 40, 26). In *A Priest to the Temple* that formulation applied specifically to the services of the Church of England. The ritual of the Book of Common Prayer was to be followed because it provided a decent, orderly, and edifying form of worship which reflected that ordered beauty of the universe to which the individual strove to conform. In daily life the same criteria applied. The command of love to God and one's neighbour meant that each action must be decent, orderly, and edifying as well as charitable. It was impossible to distinguish the aims of specific actions, for all was done to the glory of God: the aid both spiritual and physical of one's neighbour was also an act of worship of the productive life; and any individual act of public or private worship, once communicated, could become an act of edification to one's neighbour. The ultimate method of reflecting God's glory was the creation of a work of decency and order, a work of beauty, whether a church, an ordered poem, or an ordered life. This was not confined to the artist, but was the privilege and duty of every Christian. To do all actions 'as for thee' was 'The Elixir' 'That turneth all to gold.'

Herbert intended the poems in *The Temple* as expressions of his love for God as well as his neighbour. In Herbert's characteristic imagery, they are both 'fruits and flowers' of the Christian life, 'wreaths' of worship for God's altar and the harvest of 'fruits' of edification for others. As acts of worship they were to symbolize in their elaborate forms the beauty of the divine creation. As acts of edification they were to communicate to others the rational fitness of the symbolic forms, and to inflame them with the desire to follow the 'beauty of holiness.' The poems thus fulfilled for their readers the traditional classical aims, pleasure and profit. For nothing could be more pleasant than to contemplate the order of God's providence in the universe, the Church, or the personal life; and nothing could be more profitable, since such contemplation should increase the reader's faith and cause him to order his own life after the divine pattern.

Any attempt therefore to find either in individual poems or in the sequence of the poems a direct revelation of autobiography will fail, for the primary purpose of the poems was not what we understand by self-expression. There is, of course, no question of sincerity. The poems are a 'picture' of meticulously observed spiritual experience. But the self to Herbert was not the valuable thing which it became to a later age, and he desired that his poems should be burned if Ferrar did not think they could 'turn to the advantage of any dejected poor Soul.'[15] 'Personality' and personal experiences were of interest to the poet exactly in so far as they could be profitably used in the objective creations which were his poems. In his 'Dedication' to *The Temple* Herbert made a sharp distinction between his poems and himself, which still warns the reader:

> Lord, my first fruits present themselves to thee;
> Yet not mine neither: for from thee they came,
> And must return. Accept of them and me,
> And make us strive, who shall sing best thy name.
> Turn their eyes hither, who shall make a gain:
> Theirs, who shall hurt themselves or me, refrain.

For the conception which gives significance to the individual poems and to the organization of *The Temple*, a passage from one of Lancelot Andrewes's sermons is more revealing than most of the misty bits of Herbert's biography:

> So come we to have two sorts of Temples; Temples of flesh and bone, as well as Temples of lime and stone. For if our bodies be termed houses, because our souls, tenant-wise, abide and dwell in them; if because our souls dwell they be houses, if God do so they be temples: why not? why not?... But then they be so specially, when actually we employ them in the service of God. For being in His Temple, and there serving Him, then if ever they be *Templa in Templo*, 'living Temples in a Temple without life.' A body then may be a Temple, even this of ours.
>
> And if ours, these of ours I say, in which the Spirit of God dwelleth only by some gift or grace, with how much better right, better infinitely, His body, Christ's, in Whom the whole Godhead in all the fulness of it, dwelt corporally![16]

We do not need to assume that Herbert knew this particular passage, for the conception of the Temple was present everywhere in Christian thought. But the passage gives to the modern reader the key to the meaning of Herbert's title. For the temple as a building was a hieroglyph for the body, particularly the human body in the service of God and the divine body of Christ. By implication of its constructive elements, 'flesh and bone' and 'lime and stone,' the temple could become a symbol for all the types of order in the universe, both God's and man's. It is that symbol which pervades Herbert's volume.

Herbert's inclusion of many poems which refer to actual ceremonies or physical details of the English Church has led even so perceptive a critic as Helen C. White, who recognized the ambiguity of the title, to conclude that Herbert abandoned his initial plan for the organization of his poems.[17] No one would suggest that Herbert conceived of an abstract plan for something resembling 'The Christian Year.' Yet the order of the poems in the Williams MS. and the careful rearrangement of them in the Bodleian MS. and the 1633 edition indicate that Herbert did arrange the poems in what was to him a significant order which had little to do with biographical revelation.[18] If we conceive of *The Temple* as the symbolic record, written by a poet, of a 'typical' Christian life within the Church, most of Miss White's perplexities concerning the meaning of the order of the poems disappear. 'H. Baptisme,' for example,[19] is a natural meditation after 'Easter' and 'Easter-wings' for the Protestant who remembers the symbolism of the death, burial and Resurrection; and 'Nature' and 'Sinne' almost inevitably follow with the reminder that baptism does not free man from his sinful nature. 'Affliction (I)' is more personal than most of Herbert's poems, but it also naturally follows 'Sinne.' 'Repentance,' 'Faith,' 'Prayer,' and 'The H. Communion' are the means by which the Christian triumphs over affliction, and they are followed by the general rejoicing of 'Antiphon (I)' and the more specific expressions of 'Love (I)' and '(II).' The two poems called 'The Temper' are prayers that Go will not 'rack me . . . to such a vast extent,' following the exaltation of 'Love,' and indicating the inevitable emptiness after the moment of illumination. 'Jordan (I)' is Herbert's personal declaration of intent in writing his poems; the poem relates directly to the prayer of 'Love (II),' and its general significance is partially indicated by 'Employment (I),' which immediately follows. The Christian unsure of his calling turns to 'The H. Scriptures,' is moved by the account of the descent of the Holy Spirit on 'Whitsunday,' and prays that similar 'Grace' may 'Drop from above.' Not all the sequences are so easily followed, but the central plan is clear. Long before Andrewes, Paul had indicated in 1 Cor. vi. 19-20 that 'temple' had one primary meaning for the Christian. The Church of England, in its doctrines, its services, and even the physical construction of its churches, furnished spiritual sustenance for that 'temple not made with hands,' and it was filled with hieroglyphs of man's spiritual state. But it was the life of man within that Church which formed the principle of organization for Herbert's volume.

However symmetrical the ideal state of the Christian at any one moment, the pilgrimage of the Christian in time was not a broad and straight highway from the vales of sin to the Heavenly City. The very fluctuations between sorrow and joy, doubt and assurance, which caused George Herbert Palmer to believe that the arrangement of the poems was meaningless, seemed to the earlier readers of *The Temple* one of the most valuable evidences of Herbert's psychological realism. Most of the men of the seventeenth century did not believe that sorrow was totally banished or that man achieved continuous beatitude on this earth. God had constantly to 'create':

> Lord, mend or rather make us: one creation
>   Will not suffice our turn:
> Except thou make us dayly, we shall spurn
>   Our own salvation.   ('Giddinesse.')

Through Herbert's pictures of violently alternating spiritual change, however, they could perceive a deepening understanding of the 'giddie' state of man. It is significant that all of Herbert's 'Afflictions' (there are five poems so entitled, although only the first is generally known today) occur within the early part of 'The Church,' the central body of lyrics within *The Temple*. Those 'Afflictions' represent a developing spiritual maturity in the attitudes which they express. In the larger half of 'The Church' the experience earlier described as 'Affliction' is comprehended under new modes: as the 'Dulnesse,' 'Complaining,' 'Longing,' 'The Search' or 'Grief' of the individual; or as 'Discipline,' 'The

Pulley,' 'The Crosse,' part of 'Josephs coat,' the 'Bitter-
sweet' of the Christian life:

> Ah my deare angrie Lord,
> Since thou dost love, yet strike;
> Cast down, yet help afford;
> Sure I will do the like.
> I will complain, yet praise;
> I will bewail, approve:
> And all my sowre-sweet dayes
> I will lament, and love.

It was, perhaps, a perception of the pattern of *The Temple*
which led T. S. Eliot to remark that Herbert's poetry 'is
definitely an *œuvre* to be studied entire.'[20]

The form of Herbert's volume is often the key to the
understanding of individual poems. 'Love (III),' one of
Herbert's best-known poems in the anthologies, has been
generally interpreted as picturing the soul's welcome to the
Communion or to salvation on earth:

> Love bade me welcome: yet my soul drew back,
>   Guiltie of dust and sinne.
> But quick-ey'd Love, observing me grow slack
>   From my first entrance in,
> Drew nearer to me, sweetly questioning,
>   If I lack'd any thing.
>
> A guest, I answer'd, worthy to be here:
>   Love said, You shall be he.
> I the unkinde, ungratefull? Ah my deare,
>   I cannot look on thee.
> Love took my hand, and smiling did reply,
>   Who made the eyes but I?
>
> Truth Lord, but I have marr'd them: let my shame
>   Go where it doth deserve.
> And know you not, sayes Love, who bore the blame?
>   My deare, then I will serve.
> You must sit down, sayes Love, and taste my meat:
>   So I did sit and eat.

As the poem is in the Williams MS. it is probably 'early,' but both there and in the 1633 edition it is the last lyric within 'The Church' and it follows 'Death,' 'Dooms-day,' 'Judgement,' and 'Heaven.' George Ryley, who had read *The Temple* as the typical record of the Christian life, recognized that 'the matter of it is equally applicable to the entertainment we meet with in Divine ordinances'; but because of the position of the poem in *The Temple* he believed, correctly I think, that it was intended as a description of the soul's reception into heaven: 'A Christian's coming to Heaven is the effect of Divine Love. Therefore, after a contemplation on the state, it's proper to ruminate a little upon that which enstates us there.'[21] The banquet at which Love serves personally is not that of the earthly church, but that final 'communion' mentioned in Luke xii. 37, of which the present Communion is but an anticipation: 'Blessed are those seruants, whom the Lord when he commeth, shall find watching: Verily, I say vnto you, That he shall girde himselfe, and make them to sit downe to meate, and will come foorth and serue them.' However we read it the poem is moving, but it gains immensely in richness when we recognize the relationships it establishes between this world and the next, between abstracted and incarnate Love.

Within most of the individual poems the emphasis is on construction rather than pilgrimage. Herbert's imagery characteristically concerns the creator and the architect rather than the 'nests' and 'tears' of Crashaw; the 'light' of Vaughan, or Donne's imagery of death. God is specifically the '*Architect*' in 'The Church-floore,' and He is almost everywhere the builder or the artist or the musician. One of the most convincing arguments against despair derives from the nature of God as artist: 'As Creatures, he must needs love them; for no perfect Artist ever yet hated his owne worke.'[22] Herbert rings all the traditional changes on 'stone' as the chief architectural element, under its various guises as the heart of man, the tomb of Christ, the law of Moses, 'the stone that the builders rejected.' The hardness of the stone was generally recognized; it was the employment of

that hardness in the construction of a true temple which
appealed to Herbert's imagination.[23]

In 'The World,' 'Love's' work is to build a 'stately
house.' 'Fortune' attempts to disguise the house's structure;
'Pleasure' ornaments it with '*Balcones, Terraces,* Till she had
weakned all by alteration'; 'Sinne' 'The inward walls and
sommers cleft and tore'; and 'Sinne' and 'Death' combined
'raze the building to the very floore';

> But *Love* and *Grace* took *Glorie* by the hand,
> And built a braver Palace then before.

In 'Vanitie (I)' the activities of the 'fleet Astronomer,' the
'nimble Diver,' and the 'subtil Chymick,' divorced from the
search for God, are the search for death; life is found in the
discovery of God, and creation is its mark. In 'Deniall'
separation from God is compared with the 'breaking' of a
bow, of music, of a blossom, of the heart—and of rhyme and
stanzaic structure.

There was for Herbert no one architectural pattern; there
were almost as many patterns as there were experiences. But
Herbert could not conceive of such a thing as a formless
poem. 'The Collar,' one of his most popular poems today,
makes an immediate appeal to many readers with its expression of revolt and with what appears to be its daring use of
'free verse.' But the poem is not written in 'vers libres'; it
is one of Herbert's most deliberate ventures in 'hieroglyphic
form.' The object of imitation is the disordered life of self-
will which rebels against the will of God and therefore lacks
the order and harmony of art as well as of the religious life:
a strict 'imitation' would be no form at all—and no poem
at all. Herbert has given a formalized picture of chaos.

> I struck the board, and cry'd, No more.
> I will abroad.
> What? shall I ever sigh and pine?
> My lines and life are free; free as the rode,
> Loose as the winde, as large as store.
> Shall I be still in suit?
> Have I no harvest but a thorn
> To let me bloud, and not restore

90

What I have lost with cordiall fruit?
    Sure there was wine
Before my sighs did drie it: there was corn
    Before my tears did drown it.
Is the yeare onely lost to me?
    Have I no bayes to crown it?
No flowers, no garlands gay? all blasted?
    All wasted?
Not so, my heart: but there is fruit,
    And thou hast hands.
Recover all thy sigh-blown age
On double pleasures: leave thy cold dispute
Of what is fit, and not. Forsake thy cage,
    Thy rope of sands,
Which pettie thoughts have made, and made to thee
Good cable, to enforce and draw,
    And be thy law,
While thou didst wink and wouldst not see.
    Away; take heed:
    I will abroad.
Call in thy deaths head there: tie up thy fears.
    He that forbears
To suit and serve his need,
    Deserves his load.
But as I rav'd and grew more fierce and wilde
    At every word,
Me thoughts I heard one calling, *Child!*
And I reply'd, *My Lord.*

For readers accustomed to a different tradition in poetry, the picture of chaos may not at first be apparent. Except for some permissible extravagance of emotion and certain ideas which prove fallacious from the point of view of Christian doctrine, there is in the thought no obvious indication of the failure of rational control. The poem is clearly divided into four sections of argument: the original complaint of the heart, the answering assurance of the will that there is 'fruit' if the heart would seek it, the repeated complaint and statement of purpose by the heart, and the final resolution. The heart originally rebels because of lack of 'fruit,' and, as Helen White has noted,[24] after the early 'flowers' and 'garlands' the imagery becomes more vulgar as the emotion becomes 'more fierce and wilde.' But the meaning of Herbert's poem, his evaluation of that revolt and its resolution, is clearly imaged in the elaborate anarchy of the patterns of measure and rhyme. The poem contains all the elements of order in violent disorder. No line is unrhymed (a few rhymes occur as often as four times) and each line contains two, three, four, or five poetic feet. (Herbert counted syllables. All the lines have four, six, eight, or ten syllables except lines 12 and 14, with their conventional feminine rhymes, and lines 15 and 16, with their daring but still 'permissible' combination of short feet and feminine rhymes.) Although readers accustomed to Renaissance poetry might feel uncomfortable with the disorder of the first thirty-two lines, they could hardly divine the stanzaic norm which is the measure for that disorder until it is established, simultaneously with the submission of the rebel, in the final quatrain: $10^a \; 4^b \; 8^a \; 6^b$. That pattern of line lengths and rhyme does not occur until the final four lines; before those lines the elements of the pattern are arranged so as to form almost the mathematical ultimate in lack of periodicity. If we consider that the first thirty-two lines represent eight quatrains, we discover six different patterns of rhyme (the only repeated one is the unformed *a b c d*) and seven patterns of line lengths. Until the final four lines, the poem dramatizes expertly and convincingly the revolt of the heart, and its imitation of colloquial speech almost convinces us of the justice of the cause. But the disorder of the poem provides a constant implicit criticism, and with the final lines we recognize that 'The Collar' is a narrative in past tense: the message for the present concerns the necessity of order.

The Temple is almost a casebook of examples showing how 'Order' gives 'all things their set forms and houres.'[25] It reflects Herbert's belief that form was that principle by which the spiritual created existence out of chaos, and Herbert assumed that that process could be rationally apprehended. Since the principle was divine and therefore universal, the understanding of the formal organization of any one object or state or action gave a clue to the understanding of the rest. The poet's duty was to perceive and to communicate God's form. In the process he would construct out of the chaos of experience and the mass of language another object which would reflect his discovery: literary form as we understand it was but a reflection of that form which was everywhere present, although often hidden to eyes that could not 'see.' It, too, in its material embodiment appealed to man's senses and moved his affections. The rational contemplation of it should lead to an understanding of its symbolic significance.

Such an undeviating effort to answer the question, 'How are all things neat?'[26] ran the risk of over-neatness. For a person who did not scrutinize the heart, who attempted to formulate the answers before he had experienced them, such an external conception of the function of the priest and the poet would leave the craftsman and the logician admirably free, but it might also lead to triviality and inhumanity. That Herbert was deflected so rarely from the genuine was the result not only of his integrity as man and as artist, but also of the nature and depth of his experienced suffering. Suffering, both spiritual and physical, was the continuous challenge to the meaning of Herbert's existence and his art. Herbert believed that the Christian's life should be ordered in accordance with the will of God. As Austin Warren has remarked, the 'marks' of that order were joy and 'fruit' and peace.[27] When these were absent, a searching of the self and a passionate attempt at resolution were necessities. To Herbert it was not enough to present 'honestly' the ugliness and the disorder either in the worship of God or in poetry. That desperate sorrow which seemed meaningless and for which no resolution could be conceived could serve neither for worship nor for edification. But poetry was not therefore to be left to the secular 'lover's lute.'[28] Suffering for which some resolution or evaluation could be envisaged was the subject of the most moving poetry. While Herbert had experienced the joy and peace of resolution, he had also experienced its momentariness. He knew that the Christian's and the poet's forms were only approximations within time which had constantly to be renewed. The composition of the poems, imitative as they were of that ordering which he had experienced and which he hoped to experience again, was the act of the craftsman who shapes the imperfect materials of his own suffering as well as joy into a pattern symbolic of the divine order.

CHAPTER V

The Proper Language

WHATEVER a poet's theories of form, he creates his form through language. In a world where the ultimate reality often seems to be a matter of personal opinion, it is easy to believe that 'the style is the man' in a simplistic sense which most Renaissance writers would fail to comprehend. Yet most of the older writers conceived neither that personal experience was the only sanction for reality nor that personality must be 'refined out of existence.' Nor did they know of any one type of language which was suitable for all occasions. None of Herbert's many comments on how he believed language could and should be used indicate that at any time he believed 'quaintness' or obvious individuality proper linguistic ideals. In the poet's and the preacher's experiments, the chief consideration was not how to convey personal experience honestly but how to use language most effectively for the subject, the aim, and the intended audience of specific compositions. It is dangerous, therefore, to take as evidence of his experience or personality the language of an early seventeenth-century writer divorced from his intent. Such a modern judgment as 'Herbert's narrower experience not only limits his choice of subject-matter, but simplifies the texture of his poems,'[1] is without justification. Herbert quite consciously selected those aspects of his experience which he wished to use as 'subject-matter,' and he consistently subordinated metaphorical texture to the aim and structure of the individual poem. Herbert's language does not and was not intended to give a convenient metrical measure for the total range and depth of his experience; it does give valid evidence concerning his aims and his intended audience.

For over seven years the practice of rhetoric was literally Herbert's business. His official orations and letters and poems while at Cambridge were usually addresses of welcome, expressions of thanks for past favours, or requests for new ones. Herbert's letter of advice to his successor, Robert Creighton, describes his conception of the style befitting such a function.[2] First of all, the University Orator must realize that he wrote not in his own person but in the person of the University: 'But, ah, cautiously begin, restraining moreover thy style and natural genius. . . . Consider well, not so much what may be becoming to thyself writing, as what may be becoming to the University writing by thy pen.' Herbert emphasized the elevation of tone necessary for the orator, but he also warned against an excessively conceited style. An oration should be 'clear, transparent, lucid.' Without those qualities the business to be transacted would perish as vainly as Ixion's attempted intercourse with the clouds! It should also be 'brief and concise.' 'Learning' had its place, but the orator should not overdo it: 'An oration is one thing; a letter is another. Be sparing of learning in letters; in making an oration indulge in it a little—not much even then; for it is not befitting (the character of) our matron, whom it is thy place to set off to advantage. To speak once for all, a perfect speech, as a (perfect) man, is four-square—serious, elevated, transparent, concise.' We should not take too literally the remarks concerning learning (the witty observation that learning did not suit the character of the University would probably have been made only to another Cambridge man), nor should we assume that what would seem transparent and lucid to seventeenth-century Latinists will seem so to us. In his letters to Creighton, Herbert quoted easily and wittily from St John Chrysostom as well as Plato in the Greek. Herbert probably could assume that his successor would use 'ornament'; he wished to emphasize that the oration must be understood by the audience. If we can judge by Herbert's practice, the orator's chief role was to 'set off to advantage' the University, and his chief means was self-conscious flattery in conceited language. Personal sincerity was hardly more expected than in the presentation of our university kudos.

The young Latin Orator, however, was master of more

than one style. When Francis Bacon asked Dr Playfere, the distinguished Lady Margaret Professor of Divinity, to help translate *The Advancement of Learning*, Playfere's specimen translation was 'of such superfine Latinity, that the Lord Bacon did not encourage him to labour further in that work, in the penning of which he desired not so much neat and polite, as clear masculine and apt expression.'[3] Eventually Bacon had the English 'to be translated into the *Latine* Tongue by Mr *Herbert*, and some others, who were esteemed Masters in the *Roman* Eloquence.'[4] George Herbert, the author of the elegant and conceited Latin poems and orations, was able to satisfy Bacon's standards while Playfere was not. Bacon's dedication of his *Translation of Certaine Psalmes into English Verse* (1625) to 'his very good friend, Mr George Herbert' was a public acknowledgment of Herbert's services:

> The paines, that it pleased you to take, about some of my Writings, I cannot forget: which did put mee in minde, to dedicate to you, this poore Exercise of my sicknesse. Besides, it being my manner for Dedications, to choose those that I hold most fit for the Argument, I thought, that in respect of Diuinitie, and Poesie, met (whereof the one is the Matter, the other the Stile of this little Writing) I could not make better choice. So, with signification of my Loue and Acknowledgment, I euer rest
>
> > Your affectionate Frend,
> >
> > Fr: St. Alban.[5]

In so far as the practice of poetry and religion were concerned, the relationship was one in which Herbert was the master.[6]

In matters of rhetoric, however, Herbert may have learned from Bacon. Although many of Bacon's observations on language were based on accepted commonplaces, they were extremely influential, and they placed fresh emphasis on the conception of the audience as the primary source for all linguistic criteria.[7] As a realist concerned with power Bacon considered rhetoric and religion (that art and that institutionalized belief and practice which exerted so large .

a power over the will) as of primary importance for the preservation of society because of 'the nature and condition of
men, who are full of savage and unreclaimed desires of
profit, of lust, or revenge, which as long as they give ear to
precepts, to laws, to religion, sweetly touched with eloquence
and persuasion of books, of sermons, of harangues, so long
is society and peace maintained; but if these instruments be
silent, or that sedition and tumult make them not audible,
all things dissolve into anarchy and confusion.'[8] Bacon
believed the function of rhetoric was 'to apply Reason to
Imagination for the better moving of the will.'[9] However
out of place it might be in the discovery of the new knowledge, rhetoric was essential for the inculcation of virtue.
Bacon disagreed with Plato's condemnation of rhetoric
because it could make the worse appear the better: 'For
Plato said elegantly . . . "that virtue, if she could be seen,
would move great love and affection"; and it is the business
of rhetoric to make pictures of virtue and goodness, so that
they may be seen.'[10] 'Making of pictures' was largely the
source of rhetoric's power. Although there was constantly
an undercurrent of suspicion in Bacon's writings that these
pictures did not really represent truth, that they would be
unnecessary and ineffective for the truly rational man,
Bacon believed that they must be used to make the majority
accept new knowledge: 'On this account it was that in the
old times, when the inventions and conclusions of human
reason . . . were as yet new and strange, the world was full
of all kinds of fables, and enigmas, and parables, and
similitudes: and these were used not as a device for shadow-
ing and concealing the meaning, but as a method of making
it understood. . . . For as hieroglyphics came before letters,
so parables came before arguments. And even now if any
one wish to let new light on any subject into men's minds,
and that without offence or harshness, he must still go the
same way and call in the aid of similitudes.'[11] Imagery was
necessary for quick apprehension, for retentiveness of
memory, for the moving of the will, and for action. Bacon's
and Herbert's comments on language often show remarkable
similarities. A like emphasis on the audience helped to keep

both of them from the excesses of the extreme Senecans as well as the Ciceronians.

The nature of his audience became crucial for Herbert when he went to Bemerton. Walton tells that Herbert delivered his first sermon there 'after a most florid manner; both with great learning and eloquence. But at the close of this Sermon, told them, *That should not be his constant way of Preaching, for, since Almighty God does not intend to lead men to heaven by hard Questions, he would not therefore fill their heads with unnecessary Notions; but that for their sakes, his language and his expressions should be more plain and practical in his future Sermons.*'[12] However attractive the witty sermon might seem at St Paul's or at Court, it did not serve for the edification of an unsophisticated audience, and its practice therefore did not show love for them. The rejection of the 'florid' style of Andrewes and Donne did not mean, however, that the proper manner of showing love was to organize the sermon as a logical and grammatical analysis in the manner of some advocates of 'plainness': 'The Parsons Method in handling of a text consists of two parts; first, a plain and evident declaration of the meaning of the text; and secondly, some choyce Observations drawn out of the whole text, as it lyes entire, and unbroken in the Scripture it self. This he thinks naturall, and sweet, and grave. Whereas the other way of crumbling a text into small parts, as, the Person speaking, or spoken to, the subject, and object, and the like, hath neither in it sweetnesse, nor gravity, nor variety, since the words apart are not Scripture, but a dictionary, and may be considered alike in all the Scripture.'[13] A sermon at Bemerton must avoid both excessive ingenuity and chilling abstraction; it must speak directly, clearly, and movingly to all its audience.

A Priest to the Temple is a manual for almost every action of 'The Country Parson,' and it is written in that terse style which Bacon advocated for the communication of informa-.

tion. It is also in large part a manual of how the Parson should use language. For sermons and catechizing were two of the most important means by which the Parson could fulfil the three chief points of his duty: 'the one, to infuse a competent knowledge of salvation in every one of his Flock; the other, to multiply, and build up this knowledge to a spirituall Temple; and third, to inflame this knowledge, to presse, and drive it to practice, turning it to reformation of life, by pithy and lively exhortations; Catechizing is the first point, and but by Catechizing, the other cannot be attained.'[14] In his comments on preaching and catechizing Herbert continually emphasized the efficacy of 'particulars': 'particulars ever touch, and awake more than generalls'; 'exactnesse lyes in particulars.'[15] Not only should the Parson relate the 'particulars' of salvation, but he should direct his remarks to particular persons, and he should use the detailed knowledge of his parishioners' lives as a source of metaphor. Herbert's description of how man learns and how his will can be affected might have been written by Bacon: 'He [the Parson] condescends even to the knowledge of tillage, and pastorage, and makes great use of them in teaching, because people by what they understand, are best led to what they understand not.'[16]

Catechizing and sermons differed in their functions and catechizing was the better method for 'informing.' After the parishioners had memorized the Catechism, the Parson made them realize the significance of what they had learned by a judicious application of the socratic method. A man may be led to answer the question, 'Since man is so miserable, what is to be done?' by means of a question as to what he would do if he had fallen into a ditch which he could not get out of alone: 'This is the skill, and doubtlesse the Holy Scripture intends thus much, when it condescends to the naming of a plough, a hatchet, a bushell, leaven, boyes piping and dancing; shewing that things of ordinary use are not only to serve in the way of drudgery, but to be washed, and cleansed, and serve for lights even of Heavenly Truths.'[17]

Catechizing 'exceeds even Sermons in teaching,' but it cannot 'inflame': 'For questions cannot inflame or ravish, that must be done by a set, and laboured, and continued speech.'[18] When the Country Parson preaches, therefore, 'he procures attention by all possible art.'[19] The preacher artfully uses specific physical gestures, relates 'judgements of God,' warns his audience of the dangers of sermons (every man is either better or worse after one), and tells 'stories, and sayings of others,' 'for them also men heed, and remember better then exhortations; which though earnest, yet often dy with the Sermon, especially with Countrey people; which are thick, and heavy, and hard to raise to a poynt of Zeal, and fervency, and need a mountaine of fire to kindle them; but stories and sayings they will well remember.'

These are the means of gaining the attention necessary for the reception of the sermon's message: 'By these and other means the Parson procures attention; but the character of his Sermon is Holiness; he is not witty, or learned, or eloquent, but Holy.' But since even the truly holy man might not be able to communicate that quality to his audience, Herbert outlined five chief means by which the 'character' of holiness could be conveyed in a sermon: 'it is gained, first, by choosing texts of Devotion, not Controversie, moving and ravishing texts, whereof the Scriptures are full. Secondly, by dipping, and seasoning all our words and sentences in our hearts, before they come into our mouths, truly affecting, and cordially expressing all that we say; so that the auditors may plainly perceive that every word is hart-deep.' The final three methods are more obviously rhetorical: 'by turning often, and making many Apostrophes to God, as, Oh Lord blesse my people, and teach them this point'; 'by frequent wishes of the peoples good, and joying therein'; and 'by an often urging of the presence, and majesty of God.' Herbert gives examples of each practice, usually from the Bible. The modern sensibility may be shocked when he adds, 'Such discourses shew very Holy.' Yet we, rather than Herbert, may divorce appearance from reality: he recommended devices for gaining the appearance of holiness on the assumption that appearance should correspond with reality.

A Priest to the Temple continually returns to the holy life. The preacher places himself both as the speaker of God's word and as the audience for that word: '(as Saint *Paul* implyes that he ought, *Romans* 2.) hee first preacheth to himselfe, and then to others.'[20] The personal experience of the preacher is not irrelevant; it is the most important source of the sermon. Chapter xxxiii of *A Priest to the Temple* is called 'The Parson's Library,' but it has no reference to books:

> The Countrey Parson's Library is a holy Life: for besides the blessing that that brings upon it, there being a promise, that if the Kingdome of God be first sought, all other things shall be added, even it selfe is a Sermon. For the temptations with which a good man is beset, and the ways which he used to overcome them, being told to another, whether in private conference, or in the Church, are a Sermon. Hee that hath considered how to carry himself at table about his appetite, if he tell this to another, preacheth; and much more feelingly, and judiciously, then he writes his rules of temperance out of bookes. So that the Parson having studied, and mastered all his lusts and affections within, and the whole Army of Temptations without, hath ever so many sermons ready penn'd, as he hath victories. And it fares in this as it doth in Physick: He that hath been sick of a Consumption, and knows what recovered him, is a Physitian so far as he meetes with the same disease, and temper; and can much better, and particularly do it, then he that is generally learned, and was never sick. And if the same person had been sick of all diseases, and were recovered of all by things that he knew; there were no such Physician as he, both for skill and tendernesse.[21]

The passage is central to Herbert's view of the proper relationship between language and experience. A description of the temptations without 'the ways which he used to overcome them' was obviously not pertinent. Experience was not to be presented 'raw.' One must study it, analyse it, and reach an understanding of the causes and effects involved both in the struggle and the victory. The expression of individual experience was valued not for the sake of self-expression but for its didactic effectiveness; not because of its uniqueness but because of its universal applicability; not because a particular experience unfalsified by moral and rational generalizations was intrinsically valuable but because the particular furnished the most effective vehicle for such generalizations. Even without an obviously didactic aim on the part of the speaker, the relation of Christian experience inevitably functioned didactically. A pulpit was finally unessential to a sermon, nor were conflicts the only source of sermons: 'Neither is this true onely in the military state of a Christian life, but even in the peaceable also; when the servant of God, freed for a while from temptation, in a quiet sweetnesse seeks how to please his God.'[22] The chief difference in such a 'sermon' by an ordinary Christian and by the parson and the poet lay in the latter's greater consciousness of their aims and in their use of 'all Art.'

Many of the parson's criteria for the proper use of language in his professional capacity applied also to his poetry. Within *The Temple* 'The Church-porch,' for example, was intended to prepare the reader for his entrance into 'The Church.' It is a long didactic poem which wittily appeals to a semi-worldly common sense: as in the applications of the catechism, 'inflaming' is hardly to the point. Herbert's address to the 'Sweet youth' in the opening stanza neatly sums up the approach:

> Hearken unto a Verser, who may chance
> Ryme thee to good, and make a bait of pleasure.
> A verse may finde him, who a sermon flies,
> And turn delight into a sacrifice.

For such an aim Herbert used many proverbs, native as well as 'outlandish,' and he even found it pertinent to instruct the reader as to how he might improve his speech:

> In thy discourse, if thou desire to please,
> All such is courteous, usefull, new, or wittie.
> Usefulnesse comes by labour, wit by ease;
> Courtesie grows in court; news in the citie.
> Get a good stock of these, then draw the card
> That suites him best, of whom thy speech is
> heard. (st. 49.)

The 'sweet youth' to whom the poem is addressed seems to be a young aristocrat such as Herbert had been. He was expected to know the town and the Court, and to appreciate the mingling of worldly and holy advice. George Herbert, who had advised his younger brother Henry when in Paris 'even in speeches, to observe so much, as when you meet with a witty French speech, try to speak the like in English,'[23] knew how to please him.

'The Church-porch' is not at all, however, typical of the lyrics within 'The Church.' Although the audience of those poems is often difficult to define, for many of them it is that of the public prayer or the communicated meditation. Unlike the sermon, the prayer was addressed to God rather than to the congregation, yet it was delivered in the presence of the congregation, and the listeners must understand and join their silent prayers with the spoken one. (The audience for the prayer or the meditative lyric may be compared with that of the Elizabethan love poem, addressed to a mistress but circulated in manuscript or published by the poet.) Since the hearers were expected to identify with the thought and emotion of the speaker, the prayer and the religious poem must be both more 'rational' and more 'inflaming' than the sermon. For the poem as for the public prayer, art must be employed to the utmost, and it should be equalled by emotion.[24]

Although the audience of most of Herbert's poems was similar to that of the prayer, the genre differed. In secular terms the poem was both more private and more pleasant than the prayer; it was nearer to the Elizabethan love lyric. In his early sonnet Herbert had posed the problem of the relationship between contemporary love poems and the true nature of love:

> Doth Poetry
> Wear *Venus* Livery? only serve her turn?
> Why are not *Sonnets* made of thee? and layes
>   Upon thine Altar burnt? Cannot thy love
>   Heighten a spirit to sound out thy praise
> As well as any she?[25]

The question had been asked and answered before. The Jesuit Robert Southwell had made similar complaints before 1595, and he had stated his desire to remedy the situation in language often strikingly similar to Herbert's.[26] The conventional praise, plea, and lament of the love poems often furnished a frame of reference and a metaphorical texture for the religious lyrics of both Southwell and Herbert. Yet the differences between the secular and the religious lyrics are more striking than the similarities, and Herbert would probably have insisted that in matters of real import the love poets had borrowed the language of Christianity rather than that he imitated them. Language which was outrageous and even sacrilegious hyperbole when applied to women was factual, the seventeenth-century religious man believed, when addressed to God.

The conceptions of both audience and genre helped to determine the proper language for a poem, but most important of all was what the poet intended to do with the genre—how he wished to affect his audience. For Herbert, nearly all the earlier functions of the lyric were subsumed under the concept of praise. The audience for most of the meditative lyrics of 'The Church' was not so much to be ensnared by wit and worldly wisdom as to be moved by realization to praise. To praise and glorify God was man's chief duty. Man stood in relation to the rest of the universe as the priest to his congregation:

> O Sacred Providence, who from end to end
> Strongly and sweetly movest, shall I write,
> And not of thee, through whom my fingers bend
> To hold my quill? shall they not do thee right?
>
> Of all the creatures both in sea and land
> Onely to Man thou hast made known thy wayes,
> And put the penne alone into his hand,
> And made him Secretarie of thy praise.
>
> Beasts fain would sing; birds dittie to their notes;
> Trees would be tuning on their native lute
> To thy renown: but all their hands and throats
> Are brought to Man, while they are lame and mute.

Man is the worlds high Priest: he doth present
The sacrifice for all; while they below
Unto the service mutter an assent,
Such as springs use that fall, and windes that blow.

He that to praise and laud thee doth refrain,
Doth not refrain unto himself alone,
But robs a thousand who would praise thee fain,
And doth commit a world of sinne in one.   ('Providence.')

The religious poet took upon himself the burden of voicing
praise for those who could not write or sing. The poems in
The Temple continually echo the imperative of 'Antiphon (I)':
'Let all the world in ev'ry corner sing, *My God and King.*'
They also insist that although 'The church with psalms must
shout,' 'above all, the heart Must bear the longest part':

Rise heart; thy Lord is risen. Sing his praise
Without delayes.   ('Easter.')

Conversion itself, from one point of view, was simply the
addition of another soul to the chorus of those who were
praising God:

O that I might some other hearts convert,
And so take up at use good store:
That to thy chest there might be coming in
Both all my praise, and more!   ('Praise [III].')

One of the chief sources of the Christian's and the poet's
'miserie' was that he could not properly praise God. 'Lord,
let the Angels praise thy name. Man is a foolish thing, a
foolish thing,' was the cry of the individual who attempted
to praise and was overcome by his inability and his sense of
corruption. Yet the attempt must be made, for however
imperfect the gift, it was the portion which God had
accepted for His own:

My God, Man cannot praise thy name:
Thou art all brightnesse, perfect puritie;
The sunne holds down his head for shame,
Dead with eclipses, when we speak of thee:
How shall infection
Presume on thy perfection?

106

> As dirtie hands foul all they touch,
> And those things most, which are most pure and fine:
> So our clay hearts, ev'n when we crouch
> To sing thy praises, make them lesse divine.
> > Yet either this,
> > Or none, thy portion is.   ('Miserie.')

The poem of repentance and the 'complaint' miraculously became songs of praise: 'There can no discord but in ceasing be.'[27] Such imperfect praises, with their requests for additional grace, were signs that some grace had already been vouchsafed. The greater the grace granted, the more clearly could the individual glimpse the divine plan and rejoice:

> How should I praise thee, Lord! how should my rymes
> > Gladly engrave thy love in steel,
> > If what my soul doth feel sometimes,
> > My soul might ever feel!   ('The Temper [I].')

Praise expanded into the enjoyment of grace and communion with God, the final goal of Herbert's poems. The writing of a verse gave to Herbert 'The Quidditie' of the spiritual experience; it was an inevitable concomitant of vitality, of the renewed perception of the senses blessed by God:

> And now in age I bud again,
> After so many deaths I live and write;
> > I once more smell the dew and rain,
> And relish versing: O my onely light,
> > > It cannot be
> > > That I am he
> On whom thy tempests fell all night.
> > > > ('The Flower.')

Herbert concluded 'The Invitation' with the following stanza:

> Lord I have invited all,
> > And I shall
> Still invite, still call to thee.
> For it seems but just and right
> > In my sight,
> Where is All, there All should be.

Those lines might have been used as an epigraph for *The Temple*: within his poems Herbert attempted to move all souls to join in the praise of God. For such an aim certain types of language were unsuitable. From most of his poems, the language of the conventionally 'romantic' pastoral was banished along with its subject:

> Who sayes that fictions onely and false hair
> Become a verse? Is there in truth no beautie?
> Is all good structure in a winding stair?
> May no lines passe, except they do their dutie
>   Not to a true, but painted chair?
>
> Is it no verse, except enchanted groves
> And sudden arbours shadow course-spunne lines?
> Must purling streams refresh a lovers loves?
> Must all be vail'd, while he that reades, divines,
>   Catching the sense at two removes?
>
> Shepherds are honest people; let them sing:
> Riddle who list, for me, and pull for Prime:
> I envie no mans nightingale or spring;
> Nor let them punish me with losse of rime,
>   Who plainly say, *My God, My King.* ('Jordan [I].')

The fact that Herbert used in his rhetorical questions so many of the clichés which he was rejecting has caused some readers to consider the poem a 'metaphysically' obscure poem denouncing obscurity. The poem is addressed to the partisans of the pastoral love poems, and they are expected to recognize the meanings (as well as the absurdities) of their own conventions. 'Jordan (I)' is a defence of 'true beauty' (i.e. religion) as the subject of poetry and a rejection of the language and conventions of 'false beauty' for the sacred subject. The objections are specific: the pastoral allegory presents a conscious fiction and disguises the real names and personalities of its protagonists; it pictures not 'truth,' but an imaginary world in which the actions of disguised figures take place in 'enchanted groves,' 'sudden arbours' and by 'purling streams' (the literary judgment on the 'course-spunne lines' seems related to the quoted

clichés); such poetry places its prime emphasis on the ingenious 'winding stair' of its rational structure and on the
covertness of its meanings. 'He that reades, divines, Catch-
ing the sense at two removes.' The religious lyric is opposed
by implication at each point. It does not employ 'fictions'
such as Strophon and Amaryllis (or even Astrophel and
Stella), but must 'plainly say, *My God, My King.*' Its world
is the true one of experience and reality. The religious poem,
like the oration, must be 'four-square,' not 'winding.' 'He
that reades' must understand rationally before he is 'en-
flamed': language must not obscure the rational meaning;
the reader must not be forced to 'divine.'

For similar reasons Herbert condemned the search for
witty language. In its earlier version in the Williams MS.,
'Jordan (II)' was appropriately entitled 'Invention':

> When first my lines of heav'nly joyes made mention,
> Such was their lustre, they did so excell,
> That I sought out quaint words, and trim invention;
> My thoughts began to burnish, sprout, and swell,
> Curling with metaphors a plain intention,
> Decking the sense, as if it were to sell.
>
> Thousands of notions in my brain did runne,
> Off'ring their service, if I were not sped:
> I often blotted what I had begunne;
> This was not quick enough, and that was dead.
> Nothing could seem too rich to clothe the sunne,
> Much lesse those joyes which trample on his head.
>
> As flames do work and winde, when they ascend,
> So did I weave my self into the sense.
> But while I bustled, I might heare a friend
> Whisper, *How wide is all this long pretence!*
> *There is in love a sweetnesse readie penn'd:*
> *Copie out onely that, and save expense.*

'As flames do work and winde, when they ascend, So did I
weave my self into the sense' may seem to be a felicitous
description of that 'fusion of thought and feeling' which
some moderns have hoped to achieve, and it is difficult to

believe that Herbert intended to condemn the process. The poem has therefore occasionally been considered a momentary weakness, a churchly recantation of Herbert's own principles of art.[28] The statement in 'Jordan (II),' however, is thoroughly consistent with Herbert's other comments on poetry: the confusion arises from the differing evaluations which Herbert and most moderns give to the 'self.' 'Jordan (II)' follows 'Miserie,' the poem describing man's corrupt incapacity for praise. The final stanzas of 'Miserie' describe the 'self' and allow for no misinterpretation of that word in the poem which follows:

> Indeed at first Man was a treasure,
> A box of jewels, shop of rarities,
> > A ring, whose posie was, *My pleasure*:
> He was a garden in a Paradise:
> > > Glorie and grace
> > > Did crown his heart and face.

> But sinne hath fool'd him. Now he is
> A lump of flesh, without a foot or wing
> > To raise him to a glimpse of blisse:
> A sick toss'd vessel, dashing on each thing;
> > > Nay, his own shelf:
> > > My God, I mean my self.

The self was corrupt and a barrier to praise. In *The Temple* Herbert did not intend to 'weave' that 'self into the sense.' The search for 'quaint words, and trim invention,' the process of 'Curling with metaphors a plain intention,' implied a dependence on the self rather than upon God.[29] It was an evidence of '*Spirituall pride*,' the chief of '*the proper and peculiar temptations*' of the parson, '*the sicknesse that destroyeth at noone day*.'[30]

The process of copying out that 'sweetnesse' that is 'readie penn'd' in love, however, is not so simple as it sounds. 'God is love,' and love comes from God. That the universe was created and is sustained, that life exists, that Christ died for man's sins—all are but evidences of God's love. The love that the individual feels for God is also a gift from God, and it implies an understanding of God's love and gratitude for His providence. In all its manifestations, love is one. To copy the 'sweetnesse' that is in love, then, does not mean to express one's emotions honestly and precisely: the attempt to 'invent' a fitting description of 'heav'nly joyes' was exactly what had caused the poet's thoughts 'to burnish, sprout, and swell.' The poem insists, 'Do not "bustle" to invent within your own brain "quaint words," elaborate metaphors, and ingenious notions as equivalents for "heav'nly joyes." Such attempts will fail and they tarnish the theme. The individual does not have to invent arguments for such joys: God has already "invented" them in the manifestations of His love. Consider these in yourself and particularly in the world about you, and you will discover that the Christian poet has merely to "copie"; the notions and the metaphors are everywhere present, and the clear expression of them honors God more properly than any human ingenuity.' The conception includes sincerity, but it includes much more. The desire to which sincere expression is to be given does not come from the old self, but from the consumption of that self by divine love:

> Immortall Heat, O let thy greater flame
> Attract the lesser to it: let those fires
> Which shall consume the world, first make it tame;
> And kindle in our hearts such true desires
> As may consume our lusts, and make thee way.
> Then shall our hearts pant thee; then shall our brain
> All her invention on thine Altar lay,
> And there in hymnes send back thy fire again. ('Love [II].')

The style of Lord Herbert of Cherbury was not suitable to George Herbert's aims, nor was the style of John Donne when he was attempting 'to match Sir Edward Herbert in obscureness.'[31] The florid style in poetry did not serve properly for either edification or worship. The reader must understand and he must not become more interested in the poet's ingenuity than in the subject of the poem. The poem should 'speak' from the heart 'to all.'[32]

Its ability to communicate to other men, however, was

not the only, or even the most important, characteristic of the religious poem. After all, God was the primary 'audience' for the religious lyric, and from the point of view of eternity the praise of an uneducated man or of a technically deficient poet was infinitely preferable to that of an able technician whose heart was not properly turned toward God. Herbert made the clearest statement of his subordination of execution to intent in 'A true Hymne':

> My joy, my life, my crown!
> My heart was meaning all the day,
> Somewhat it fain would say:
> And still it runneth mutt'ring up and down
> With onely this, *My joy, my life, my crown.*
>
> Yet slight not these few words:
> If truly said, they may take part
> Among the best in art.
> The finenesse which a hymne or psalme affords,
> Is, when the soul unto the lines accords.
>
> He who craves all the minde,
> And all the soul, and strength, and time,
> If the words onely ryme,
> Justly complains, that somewhat is behinde
> To make his verse, or write a hymne in kinde.
>
> Whereas if th' heart be moved,
> Although the verse be somewhat scant,
> God doth supplie the want.
> As when th' heart sayes (sighing to be approved)
> *O, could I love!* and stops: God writeth, *Loved.*

We should not be surprised that when Herbert described his inability to express himself and the relative unimportance of technique, he wrote a logically constructed poem in an elaborate metrical pattern. God truly 'doth supplie the want' for the individual who cannot create an artful hymn of praise because of natural or momentary inability or lack of training; such a 'movement' of the heart is infinitely preferable to the 'wit' which jags 'his seamlesse coat . . . With curious questions and divisions,'[33] whether in divinity or poetry. Yet this does not imply that religious poetry should be simple-minded nor that the poet should disregard technique. God craves 'all the minde, And all the soul, and strength, and time.'[34] The man who is granted poetic ability must use it in the praise of God. Such praise requires the best workmanship of which the individual is capable:

> Wherefore with my utmost art
> I will sing thee. ('Praise [II].')

The poet who attempted to enlighten and inflame without the aid of the secular allegorical machinery, without witty language of personal ingenuity, and without references to the worlds of Greece and Rome,[35] had need of the 'utmost art.' Yet there was no need to banish finally either allegory or wit or mythology, for God had infinitely provided all three in the 'two books' of His revelation and His work. Of those 'books,' the first was the more important for the poetry, for it showed how properly to interpret the second. Herbert assumed an intimate knowledge of the Bible on the part of his readers. He had no concern with avoiding obscurity for an audience which did not possess such knowledge. He intended, I believe, that a literate reader who knew the Bible and the ordinary worlds of nature and business and communication should be able to understand and respond to his poems after careful reading and meditation. If, occasionally, that was not true, Herbert would have considered himself at fault. The enormous popularity of *The Temple* in the mid-seventeenth century indicates that in general he achieved his aim.

A knowledge of the Bible and of the seventeenth-century English world was hardly parochial. God had shown how the poet could use the worldly knowledge which people understand to lead them to the knowledge of the spirit which 'they understand not.' In the Bible He had graciously 'accommodated' His manner of speech to man's understanding: the parables of Jesus, the metaphysical teachings.

of St Paul, the imagery of the Psalms, revealed divine truths to man in the terms of his daily experience. He had presented the central doctrine of salvation, the Doctrine of the Covenant, in those very terms of farming, tenancy, contract, and debt which were most commonly within the experience of the ordinary man. The poet could use such terms with the assurance that they would be immediately recognized and understood. In many of Herbert's poems, the images of the market-place and the images of divine wisdom coincide.

Repeatedly one discovers that what seem to be difficult or strained 'conceits' in *The Temple* have specific sources either in the Bible or in theological commonplaces: they would have been as readily understood by students of the Bible as by the wits at Court. The final figure of 'The Dawning,' for example, has been considered one of the most tasteless examples of the 'metaphysical conceit':

> Awake sad heart, whom sorrow ever drowns;
> Take up thine eyes, which feed on earth;
> Unfold thy forehead gather'd into frowns:
> Thy Saviour comes, and with him mirth?
> Awake, awake;
> And with a thankfull heart his comforts take.
> But thou dost still lament, and pine, and crie;
> And feel his death, but not his victorie.
>
> Arise sad heart; if thou doe not withstand,
> Christs resurrection thine may be:
> Do not by hanging down break from the hand,
> Which as it riseth, raiseth thee:
> Arise, arise;
> And with his buriall-linen drie thine eyes:
> Christ left his grave-clothes, that we might, when grief
> Draws tears, or bloud, not want a handkerchief.

Part of the incongruity for the modern reader derives from the feeling that 'handkerchief,' as word and object, is essentially trivial and slightly ludicrous. The word does not seem to have possessed such connotations in the early seventeenth century. In the Authorized Version of the Bible

'handkerchiefs' were the miraculous means of Paul's healing:
'And God wrought speciall miracles by the hands of Paul:
So that from his body were brought vnto the sicke handkerchiefs or aprons, and the diseases departed from them, and
the euill spirits went out of them' (Acts xix. 11-12). A more
serious objection may be that, after the modern reader has
grasped the surface meaning of the lines, Christ's 'grave-
clothes' and 'a handkerchief' seem only artificially equated.
They did not seem so to Herbert, and he expected his
readers to perceive their inherent (i.e. biblical) relationship.
The poem concerns the proper celebration of Easter. It was
probably written after 'Easter' and 'Easter-wings,' and it
echoes those poems:[36] 'Easter' was a 'praise' and 'Easter-
wings' a prayer for the ability to praise. 'The Dawning' is
addressed to the sorrowful heart rather than to God, and it
states the reasons for rejoicing so that the heart will give
up its sorrow and join the chorus of praise. Christ's resurrection is a sign that His followers will also arise:

> Arise sad heart; if thou doe not withstand,
> Christs resurrection thine may be.

Herbert expected his readers to remember the prophecies
and the descriptions of the divine event, and they told of the
banishment of grief for joy: 'He will swallow vp death in
victorie, and the Lord God wil wipe away teares from off al
faces' (Isa. xxv. 8). Mary had wept on the morning of the
Resurrection when she found the tomb empty, but the
appearance of Jesus had changed her tears to joy. The joy
of Christians at Easter is a type of that final rejoicing in
heaven when 'they which came out of great tribulation' shall
cry, 'Saluation to our God, which sitteth vpon the Throne,
and vnto the Lambe': 'For the Lambe, which is in the
middest of the throne, shall feede them, and shall leade them
vnto liuing fountaines of waters: and God shal wipe away
all teares from their eyes' (Rev. vii. 10-17). It is a foretaste
of the joys of the 'new Hierusalem': 'And God shall wipe
away all teares from their eyes; and there shall bee no more
death, neither sorrow, nor crying, neither shall there bee
any more paine: for the former things are passed away'

(Rev. xxi. 4). Knowledge of the Resurrection is the instrument God uses to 'wipe away all tears' and cause rejoicing before that final victory. The discovery of the 'grave-clothes' was the first sign that Christ had truly arisen rather than that His body had been carried away. The presence of the grave-clothes in the sepulchre caused the disciple 'whom Jesus loved' to believe: 'Then commeth Simon Peter following him, and went into the Sepulchre, and seeth the linnen clothes lie, And the napkin that was about his head, not lying with the linnen clothes, but wrapped together in a place by it selfe. Then went in also that other disciple which came first to the Sepulchre, and he saw, and beleeued' (John xx. 6-8). The 'conceit' was there for the finding, and it was of the fullest possible significance.

Any metaphor or scheme was acceptable to Herbert so long as it represented 'God's art,' was likely to be understood, and did not endanger the poem's unity. Without appreciable loss, a reader of a lover's 'Valediction' to his mistress might become more interested in a figure of 'stiffe twin compasses' than in the plight of the lovers; but the possibility of such a reading must be avoided if the 'lover' addressed God. Herbert simultaneously achieved richness and prevented imagery from obscuring or deflecting the rational structure of his poems by two characteristic methods. The first (and most generally recognized today) was to construct the poem as a meditation on a central 'hieroglyph,' often identified by the poem's title. His second method was to reduce the 'conceit' to a concise statement (often within one line of the poem), and to limit severely its logical function. 'Vertue' conveniently illustrates the second practice:

> Sweet day, so cool, so calm, so bright,
> The bridall of the earth and skie:
> The dew shall weep thy fall to night;
>   For thou must die.
>
> Sweet rose, whose hue angrie and brave
> Bids the rash gazer wipe his eye:
> Thy root is ever in its grave,
>   And thou must die.

Sweet spring, full of sweet dayes and roses,
A box where sweets compacted lie;
My musick shows ye have your closes,
    And all must die.

Onely a sweet and vertuous soul,
Like season'd timber, never gives;
But though the whole world turn to coal,
    Then chiefly lives.

The poem is full of 'conceits,' but each is limited to one line of verse and to the illustration of its relationship to mortality. The most daring of the 'conceits,' 'A box where sweets compacted lie,' has been partially prepared for by 'full of sweet dayes and roses' in the preceding line. Its connotations are not developed, but are blocked by 'My musick shows ye have your closes': by means of an additional 'conceit' the focus is effectively shifted back to 'Spring' and death. Similarly, in the last stanza 'season'd timber' is limited to its one point of resemblance to the 'vertuous soul,' that it 'never gives.' The last two lines concerning the Judgment (in which 'season'd timber' would certainly 'turn to coal' along with the rest of the world) move firmly to the immortality of the 'vertuous soul,' for which no metaphor is possible except the contrast with the mortality of 'the whole world.'

The care which Herbert brought to 'Vertue' and to most of his other poems was the care of a lover. Herbert was a poet before he was a priest; he loved 'sweet phrases' and 'lovely metaphors' so much, he felt and understood their powers of enchantment so deeply, that he recognized their dangers. The 'wanton lovers' had proved that language could be used to ensnare rather than to illumine. There was the particular risk that the religious poet might be enchanted by his own metaphors, that he might forget his heavenly aims in his earthly love for language. Yet language was the chief instrument which God had chosen for the conversion of souls to Him, it was the medium of rational praise, and in its very sounds and spellings one could discover fresh evidences of the illimitable connections between the universe and God.[37] The answer to the sensuous dangers was to be found not in rejecting the earthly instrument but in mastering it.

Herbert's mastery is continually manifested in the extraordinary range of language within *The Temple*. At one extreme, the language of the fine poem 'Discipline' imitates the title of the poem, and the result is a bareness of statement rare in English poetry:

> Throw away thy rod,
> Throw away thy wrath:
> O my God,
> Take the gentle path.

In 'The Pearl's' witty survey of all the 'wayes' of Learning, Honour, and Pleasure, the language is as complex as the subject. The one constant is that words and metaphors are suited to the subject and intent of the poem. For most of his subjects and most of his aims, Herbert desired and obtained disciplined richness rather than bareness or great complexity.

'The Forerunners' is Herbert's survey of his poetic achievement in the light of approaching age and death. With allowance made for the quantity of metaphor necessary to describe the effects of poetry, the poem is characteristic of Herbert's disciplined richness:

> The harbingers are come. See, see their mark;
> White is their colour, and behold my head.
> But must they have my brain? must they dispark
> Those sparkling notions, which therein were bred?
> Must dulnesse turn me to a clod?
> Yet have they left me, *Thou art still my God.*

> Good men ye be, to leave me my best room,
> Ev'n all my heart, and what is lodged there:
> I passe not, I, what of the rest become,
> So *Thou art still my God*, be out of fear.
> He will be pleased with that dittie;
> And if I please him, I write fine and wittie.

Farewell sweet phrases, lovely metaphors.
But will ye leave me thus? when ye before
Of stews and brothels onely knew the doores,
Then did I wash you with my tears, and more,
      Brought you to Church well drest and clad:
My God must have my best, ev'n all I had.

Lovely enchanting language, sugar-cane,
Hony of roses, whither wilt thou flie?
Hath some fond lover tic'd thee to thy bane?
And wilt thou leave the Church, and love a stie?
      Fie, thou wilt soil thy broider'd coat,
And hurt thy self, and him that sings the note.

Let foolish lovers, if they will love dung,
With canvas, not with arras, clothe their shame:
Let follie speak in her own native tongue.
True beautie dwells on high: ours is a flame
      But borrow'd thence to light us thither.
Beautie and beauteous words should go together.

Yet if you go, I passe not; take your way:
For, *Thou art still my God*, is all that ye
Perhaps with more embellishment can say.
Go birds of spring: let winter have his fee;
      Let a bleak palenesse chalk the doore,
So all within be livelier then before.

It is all there: the love for language and the rational control, the insistence on propriety and the equal insistence that language is finally unimportant when compared with the spirit. In the poem, as in Herbert's career, is the implication that the beauty of language, like the soul's, can live only if it is 'lost' to the proper object; that the craftsman maintains his mastery of beauty only upon the condition of his willingness to surrender it.

III

CHAPTER VI

The Poem as Hieroglyph

TOO often Herbert is remembered as the man who possessed the fantastic idea that a poem should resemble its subject in typographical appearance, and who therefore invented the practice of writing poems in shapes such as wings and altars. Herbert, of course, no more invented the pattern poem than he invented 'emblematic poetry' or the religious lyric: his originality lies in his achievement with traditional materials. 'The Altar' and 'Easter-wings,' his two most famous pattern poems, are not exotic or frivolous oddities; they are the most obvious examples of Herbert's religious and poetic concern with what we may call the hieroglyph.

A hieroglyph is 'a figure, device, or sign having some hidden meaning; a secret or enigmatical symbol; an emblem.'[1] In the Renaissance 'hieroglyph,' 'symbol,' 'device,' and 'figure' were often used interchangeably. Because of special meanings which have become associated with the other words, 'hieroglyph' seems more useful than the others today, and even in the seventeenth century it was often considered the most inclusive term.[2] 'Hieroglyphic,' the older form of the noun, was derived from the Greek for 'sacred carving,' and the root usually retained something of its original religious connotation. Ralph Cudworth used it in its generally accepted meaning when he said in a sermon, 'The Death of Christ . . . Hieroglyphically instructed us that we ought to take up our Cross likewise, and follow our crucified Lord and Saviour.'[3] The hieroglyph presented its often manifold meanings in terms of symbolic relationships rather than through realistic representation. Francis Quarles's anatomy of the hieroglyphic significance of the rib is an extreme example of the general hieroglyphic state of mind:

Since of a Rib first framed was a Wife,
Let Ribs be Hi'rogliphicks of their life:
Ribs coast the heart, and guard it round about,
And like a trusty Watch keepe danger out;
So tender Wiues should loyally impart
Their watchfull care to fence their Spouses' heart:
All members else from out their places roue
But Ribs are firmely fixt, and seldom moue:
Women (like Ribs) must keepe their wonted home,
And not (like *Dinah* that was rauish't) rome:
If Ribs be ouer-bent, or handled rough,
They breake; If let alone, they bend enough:
Women must (vnconstrain'd) be plyent still,
And gently bending to their Husband's will.[4]

Quarles's poem suggests that wherever the poet found his hieroglyphs, their 'meanings' tended to substantiate his own point of view. The central meanings for the serious religious poet were usually already established by the Bible and Christian tradition.

Aside from the metaphorical use of hieroglyphs common to almost all the poets of the time, the religious lyric poet could most obviously make his poem a meditation on one of the innumerable hieroglyphs in nature, art, or the Church, or he could use the hieroglyph as the central image in a meditation on some doctrine or experience. Quarles's poem and most of the poems written for the emblem books typify the first practice: the moral applications are drawn from the image point by point. Herbert never wrote a poem quite so crudely. 'The Church-floore' is as close as he ever came, and that poem's departures from tradition are instructive. The first eighteen lines describe the hieroglyphic meanings of the 'Church-floore':

> Mark you the floore? that square & speckled stone,
> Which looks so firm and strong,
> Is *Patience*:
>
> And th' other black and grave, wherewith each one
> Is checker'd all along,
> *Humilitie*:

The gentle rising, which on either hand
Leads to the Quire above,
Is *Confidence*:

But the sweet cement, which in one sure band
Ties the whole frame, is *Love*
And *Charitie*.

Hither sometimes Sinne steals, and stains
The marbles neat and curious veins:
But all is cleansed when the marble weeps.
Sometimes Death, puffing at the doore,
Blows all the dust about the floore:
But while he thinks to spoil the room, he sweeps.

An elaborate and promising hieroglyph is described, but in spite of many hints its meaning is both abstract and ambiguous. We are told that the elements which compose the floor are Patience, Humilitie, Confidence, and Charitie, and that Sinne and Death attempt (and fail) to deface it; but we are not told to what the floor is being compared. From the title of the poem the reader might assume that the floor is a hieroglyph of the Church's foundation, which is based on the theological virtues (Patience and Humilitie may be considered as defining Faith in action), and against which the 'gates of Hell' (Sinne and Death) shall not prevail. Such an interpretation would be thoroughly conventional, and the first eighteen lines might almost serve as an unusually successful 'explanation' of an emblem which made that point. But Herbert's characteristic final couplet changes that 'explanation' and makes the poem:

Blest be the *Architect*, whose art
Could build so strong in a weak heart.

We discover with the last word of the poem that the principal referent of the hieroglyph is not the institution of the Church but the human heart. Patience, Humilitie, Confidence, and Charitie are the materials with which God builds the structure of salvation within the heart. God has built so that the 'marble' heart will weep with repentance and cleanse Sinne's stains. Death's intended triumph in

blowing 'all the dust about the floore' only 'sweeps' away
the imperfections of that flesh which is dust. Herbert nearly
always presents the institutional as a hieroglyph of the
personal rather than *vice versa*, and the hieroglyph of 'The
Church-floore' has pictured primarily the marvellous art of
God in decreeing the perseverance of the saints rather than
His art in the construction of the Church. Yet those two
arts are related; once raised, the image of the 'Church-
floore' as the foundation of Christ's Church is relevant. The
final couplet is a dramatic reminder to the meditator that
'the most high dwelleth not in temples made with hands'
(Acts vii. 48), 'that yee are the Temple of God, and that the
Spirit of God dwelleth in you' (1 Cor. iii. 16). But in
relation to the subject of the meditation, the title of the
poem, the couplet is also a reminder that the structure which
God has built within the heart is truly the 'floore' of both
the Church Militant and the Church Triumphant; that the
conviction within the 'weak heart' that 'Thou art the Christ,
the sonne of the liuing God' is the 'rocke' upon which
Christ built His Church.[5] The artful '*Architect*' has built
within the individual heart, equally indestructibly, the salvation of the individual and the foundation of His Church.
The structure, moreover, is one. Such a complex unfolding of meanings is far removed from the practice of the
emblematists, but it is characteristic of Herbert.

In 'The Bunch of Grapes' Herbert used the hieroglyph
in the second obvious fashion, as the central image in a
meditation on a personal experience. The title of the poem
indicates the hieroglyph, but the 'cluster' is not mentioned
until the end of the third stanza. The subject of meditation
is the problem of the absence of joy from the Christian's life:

> Joy, I did lock thee up: but some bad man
> Hath let thee out again:
> And now, me thinks, I am where I began
> Sev'n yeares ago: one vogue and vein,
> One aire of thoughts usurps my brain.
> I did towards Canaan draw; but now I am
> Brought back to the Red sea, the sea of shame.

Joy, once possessed, has now escaped. Herbert prevents any misunderstanding of the traditional imagery of Canaan and the Red Sea by explaining in the next stanza Paul's teaching that every event during the wandering of the Children of Israel from Egypt to the Promised Land was a type of the Christian's experiences in his journey between the world of sin and heaven:[6] we may discover within the ancient history the heavenly evaluations and solutions for our problems. With the third stanza, Herbert enumerates some of the parallels:

> Then have we too our guardian fires and clouds;
>> Our Scripture-dew drops fast:
> We have our sands and serpents, tents and shrowds;
>> Alas! our murmurings come not last.
>> But where's the cluster? where's the taste
> Of mine inheritance? Lord, if I must borrow,
> Let me as well take up their joy, as sorrow.

Joy may not be fully achieved until we reach the Promised Land, but the Christian should at least experience a foretaste of it, such a rich proof of its existence as was the cluster of Eshcol to the Children of Israel. But the introduction of Eshcol provides the answer. That 'branch with one cluster of grapes,' which was so large that 'they bore it betweene two vpon a staffe,' had represented a joy which the Israelites refused. To them the bunch of grapes substantiated the report that it was 'a land that eateth vp the inhabitants thereof, and all the people that we saw in it, are men of a great stature. And there we saw the giants, the sonnes of Anak, which come of the giants: and wee were in our owne sight as grashoppers, and so wee were in their sight' (Num. xiii. 32-33). From fear they turned to the rebellion which caused God to decree the wandering of forty years. Of all the adults who saw the grapes, only Caleb and Joshua entered the Promised Land. The image of the bunch of grapes suggests, then, not only the foretastes of Canaan and heaven, but also the immeasurable differences between those foretastes under the Covenant of Works and the Covenant of Grace:

But can he want the grape, who hath the wine?
　　　I have their fruit and more.
Blessed be God, who prosper'd *Noahs* vine,
　　　And made it bring forth grapes good store.
　　　But much more him I must adore,
Who of the Laws sowre juice sweet wine did make,
Ev'n God himself being pressed for my sake.

The bunch of grapes is a type of Christ and of the Christian's communion. 'I have their fruit and more,' for the grapes, of which the promise was conditional upon works, have been transformed into the wine of the New Covenant: 'I' have both the foretaste and the assurance of its fulfilment. The prospering of '*Noahs* vine,' like the cluster of Eshcol, was a sign of God's blessing. It was a partial fulfilment of 'Bee fruitfull and multiply, and replenish the earth,' and of God's covenant with all flesh: 'neither shall there any more be a flood to destroy the earth' (Gen. ix. 1, 11). Yet, as at Eshcol, God's blessings under the Law could become man's occasion for the renewal of sin and the curse: Noah's misuse of the vine resulted in the curse on Ham. The bunch of grapes has furnished the image of the poet's lost joy, the image of blessings refused or perverted, and also the image of the Christian's source of joy, ever present if he will cease his murmurings. The Holy Communion is a constant reminder of Christ's sacrifice which established the joyful Covenant of Grace; it is the instrument of present grace; and it foretells the joy of heavenly communion. The examination of the Christian's lack of joy has resolved rather than explained the original problem. The blessing and adoration of the final lines indicate that joy is no longer lost.

　Herbert frequently used a hieroglyph to crystallize, explain, or resolve the central conflict in a poem. 'Josephs coat,' a strange sonnet with an unrhymed first line, concerns the mixture of joy and sorrow in the Christian life, and Joseph is not mentioned in the text. The conclusion, 'I live to shew his power, who once did bring My *joyes* to *weep*, and now my *griefs* to *sing*,' is an acknowledgment of God's power, but without the title it might be construed as an acknowledgment of a powerful and inexplicable Fate. The title, a reference to a traditional Christian type, gives Herbert's interpretation of the experience of contradictory joys and sorrows. Joseph's 'coat of many colours' was the sign of his father's particular love.[7] It was also the immediate occasion for his brothers' jealousy and hatred and for his slavery and suffering; but the presentation of the coat was, finally, the initial incident in the long chain of causes which led to the preservation of the Children of Israel in Egypt. After all the suffering, the sign of Jacob's love ended in beatitude. The extraordinary mixture of joy and sorrow in the Christian's life is a particular sign of God's love. Joy has been made 'to *weep*' to forestall that self-sufficience which leads to wilful pride, and '*griefs*' have been made 'to *sing*' to preserve the soul and body from despair and death. God's 'Cross-Providences' also lead to beatitude. For Herbert, 'Joyes coat,' with which anguish has been 'ticed' was evidenced by his ability to 'sing,' to compose lyrics even when the subject was grief.

At first reading 'Church-monuments' appears to belong to the group of poems which are explanations of a hieroglyph. For once the modern reader could surmise the title from the contents, for the poem is a considered meditation on 'Church-monuments' in which all their hieroglyphic applications are drawn.

> While that my soul repairs to her devotion,
> Here I intombe my flesh, that it betimes
> May take acquaintance of this heap of dust;
> To which the blast of deaths incessant motion,
> Fed with the exhalation of our crimes,
> Drives all at last. Therefore I gladly trust
>
> My bodie to this school, that it may learn
> To spell his elements, and finde his birth
> Written in dustie heraldrie and lines;

Which dissolution sure doth best discern,
Comparing dust with dust, and earth with earth.
These laugh at Jeat and Marble put for signes,

To sever the good fellowship of dust,
And spoil the meeting. What shall point out them,
When they shall bow, and kneel, and fall down flat
To kisse those heaps, which now they have in trust?
Deare flesh, while I do pray, learn here thy stemme
And true descent; that when thou shalt grow fat,

And wanton in thy cravings, thou mayst know,
That flesh is but the glasse, which holds the dust
That measures all our time; which also shall
Be crumbled into dust. Mark here below
How tame these ashes are, how free from lust,
That thou mayst fit thy self against thy fall.

The first stanza states the purpose of the meditation, that 'my flesh . . . betimes May take acquaintance of this heap of dust.' Most obviously, the monuments form a hiero-glyph worthy of the flesh's 'acquaintance' because they contain the dust of formerly living flesh. Yet, with the identification of 'heap of dust' as that 'To which the blast of deaths incessant motion . . . Drives all at last,' the meaning expands to include the dissolution of all earthly things. Through contemplating the monuments the 'bodie' 'may learn To spell his elements.' The ambiguous 'spell' (mean-ing both to 'divine' the elements and to 'spell out' the inscriptions) introduces as part of the hieroglyph the inscrip-tions on the monuments. Their 'dustie' physical state (which makes them difficult to decipher) and their intended verbal meaning cause them to serve as intermediate symbols relating the flesh of man and the contents of the tomb. The 'dustie heraldrie and lines' factually tell the genealogies of the deceased and include some conventional version of 'for dust thou art, and vnto dust shalt thou returne.' ('Lines,' associated with 'birth' and 'heraldrie' seems to signify genealogical 'lines' as well as the lines of engraving.) The

monuments are an ironic commentary on mortality; their
states and messages mock at their composition of 'Jeat and
Marble'—too obviously fleshly attempts to deny the dissolution of the bodies which they contain. Can there be
monuments to monuments? Can monuments hope for a
memorial 'When they shall bow, and kneel' as the body of
the meditator is doing, or 'fall down flat' in dissolution, as
his body will do and as the bodies within the monuments
have already done? The flesh can learn its 'stemme And
true descent' both in its origin in dust and in its decline
into dust.

The figure of the hour-glass summarizes what 'thou
mayst know' from the contemplation of the monuments
and further enriches the meaning:

> That flesh is but the glasse, which holds the dust
> That measures all our time; which also shall
> Be crumbled into dust.

It is one of Herbert's most successful condensations, and
it is difficult only if we have failed to follow the careful
preparation for its introduction. The hour-glass defines the
flesh in terms of what has been learned from the monuments.
The monuments, like the traditional *memento mori*, have told
of more than physical death. It is 'the exhalation of our
crimes' which 'feeds' 'the blast of deaths incessant motion';
and the monuments, like the 'grasse' of the Psalmist and
Isaiah and the New Testament,[8] have served to exemplify
the vain dust of the sin and the 'goodlinesse' and 'glory' of
living flesh as well as that flesh's final dissolution. The
function of proud flesh and proud monument is the same:
to hold 'the dust That measures all our time,' whether it is
the figurative dust of our vain goodliness and glory and
sinful wills or the actual dust of our bodies. Dust is the true
measure of 'all our time' (not our eternity): the vanity and
endurance of our lives and of our ashes provide the sole
significances to the flesh and the monument. Finally, the
flesh and the monuments, the containers, 'shall Be crumbled
into dust,' both symbolic of and undifferentiable from the

dust contained. The closing address directs the flesh's attention to the 'ashes' rather than to the monuments:

> Mark here below
> How tame these ashes are, how free from lust,
> That thou mayst fit thy self against thy fall.

The flesh can escape neither its measuring content nor its final goal. The knowledge it has gained may, however, serve as bridle to 'tame' its lust. The flesh may 'fit' itself 'against' its 'fall' in that, in preparation for its known dissolution, it may oppose its 'fall' into pride and lust.[9]

Such an analysis indicates the manner in which Herbert explained the complex meanings of the hieroglyph, but it does not explain 'Church-monuments.' The movement of the words and the lines, of the clauses and the sentences, conveys even without analysis a 'meaning' which makes us recognize the inadequacy of any such prose summary. Yvor Winters has called 'Church-monuments' 'the greatest poem by George Herbert': 'George Herbert's *Church Monuments*, perhaps the most polished and urbane poem of the Metaphysical School and one of the half dozen most profound, is written in an iambic pentameter line so carefully modulated, and with its rhymes so carefully concealed at different and unexpected points in the syntax, that the poem suggests something of the quiet plainness of excellent prose without losing the organization and variety of verse.'[10] The effect which Winters praised is achieved largely through the extraordinary use of enjambment and the looseness of the syntax. Only three lines of the poem come to a full stop, and nine of the twenty-four lines are followed by no punctuation. Many of the semi-cadences indicated by the punctuation, moreover, prove illusory: the syntax demands no pause, and the commas serve as fairly arbitrary directions for a slight voice rest, obscuring rather than clarifying the simple 'prose' meaning. Winters seems to praise 'Church-monuments' for practices which are found in no other poem in *The Temple*. Herbert characteristically considered his stanzas as inviolable architectural units. Each usually contained a complete thought, representing one unit in the logic of the 'argument,' and the great majority of his stanzas end with full stops.[11] In the form in which it was printed in 1633 'Church-monuments' provides the only example of complete enjambment between stanzas in *The Temple*, and two of the three examples of stanzas in which the final points are commas.[12] When Herbert departs so dramatically from his usual consistent practice, it is advisable to look for the reason. It cannot be found, I believe, in an intent to suggest 'something of the quiet plainness of excellent prose without losing the organization and variety of verse.' These straggling sentences fulfil the criteria for excellence by neither Ciceronian nor Senecan nor Baconian standards of prose. They possess neither the admired periodicity, nor trenchant point, nor ordinary clarity. The series of clauses and participial phrases, each relating to a word in some preceding clause or phrase, threaten to dissolve the sentence structure. The repetitions of 'that' and 'which' give the effect of unplanned prose, a prose which seems to function more by association than by logic.

The poem is a meditation upon a *memento mori*, the hieroglyph of the monuments. One reason for the slowness of the movement and the 'concealed' rhymes might be that the tone of the meditation was intended to correspond to the seriousness of its object. The most important clue, however, is in the manuscripts: in neither the Williams nor the Bodleian MSS. is the poem divided into stanzas at all. As F. E. Hutchinson remarked, 'the editor of *1633* recognized that the rhyme-scheme implies a six-line stanza,'[13] and subsequent editors followed the original edition and printed the poem in stanzas. But the manuscript arrangement was not the result of accident or carelessness. In the Williams MS., which Herbert corrected, the non-stanzaic form is emphasized by the indentation of line 17 to indicate a new paragraph.[14] The fact that Herbert established a six-line stanzaic rhyme scheme but did not create stanzas, either formally or typographically, is a minor but a convincing evidence that he intended the poem itself to *be* a *memento mori*, to function formally as a hieroglyph. The dissolution of the body and the monuments is paralleled by the dissolution of the sentences and the stanzas.

The movement and sound of the poem suggest the 'falls' of the flesh and the monuments and the dust in the glass. The fall is not precipitous; it is as slow as the gradual fall of the monuments, as the crumbling of the glass, as the descent of the flesh from Adam into dust. Every cadence is a dying fall. Even the question of stanza 3 contains three commas and ends with the descriptive clause, 'which now they have in trust,' carrying no interrogation. Part of the effect is achieved by obvious 'prose' means. 'Dust' re-echoes seven times in the poem, and the crucial words and phrases describe or suggest the central subject: 'intombe'; 'blast of deaths incessant motion'; 'dissolution'; 'earth with earth'; 'bow, and kneel, and fall down flat'; 'descent'; 'measures'; 'crumbled';[15] 'ashes'; 'fall.' Herbert has also used every means to slow the movement of the neutral words. With the clusters of consonants, it is impossible to read the poem rapidly.[16] The related rhymes, with their internal echoes and repetitions, both give phonetic continuity to the poem and suggest the process of dissolution: 'devotion' and 'motion' are mocked by 'exhalation' and 'dissolution'; 'betimes' and 'crimes' modulate to 'lines' and 'signes' as do 'learn' and 'discern' to 'birth' and 'earth.' 'Trust' and 'lust' are echoed incessantly by 'dust,' and, internally, by 'blast,' and 'last.' Continual internal repetition deprives the end-rhymes of any chime of finality: 'blast-last,' 'earth with earth,' 'bow-now,' 'they-pray,' 'that-that,' 'which-which' disguise and almost dissolve the iambic pentameter line. Three of the six sentences in the poem take up five and a half lines each, but, straggling as they are, each is exhausted before it reaches what should be the end of the stanza. Although the sentences are hardly independent (the many pronominal forms create a complex of interdependent meanings), the expiration of each sentence marks a break which requires a new beginning: after the opening of the poem, each new sentence begins with a long syllable which usually causes a break in the iambic rhythm. The sentences sift down through the rhyme-scheme skeleton of the stanzas like the sand through the glass; and the glass itself has already begun to crumble.

'Church-monuments' differs in kind as well as degree from such poems as 'The Church-floore' and 'The Bunch of Grapes.' The natural or religious hieroglyph was an eminently pleasant and profitable subject for a poem, and it could be used either as the object which the poem explained or as the image which explained the poem. Yet Herbert seems to have believed that it was more pleasant and profitable to make the poem itself a hieroglyph. To construct the poem so that its form imaged the subject was to reinforce the message for those who could 'spell'; for the others it would not distract from the statement—and if they read and meditated long enough, surely they would discover the mirroring of the meanings within the form of the poem!

There were fewer readers who could not 'spell' in Herbert's day than in ours. The attempt to make formal structure an integral part of the meaning of a poem assumed a general consciousness of traditional formal conventions. The disturbances of the rhyme schemes in 'Grief' and 'Home,' for example, depend for their effects on the reader's firm expectation of a conventional pattern. Such an expectation could be assumed in readers accustomed to Renaissance English poetry, whether the poetry of the Court or the hymns of the Church or the doggerel of the broadsides. In his hieroglyphs Herbert never attempted to abandon rational control for an 'identity' with a natural object: the poems always embody or assume a firm pattern of logic, rhyme, and rhythm. The formal organization of the subject was imitated by the formal organization of the poem.

The poems in which Herbert's 'imitations' are obvious are those which are likely to draw the fire of strict advocates either of that art which conceals art or of that upwelling inspiration which is oblivious of form. But Herbert often intended the form of a poem to be obvious. The opening

stanzas of 'Deniall,' for example, picture the disorder which
results when the individual feels that God denies his
requests:

> When my devotions could not pierce
> Thy silent eares;
> Then was my heart broken, as was my verse:
> My breast was full of fears
> And disorder:

> My bent thoughts, like a brittle bow,
> Did flie asunder:
> Each took his way; some would to pleasures go,
> Some to the warres and thunder
> Of alarms.

The final stanza, with its establishment of the normal
pattern of cadence and rhyme, is the symbol of reconstructed
order, of the manner in which men (and the poem) function
when God grants the request:

> O cheer and tune my heartlesse breast,
> Deferre no time;
> That so thy favours granting my request,
> They and my minde may chime,
> And mend my ryme.

The stanza which had been the symbol of the flying asunder
of a 'brittle bow' has become a symbol for the achievement
of order. The form of the final prayer indicates that its
request has already been answered. The individual and the
poem have moved from fear through open rebellion and
'unstrung' discontent. 'Deniall' is overcome through renewal of prayer: the ordered prayer provides the evidence.

Of Herbert's many other formal hieroglyphs ('Sinnes
round,' 'A Wreath,' 'Trinitie Sunday,' etc.) 'Aaron' is one
of the most effective.

> Holinesse on the head,
> Light and perfections on the breast,
> Harmonious bells below, raising the dead
> To leade them unto life and rest:
> Thus are true Aarons drest.

136

Profanenesse in my head,
Defects and darknesse in my breast,
A noise of passions ringing me for dead
Unto a place where is no rest:
Poore priest thus am I drest.

Onely another head
I have, another heart and breast,
Another musick, making live not dead,
Without whom I could have no rest:
In him I am well drest.

Christ is my onely head,
My alone onely heart and breast,
My onely musick, striking me ev'n dead;
That to the old man I may rest,
And be in him new drest.

So holy in my head,
Perfect and light in my deare breast,
My doctrine tun'd by Christ, (who is not dead,
But lives in me while I do rest)
Come people; Aaron's drest.

Herbert may have chosen the five stanzas of five lines each partially because of the five letters in 'Aaron'; if so, the technical problem may have been of importance to the poet, but it does not matter particularly to the reader. Nor does it seem that Herbert primarily intended that each stanza should 'suggest metrically the swelling and dying sound of a bell':[17] the 'bells' and the 'musick' occur only in the third line of each stanza, and the rhymes are hardly bell-like. The central meaning of those identical rhymes and those subtly transformed stanzas[18] is clearly stated in the poem. The profaneness in man's head, the defects and darkness in his heart, the cacophonous passions which destroy him and lead him to a hell of 'repining restlessnesse'[19] *can* be transformed through the imputed righteousness of Christ into the ideal symbolized by Aaron's ceremonial garments.[20] The 'clay'[21] (like the stanzas) retains its outward form, but inwardly all is changed in the divine consumption of the self. As the 'Priest for euer after the order of Melchisedec' 'dresses' the new Aaron with the inward reality for which the first Aaron's garments were but the hieroglyphs, the poem moves with a ritualistic gravity from opposition to a climatic synthesis.

When we have understood Herbert's use of form in these poems, or, say, his extraordinarily formal picture of anarchy in 'The Collar' and his divine numerology in 'Trinitie Sunday' we may see the poems which derive from the Elizabethan acrostics and anagrams in a different light. Aside from the courtiers to whom any exercise in ingenuity was welcome, this type of poem had its serious religious adherents in the seventeenth century. If biblical exegesis demanded the solution of anagrams,[22] and if the good man was truly 'willing to spiritualize everything,' the composition of such poetry was a logical result. With due appreciation of the wit involved, the good man was likely to treat such poetry seriously. The seriousness depended on a religious subject and on the assumption that the poet would draw 'true' meanings from his word-play. Herbert abided by the rules, and he never repeated the various forms. In *The Temple* there is one true anagram (labelled as such), one echo poem, one 'hidden acrostic,' one poem based on the double interpretation of initials, one based on a syllabic pun, and 'Paradise,' which can only be described as a 'pruning poem.' For his unique example of each type, Herbert usually chose that Christian subject which was most clearly illuminated by the device.

In some of these poems typography becomes a formal element. In 'Paradise,' for example, the second and third rhymes of each stanza are formed by 'paring' off the first consonant of the preceding rhyme:

> I blesse thee, Lord, because I GROW
> Among thy trees, which in a ROW
> To thee both fruit and order OW.
>
> What open force, or hidden CHARM
> Can blast my fruit, or bring me HARM,
> While the inclosure is thine ARM?

The device is artificial in the extreme, and it requires some wrenching of orthography. As an abstract form it is hardly satisfactory. But Herbert never used forms abstractly, and we are left in no doubt as to the reason for the form of this particular poem:

Inclose me still for fear I START.
Be to me rather sharp and TART,
Then let me want thy hand & ART.

When thou dost greater judgements SPARE,
And with thy knife but prune and PARE,
Ev'n fruitfull trees more fruitfull ARE.

Such sharpnes shows the sweetest FREND:
Such cuttings rather heal then REND:
And such beginnings touch their END.

Except for the third stanza, the poem survives brilliantly the test of oral reading: its success does not depend upon the construction of the rhymes. Yet the 'pruned' rhymes do compel the reader to 'see' what the poem is saying concerning the positive function of suffering. The meaning is traditional, of course. The fate of the 'unprofitable vineyard' was destruction rather than pruning. By changing the image from the vine to the English orchard, Herbert related the 'pruning' more immediately to his readers' experience, but the point is the same: the surgical knife is necessary for the order which produces fruit. The final line of the poem is 'naturally' ambiguous. For the religious man of the seventeenth century 'end' nearly always implied purpose as well as finality. 'And such beginnings touch their END' means that God's pruning causes the fruits of righteousness which are the end of man's creation. It also implies that the cutting away of the fruitless branches images the final 'cutting away' of the body and the release of the soul at death.

In 'The Altar' and 'Easter-wings' Herbert extended the principle of the hieroglyph to a third level. If the natural or religious hieroglyph was valuable as content (used either as the object which the poem explained or as the image which crystallized the meaning of the poem), and if the poem could be constructed as a formal hieroglyph which mirrored the structural relationships between the natural hieroglyph, the poem, and the individual's life, it was but a further step to make the poem a visual hieroglyph, to create it in a shape which formed an immediately apparent image relevant both to content and structure.

Neither the conception of the pattern poem nor the two shapes which Herbert used were at all novel.[23] The Greek Anthology had included six pattern poems (including a pair of wings and two altars), and those patterns were widely imitated in the sixteenth century. Although Thomas Nashe, Gabriel Harvey, and Ben Jonson denounced such poems, the practice flourished.[24] After the appearance of *The Temple* patterns were published in profusion. Wither, Quarles,[25] Benlowes, Joseph Beaumont, Herrick, Christopher Harvey, and Traherne were among the practitioners. Both before and after 1633 the literary quality of most of these poems was notoriously low. The poets seemed usually to consider the shapes as a superficial or frivolous attraction for the reader. As the Renaissance poets and critics never tired of reiterating, pleasure *could* be made a bait for profit, but a superficial conception of the 'bait' often resulted in very bad poems. Many of the patterns depended largely on wrenched typography, and it was a common practice to compose a poem in ordinary couplets, then chop the lines to fit the pattern.

Herbert's poems are another matter. From his knowledge of both the Greek originals and English practice,[26] Herbert chose the two patterns which could be most clearly related to the purposes of his Christian poetry. His patterns are visual hieroglyphs. The interpretation of them as naïve representations of 'real' objects has resulted in the citation of 'The Altar' as additional proof of Herbert's extreme Anglo-Catholicism. An examination of the poem in the light

of its tradition and Herbert's formal practice shows it to be
artistically complex and religiously 'low.'

> A broken A L T A R, Lord, thy servant reares,
> Made of a heart, and cemented with teares:
> Whose parts are as thy hand did frame;
> No workmans tool hath touch'd the same.
> A H E A R T alone
> Is   such   a   stone,
> As   nothing   but
> Thy pow'r doth cut.
> Wherefore each part
> Of my hard heart
> Meets in this frame,
> To praise thy Name:
> That, if I chance to hold my peace,
> These stones to praise thee may not cease.
> O let thy blessed[27] S A C R I F I C E be mine,
> And sanctifie this A L T A R to be thine.

When one reads 'The Altar' it is well to remember that
the word 'altar' was not applied to the Communion Table
in the Book of Common Prayer, and that the canons of
Herbert's time directed that the Table should be made of
wood rather than stone. Throughout his English writings
Herbert always used 'altar' and 'sacrifice' according to the
'orthodox' Protestant tradition of his time: 'altar' is never
applied to the Communion Table nor is the Holy Communion ever called a 'sacrifice.'[28] Yet Herbert and his contemporaries cherished the conception of the altar and the
sacrifice. The Mosaic sacrifices were considered types of the
one true Sacrifice, in which Christ had shed blood for the
remission of sins once for all time. To man were left the
'sacrifices' of praise, good works, and 'communication'
(Heb. xiii. 15-16). The Hebrew altar which was built of
unhewn stones was a type of the heart of man, hewn not by
man's efforts but by God alone. The engraving on those
stones with which 'all the words of this Law' were written
'very plainely' (Deut. xxvii. 8) was a type of the 'Epistle of
Christ,' the message of salvation engraved on the Christian

heart (2 Cor. iii. 3). Herbert's conceptions that the broken and purged heart is the proper basis for the sacrifice of praise and that even stones may participate in and continue that praise were firmly biblical. In his psalm of repentance (Ps. li.) David had stated that the true sacrifices of God are 'a broken and a contrite heart'; Christ had promised that 'the stones' would cry out to testify to Him (Luke xix. 40); and Paul had stated that 'Ye also as liuely stones, are built vp a spirituall house . . . to offer vp spirituall sacrifice' (1 Pet. ii. 5).

There is hardly a phrase in 'The Altar' which does not derive from a specific biblical passage. Yet the effect of the poem is simple and fresh. In an important sense this, the first poem within 'The Church' (the central section of *The Temple*), *is* the altar upon which the following poems (Herbert's 'sacrifice of praise') are offered, and it is an explanation of the reason for their composition. God has commanded a continual sacrifice of praise and thanksgiving made from the broken and contrite heart. The condition of mortality as well as the inconstancy of the human heart requires that such a sacrifice be one of those works which 'doe follow them' even when they 'rest from their labours.' For the craftsman and poet, construction of a work of art resulted in that continual sacrifice and introduced the concept of the altar: the poem is a construction upon which others may offer their sacrifices; it is a 'speaking' altar which continually offers up its own sacrifice of praise. The shape of Herbert's poem was intended to hieroglyph the relevance of the old altar to the new Christian altar within the heart. It was fittingly, therefore, a modification of the traditional shape of a classic altar rather than of what Herbert knew as the Communion Table.[29] F. E. Hutchinson's description of the changes in the printing of the poem furnishes a miniature history of progressive misinterpretation.[30] From 1634 to 1667 the shape was outlined merely to draw the reader's attention to its significance. The change in religious temper and vocabulary by 1674 was indicated by 'an engraving of a full-length Christian altar under a classical canopy, with the poem set under the canopy': the assumption was that Herbert had attempted to image a 'Christian altar.' The final liturgical representation of the poem did not, however, occur until the nineteenth century: 'In 1809 there is Gothic panelling and canopy-work behind a modest altar with fringed cloth, fair linen cloth, and the sacred vessels.' Herbert's attempt to use the shape of a classical altar as a hieroglyph of his beliefs concerning the relationships between the heart, the work of art, and the praise of God failed to communicate its meaning to a number of generations. While not one of Herbert's greatest poems, 'The Altar' within its context in *The Temple* is still an effective poem if we take the pains to understand it.

'Easter-wings' has been subject to fewer misinterpretations than 'The Altar.' In the last twenty years particularly it has generally been considered a good poem, although there has been little agreement as to the meaning and effectiveness of its pattern. It is the final poem in the group concerning Holy Week, and to read it within its sequence helps to explain some of the difficulties for the modern reader.

Lord, who createdst man in wealth and store,
Though foolishly he lost the same,
Decaying more and more,
Till he became
Most poore:
With thee
O let me rise
As larks, harmoniously,
And sing this day thy victories:
Then shall the fall further the flight in me.

My tender age in sorrow did beginne:
And still with sicknesses and shame
Thou didst so punish sinne,
That I became
Most thinne.
With thee
Let me combine
And feel this day thy victorie:
For, if I imp my wing on thine,
Affliction shall advance the flight in me.

The pattern is successful not merely because we 'see' the wings, but because we see how they are made: the process of impoverishment and enrichment, of 'thinning' and expansion which makes 'flight' possible. By that perception and by the rhythmical falling and rising which the shaped lines help to form, we are led to respond fully to the active image and to the poem. The first stanza is a celebration of the *felix culpa*. Man was created in 'wealth and store,' with the capacity for sinlessness. Through Adam's sin Paradise was lost, yet from one point of view the loss was not unhappy: 'where sinne abounded, grace did much more abound' (Rom. v. 20). If man 'rises' in celebration of Christ's victories, the fall will indeed further his flight to God. The second stanza concerns the reduction of the individual by God's punishment for sins. Again, if we 'combine' with Christ 'And feel this day thy victorie,' affliction can prove an advance to flight, for it is through such affliction that souls are led to 'waite vpon the Lord' and 'renew their strength,' and the promise is specific: 'they shall mount vp with wings as Eagles, they shal runne and not be weary, and they shall walke, and not faint' (Isa. xl. 31). The New Testament had related the death and resurrection of the spirit and the body to the germinal cycle of nature, and the favourite English pun on 'son-sun' seemed to acquire a supernatural sanction from Malachi iv. 2: 'But vnto you that feare my Name, shall the Sunne of righteousnesse arise with healing in his wings.' The 'decaying' of the first stanza of Herbert's poem implies the fruitful image of the grain, and the conclusion of that stanza broadens to include the rise of the 'Sun,' the 'harmonious' ascent both of the flight and the song of the larks.[31] The triumphant dichotomies are implied throughout the poem: sickness and health, decay and growth, poverty and wealth, foolishness and wisdom, punishment and reward, defeat and victory, the fall and rise of song and wings and spirit, sin and righteousness, burial and resurrection, death and life. These states are not in polar opposition. The poem and its pattern constantly insist that for man only through the fall is the flight possible; that the victory, resurrection, whether in this life or the next, can come only through the death of the old Adam.

The pattern poem is a dangerous form, and its successful practitioners before and after Herbert were few. The conception behind it, however, is neither so naïve nor so dated as some critics have assumed: writing with intentions differing greatly from Herbert's, E. E. Cummings and Dylan Thomas have created successful contemporary pattern poems.[32] For Herbert such poetry was a natural extension of his concern with the hieroglyph. Most of the other poets of his time, whether followers of Spenser, Jonson, or Donne, characteristically used hieroglyphs as the basis for their imagery in either short or extended passages. Herbert's distinction lies in his successful development of the conceptions that the entire poem could be organized around a hieroglyph and that the poem itself could be constructed as a formal hieroglyph.

The hieroglyph represented to Herbert a fusion of the spiritual and material, of the rational and sensuous, in the essential terms of formal relationships. It may have been that his delight in the power and beauty of the hieroglyphic symbol helped to keep his poems from becoming only rational exercises or pious teachings. Yet reason and piety were central, for to Herbert the hieroglyph did not exist as a total mystery or as isolated beauty, but as a beauty and mystery which were decipherable and related to all creation. The message was precise and clear even if complex and subtle. A differing conception of the religious hieroglyph led Crashaw to ecstatic adoration and worship. For Herbert, however, celebration could never be divorced from examination. The hieroglyphs, whether of God's or of man's creation, were to be 'read' rather than adored, and they sent the reader back to God. The chief tool for such reading was the logical use of man's reason.

It was, moreover, delightful as well as edifying for the

poet to imitate God in the construction of hieroglyphs. As Sir Philip Sidney had remarked long before, the way in which God had worked in the creation of nature was not so mysterious as marvellous; man could observe and could imitate:

Neither let it be deemed too saucy a comparison, to balance the highest point of man's wit with the efficacy of nature; but rather give right honour to the heavenly Maker of that maker, who having made man to his own likeness, set him beyond and over all the works of that second nature; which in nothing he showeth so much as in poetry; when, with the force of a divine breath, he bringeth things forth surpassing her doings, with no small arguments to the incredulous of that first accursed fall of Adam; since our erected wit maketh us know what perfection is, and yet our infected will keepeth us from reaching unto it.[33]

CHAPTER VII

Verse and Speech

MOST poets care as much about verse as about patterns of imagery or concepts of form, but a poet who desired to create an individual form for every poem was challenged to be an extraordinary metrical innovator. George Herbert was the most consistent and interesting experimenter in the English lyric between Sidney and Yeats.

In the most detailed study of Herbert's metrics yet made,[1] Albert McHarg Hayes gave the name of 'counterpoint' to one of Herbert's characteristic devices, and claimed that Herbert was the first poet who recognized and experimented with its potentialities: 'and this is precisely Herbert's experiment—to construct the pattern of his line lengths independently of the pattern of his rimes.'[2] The majority of English lyrics both before and after Herbert were written either in stanzas in which the lines were of equal length or in which the pattern of rhymes coincided with the pattern of line lengths: if a quatrain was constructed with alternate lines of eight and ten syllables, for example, the usual rhyme scheme would be *a b a b*. Occasionally in longer stanzas one pair of rhyming lines would differ in length, but the prevailing pattern still emphasized the recurrence of the rhymes at regular rhythmical intervals. Approximately half of Herbert's poems are written in these conventional patterns, but the other half are not at all conventional. About one-quarter of the poems in *The Temple* are either in patterns in which no lines of the same length rhyme (20) or in which, in an elaborate rhyme scheme, only one pair of lines of the same length rhyme (12).[3]

'Counterpoint' is a useful term, but the musical analogy cannot be pushed very far.[4] Although it is true that no poet before Herbert wrote so many 'contrapuntal' poems, there were a number of Elizabethan and early seventeenth-century examples. As one would expect, Sidney, the greatest of the Elizabethan experimenters in the lyric and one of the few poets whom Herbert obviously echoed, anticipated Herbert's experiments.[5] *The Psalmes of David*, begun by Sidney and completed by the Countess of Pembroke, is almost a handbook of poetic experimentation.[6] Among the various poems in classical and traditional metres, there are fourteen 'contrapuntal' or 'approximately contrapuntal' poems.[7] Their rhythms often resemble Herbert's:

> Lord, while that thy rage doth bide,
> > Do not chide:
> Nor in anger chastise me,
> For thy shafts have peirc'd me sore,
> > And yet more
> Still thy handes upon me be.[8]

> O Lord, my praying heare:
> Lord, lett my cry come to thine eare,
> > Hide not thy face away,
> But haste, and aunswer me,
> > In this my most, most, miserable day,
> Wherein I pray and cry to thee.[9]

It seems likely that Herbert knew Sidney's and Pembroke's *Psalmes*,[10] but one does not need to assume such knowledge to account for Herbert's practice. 'Counterpoint' was, after all, a fairly natural experiment for a poet concerned with metrics to make—particularly for a poet who desired to achieve an individual music for almost every poem. If the line lengths were varied independently of the rhyme schemes, the number of possible stanza forms increased almost infinitely. Herbert used twenty-nine different patterns with the simple *a b a b* rhyme scheme.[11]

I have been unable to discover any device which Herbert used for one specific effect. In a poem such as 'The Pilgrimage,' one might say that Herbert used 'counterpoint' from a desire 'to focus attention upon sense rather than sound'[12]—if one were sure he could firmly separate the two:

> That led me to the wilde of Passion, which
> Some call the wold;
> A wasted place, but sometimes rich.
> Here I was robb'd of all my gold,
> Save one good Angell, which a friend had ti'd
> Close to my side.

But on the other hand, some of Herbert's most conversational poems, poems in which the rhymes are most cunningly hidden, are in the strict form of the sonnet. And Herbert was capable of using 'counterpoint' to *increase* the musical effect, to focus attention upon sound even more insistently than conventional schemes would allow:

> *Chor*. Praised be the God of love,
> *Men*. Here below,
> *Angels*. And here above:
> *Chor*. Who hath dealt his mercies so,
> *Angels*. To his friend,
> *Men*. And to his foe.   ('Antiphon [II].')[13]

'Complaining' differs completely from 'Antiphon (II)' in tone, but again the 'counterpoint' emphasizes rather than subordinates the pattern of sound:

> Do not beguile my heart,
> Because thou art
> My power and wisdome. Put me not to shame,
> Because I am
> Thy clay that weeps, thy dust that calls.[14]

Generalizations crumble before the practice of a particularist such as Herbert. The only justifiable generalization is that every poem required a new beginning, a new form, a new rhythm.

One of Herbert's primary (and most delightful) methods of gaining individuality for his poems was his creation of 'speech' by means of his subtle handling of rhythm, sound, and diction. The fictional speakers of his poems have many voices. If we hear them at all well, we can no longer share the popular contemporary beliefs that 'dramatic irony' is the most profitable tone for all poems, nor that (strange reversal of Dryden!) 'wit' *must* 'shine Thro' the harsh cadence of a rugged line.' For Herbert valued the 'rugged line' as one device among many to achieve specific aims. He conceived and created many more varieties of speech rhythms than simply those suitable to anger, impatience, frustration, or hasty passion.

The rhythms of 'The Church Militant,' for example, are as 'natural' as those of 'The Collar,' but they belong to a different speaker. 'The Church Militant' is a witty and prophetic narrative of the westward course of both the Church and Sin. In a poem of such length there must be passages of contrasting tempo and intensity, but the predominant tone is that of bantering speech. Herbert sometimes used the end-stopped couplet for neo-classical point: 'For gold and grace did never yet agree: Religion alwaies sides with povertie' (ll. 251-252) was written before the Augustan age. He also occasionally overrode the couplets for a freer, almost indolent effect of equal wit:

> Sinne being not able to extirpate quite
> The Churches here, bravely resolv'd one night
> To be a Church-man too, and wear a Mitre:
> The old debauched ruffian would turn writer.
> I saw him in his studie, where he sate
> Busie in controversies sprung of late.
> A gown and pen became him wondrous well:
> His grave aspect had more of heav'n then hell:
> Onely there was a handsome picture by
> To which he lent a corner of his eye.   (ll. 161-170.)

If we know only the more frequently anthologized poems from *The Temple*, the tone and rhythm of such a passage are not what we expect from Herbert. Neither do the sixty-three incantatory stanzas of 'The Sacrifice,' in which Christ Himself is the speaker, fulfil our preconceptions:

But now I die; now all is finished.
My wo, mans weal: and now I bow my head.
Onely let others say, when I am dead,
> Never was grief like mine.
>> (ll. 249-252.)

'The Church Militant' and 'The Sacrifice' are typical
only of Herbert's variety. Even those poems in which he
directly and dramatically addresses God differ radically as
they are conceived as laments or praises, rebellions or sub-
missions, demands or requests, prayers or conversations.
'The Pearl. Matth. 13. 45' is addressed to God, but the
speaker is a courtier who hardly acknowledges the object of
his address for the first three stanzas. In them he proclaims
his knowledge of 'the wayes' of Learning, Honour, and
Pleasure, the courtly trinity, with his rejection implied only
in the refrain line, 'Yet I love thee.' The speech is witty,
proving the knowledge, and the accents are proper to such
speech. Certain effects resemble Donne's:

I know the wayes of Learning; both the head
And pipes that feed the presse, and make it runne;
What reason hath from nature borrowed,
Or of it self, like a good huswife, spunne
In laws and policie; what the starres conspire,
What willing nature speaks, what forc'd by fire;
Both th' old discoveries, and the new-found seas,
The stock and surplus, cause and historie:
All these stand open, or I have the keyes:
> Yet I love thee.

But after the descriptions of the speaker's knowledge, the
poem abandons courtly boasting for grave address. The
heightened speech of the conclusion finally establishes the
iambic norm:

Yet through these labyrinths, not my groveling wit,
But thy silk twist let down from heav'n to me,
Did both conduct and teach me, how by it
> To climbe to thee.

151

The resolution of the last two lines is all the more conclusive after the daring rhythmical evocation of the labyrinths.[15]

In Herbert's poems subject and image do not determine speech; they are transformed by it. The rose represents the false and 'biting' beauty of worldly pleasure in 'The Rose'; in 'Vertue' it is the image of the good but transient beauty of the world; in 'Life' it is the symbol for the Christian life,

> Fit, while ye liv'd, for smell or ornament,
> > And after death for cures.

Speech and rhythm vary accordingly. Similarly, the thought of death can be an occasion for 'Mortification,' or, as in the poem 'Death,' it can be gaily mocked in an immediate and cavalier version of the Christian's victory: 'O death, where is thy sting?'

'Mortification' is a meditation upon 'How soon doth man decay!' and its final lines are a prayer:

> How soon doth man decay!
> When clothes are taken from a chest of sweets
> > To swaddle infants, whose young breath
> > > Scarce knows the way;
> > These clouts are little winding sheets,
> Which do consigne and send them unto death.

> When boyes go first to bed,
> They step into their voluntarie graves,
> > Sleep bindes them fast; onely their breath
> > > Makes them not dead:
> > Successive nights, like rolling waves,
> Convey them quickly, who are bound for death.

> When youth is frank and free,
> And calls for musick, while his veins do swell,
> > All day exchanging mirth and breath
> > > In companie;
> > That musick summons to the knell,
> Which shall befriend him at the houre of death.

When man grows staid and wise,
Getting a house and home, where he may move
Within the circle of his breath,
Schooling his eyes;
That dumbe inclosure maketh love
Unto the coffin, that attends his death.

When age grows low and weak,
Marking his grave, and thawing ev'ry yeare,
Till all do melt, and drown his breath
When he would speak;
A chair or litter shows the biere,
Which shall convey him to the house of death.

Man, ere he is aware,
Hath put together a solemnitie,
And drest his herse, while he has breath
As yet to spare:
Yet Lord, instruct us so to die,
That all these dyings may be life in death.

A rhythm of dramatic direct address is the last thing desired for this poem; rather, the elaborately 'counterpointed' stanzas slowly repeat the ritual of mortification. The *c* rhymes are represented by 'breath' and 'death' throughout the poem, and the sounds of those two words, repeated at the end of every third line, reinforce their meanings: they seem to imitate the slow inhalation and exhalation of man, continually foreshadowing his own death. Yet too great an accentuation of those rhymes would run the risk of blunting the meaning and would cause the stanzas to fall apart; the occurrences of 'breath,' therefore, are blurred rhythmically and logically so as to break the chime. The pattern of sound is enormously complex and full analysis would be tedious. The use of related sounds at the same point within each stanza, however, accentuates the repetitive aspect of each age. The final lines of the first five stanzas (concerning the five ages of man), for example, end with 'death' and also contain the following words:

1	consign	send	
2	Convey		bound
3		befriend	houre
4	coffin	attends	
5	convey		house

In addition, 'them,' 'him,' or 'his' always occurs in these lines, following the elaborate pattern of *s*'s in the fifth lines. Herbert's schematic care for sound does not obtrude itself upon our consciousness as a 'scheme,' but at every moment the sounds which we hear contribute to the meaning of the poem.[16]

The language of 'Mortification' does not imitate 'speech' at all, but rather an inward musing and prayer. The speaker of 'Death,' however, addresses his defeated enemy directly in a most irreverent fashion:

> Death, thou wast once an uncouth hideous thing,
>> Nothing but bones,
>> The sad effect of sadder grones:
> Thy mouth was open, but thou couldst not sing.

The poem contrasts the appearances of Death when viewed 'on this side of thee' and when viewed from the vantage point of the Judgment:

> For we do now behold thee gay and clad,
>> As at dooms-day;
>> When souls shall wear their new array,
> And all thy bones with beautie shall be clad.

If we feel the 'metaphysical shudder' or the 'traditional charnel-house atmosphere' it is from our own preconceptions, not from the poem. The speech moves firmly from witty bantering, through almost affectionate condescension, to an expression of final indifference.

In its imitation of the rhetorically impatient speech of direct address, the opening of 'Conscience' seems most like a poem of Donne's:

Peace pratler, do not lowre:
Not a fair look, but thou dost call it foul:
Not a sweet dish, but thou dost call it sowre:
Musick to thee doth howl.
By listning to thy chatting fears
I have both lost mine eyes and eares.

The poem is addressed to no 'unruly Sunne,' but to that over-nice conscience (literarily associated with the Puritans, but a danger to most of the devout) which allows for no joy in the Christian life. In the first stanza, the liberal trochees and spondees dislocate the iambic rhythm in a manner similar to Donne's. The intricate pattern of sound, however, concerns much more than speech rhythms. The alliterations and repetitions of the first three lines first strike one's ear, but that is only the beginning. 'Thou,' 'thee,' and 'thy' occur in the second or third foot of lines 2 through 5. 'Listning' and 'lost' relate lines 5 and 6 by both meaning and alliteration. The long *i*'s cluster in the last two lines: 'By,' 'thy,' 'I,' 'mine,' 'eyes.' The *ow*'s of both the *a* and *b* rhymes are echoed insistently by 'thou.' Each pair of rhymes is related to another pair: 'lowre' and 'sowre' are intermingled with the assonant 'foul' and 'howl' and followed by the false rhymes of 'fears' and 'eares.'[17] In conjunction with their meanings in the first stanza, 'lowre,' 'foul,' 'sowre,' and 'howl' have an obvious onomatopoetic function which the fourth line makes unmistakable: 'Musick to thee doth howl.' Those lines give a clue to a major aspect of Herbert's practice. Although the rhythms of speech were essential for many of his aims, they were not the source of his concern for pattern and euphony. 'Howling' and 'chatting,' like dissonance and broken rhythms, were necessary for specific effects, but they were only devices in a musical pattern. The poetry of Herbert is that of a man to whom music was second only to poetry—when he made the separation at all.

CHAPTER VIII

Music

IN the *Life* Izaak Walton described in detail Herbert's devotion to music. During Herbert's years at Cambridge, 'all, or the greatest diversion from his Study, was the practice of Musick, in which he became a great Master; and of which, he would say, "That it did relieve his drooping spirits, compose his distracted thoughts, and raised his weary soul so far above Earth, that it gave him an earnest of the joys of Heaven, before he possest them."'[1] Later, at Bemerton,

> His chiefest recreation was Musick, in which heavenly Art he was a most excellent Master, and did himself compose many *divine Hymns* and *Anthems*, which he set and sung to his *Lute* or *Viol*; and, though he was a lover of retiredness, yet his love to *Musick* was such, that he went usually twice every week on certain appointed days, to the *Cathedral Church* in *Salisbury*; and at his return would say, *That his time spent in Prayer, and Cathedral Musick, elevated his Soul, and was his Heaven upon Earth*: But before his return thence to *Bemerton*, he would usually sing and play his part, at an appointed private Musick-meeting; and, to justifie this practice, he would often say, *Religion does not banish mirth, but only moderates, and sets rules to it.*[2]

It is pleasant to know that Herbert occasionally missed services at Bemerton in order to attend his music meetings.[3] Walton's climatic scene relates the poems in *The Temple* directly to Herbert's music:

> The *Sunday* before his death, he rose suddenly from his Bed or Couch, call'd for one of his Instruments, took it into hand, and said—

> > *My God, My God,*
> > *My Musick shall find thee,*
> > *and every string*
> > *Shall have his attribute to sing.*

And having tun'd it, he play'd and sung:

> *The Sundays of Mans life,*
> *Thredded together on times string,*
> *Make Bracelets, to adorn the Wife*
> *Of the eternal glorious King:*
> *On Sundays, Heavens dore stands ope;*
> *Blessings are plentiful and rife,*
> *More plentiful than hope.*

Thus he sung on Earth such Hymns and Anthems, as the Angels and he, and Mr *Farrer*, now sing in Heaven.[4]

Walton believed that Herbert's poems provided splendid texts for the heavenly choirs to sing. He certainly realized that many of those poems demand at least an imagined music.

About a fourth of the poems in *The Temple* concern music directly; one could surmise without Walton's comments that many of them were inspired by music and that some of them were intended to be sung. As a good churchman Herbert might have written of matins, evensong, the Holy Communion, and Christmas, Easter, and Whitsunday; but that the first three were 'the three Services in the Book of Common Prayer with which a Cathedral choir is mainly concerned,' and that the latter were three of the four great days which were most celebrated by music and for which the 'Proper Psalms' were usually set to music,[5] is relevant to the composition and understanding of Herbert's 'Mattens,' 'Even-song,' 'The H. Communion,' 'Christmas,' 'Easter,' and 'Whitsunday.' 'Whitsunday' begins with 'Listen, sweet Dove unto my song,' and the second sections of 'The H. Communion,' 'Easter,' and 'Christmas' are literally songs. Although we may associate psalm-singing at work with the Puritans, Herbert advised the Country Parson to inquire whether his parishioners were in the habit of 'singing of Psalms at their work, and on holy days,' and wished to encourage the practice.[6] Herbert's own 'The 23d Psalme' was not intended to surprise in language or rhythm, but it was intended to be sung.[7]

Some of Herbert's most memorable lines depend for their·

full effect upon the reader's understanding of musical metaphor:

> I am no link of thy great chain,
> But all my companie is a weed.
> Lord place me in thy consort; give one strain
> To my poore reed.
>
> ('Employment [I].')

> Come away,
> Help our decay.
> Man is out of order hurl'd,
> Parcel'd out to all the world.
> Lord, thy broken consort raise,
> And the musick shall be praise.   ('Dooms-day.')

> Oh take thy lute, and tune it to a strain,
> Which may with thee
> All day complain.
> There can no discord but in ceasing be.
>
> ('Ephes. 4. 30. *Grieve not the Holy Spirit*, &c.')

We can understand the pun on 'strain,' and most readers today will probably recognize the musical meaning of 'broken consort.' We may need to be reminded, however, that the vitality and interest of a musical composition depend in large part upon dissonances which are resolved before the cadence; dissonances are not truly 'discords' unless they occur at the end of a phrase or a composition. 'Ephes. 4. 30. *Grieve not the Holy Spirit*, &c.' insists that man's only true 'discord' occurs when he ceases his song to God, either of praise or of grievous complaining; tears too are a sign of life and are opposed to death, 'drie as dust.'

Occasionally, as in the third stanza of 'The Pearl,' Herbert's allusions are so much those of a familiar practitioner of early seventeenth-century music that we need a musician's aid:

> I know the wayes of Pleasure, the sweet strains,
> The lullings and the relishes of it;
> The propositions of hot bloud and brains;
> What mirth and musick mean; what love and wit

Have done these twentie hundred yeares, and more:
I know the projects of unbridled store:
My stuffe is flesh, not brasse; my senses live,
And grumble oft, that they have more in me
Than he that curbs them, being but one to five:
Yet I love thee.

Edward W. Naylor[8] has identified the musical terms in the opening lines: 'strains' were 'eight bars (or, perhaps, twelve or sixteen) of a Pavan, maybe'; '"relish" double or single,' was the technical word for an 'ornament in playing the lute or viol';[9] 'propositions' is 'a form of *Proposta*, subject, *Risposta*, answer, of a fugue or movement of fugal character'; '"Lullings" we may pass over as being too general in its character to need explanation, though it is used in a musical sense here.' Herbert chose exactly those musical terms which derive from or relate to the 'wayes of Pleasure,' and each of the words is used in both its musical and its sensuous sense.[10]

We also need the help of the musicologists to understand fully the opening stanzas of 'Easter,' with their magnificent imperatives to heart and lute and song:

Rise heart; thy Lord is risen. Sing his praise
Without delayes,
Who takes thee by the hand, that thou likewise
With him mayst rise:
That, as his death calcined thee to dust,
His life may make thee gold, and much more, just.

Awake, my lute, and struggle for thy part
With all thy art.
The crosse taught all wood to resound his name,
Who bore the same.
His stretched sinews taught all strings, what key
Is best to celebrate this most high day.

Consort both heart and lute, and twist a song
Pleasant and long:

Or, since all musick is but three parts vied
        And multiplied,
O let thy blessed Spirit bear a part,
And make up our defects with his sweet art.

We need to know, for example, that 'the choice of keys was significant because the doctrine of affections coordinated certain keys with certain affections,'[11] and that the pitch of church music was 'practically a minor third higher than it now is' while secular vocal music approximated modern pitch.[12] The higher pitch was of recognized iconological significance. The lute was made of wood and its strings were of gut (the 'sinew' which can stretch).[13] We should know that the common triad is the basis for all harmony, and it is probably not irrelevant that much of medieval music was written in triple rhythm and in three parts because of the symbolism of the Trinity. We should recognize that 'twist a song' is 'specially appropriate to polyphonic music,'[14] in which each voice 'bears' a distinct 'part.'

Music did more for Herbert's poems, however, than merely furnish them with a rich field of imagery. Since none of Herbert's settings has survived,[15] we cannot discuss the poems in relationship to specific accompaniments. But the practice of music in Herbert's time furnishes many hints for our non-musical reading of his poems. The traditions of vocal music help us to understand the rhythms, the sound patterns, the tone, and the form of many of the poems in *The Temple*.

English musical practice during the time of Herbert's maturity was not simply behind that of the continent: the old and the new existed side by side, and both were gradually changed. The styles and the genres were manifold.[16] The elaborate settings of the service which Herbert heard at Westminster and Salisbury[17] (and probably at Cambridge) were usually written in that sixteenth-century polyphony of which Byrd was master, but the anthems had begun to

include solo sections as well.[18] Perhaps more important for
Herbert was the increasing popularity of music for private
devotion, composed to non-liturgical texts.[19] This music partook of various styles, religious and secular. Like the
'chamber music,' much of it was written for voices and
instruments in a mixed ensemble, and the texts chosen were
often far from the 'sensuous,' 'simple,' and 'graceful' poems
which we sometimes consider intrinsic to the vocal music of
that time.[20] William Byrd's *Psalmes, Sonets, and Songs* (1588)
established the common practice of printing sacred compositions in the same volume with secular 'madrigals'[21] and
with airs.

John Dowland and his two most distinguished followers,
John Daniel and Thomas Campion, developed the air in
England, the secular form most relevant to Herbert's poems.
The madrigal, with its elaborately contrapuntal treatment
and its development of small phrases of the text, was almost
necessarily limited to one or two stanzas of verse. The air
was conceived stanzaically and therefore made possible the
setting of longer lyrics. The poets preferred it also because
its simpler counterpoint and instrumental accompaniment
gave a better hearing to complex verse.[22] Secular love songs
provided the most popular texts for the airs as well as the
madrigals:

> Where are my lines then? my approaches? views?
> Where are my window-songs?
> Lovers are still pretending, & ev'n wrongs
> Sharpen their Muse. ('Dulnesse.')

But songs of sacred love often followed the secular conventions, and simplicity could be a virtue both in melody and
text. Herbert's 'The Rose' seems to be conceived in the
tradition of the most popular type of air. It is a song of
courteous refusal addressed to the worldly advocate of
pleasure, and its clarity and courtly tone are essential:

> But I health, not physick choose:
> Onely though I you oppose,
> Say that fairly I refuse,
> For my answer is a rose.

Throughout the poem the rhythm is usually regular, but it is not mechanical; each line maintains its integrity without insistence. 'The Rose' moves with an extraordinarily delicate grace, equally distant from the witty conversation of 'The Pearl' or the congregational hymn of 'The 23d Psalme.' The air was not, however, necessarily simple. Both Dowland and Daniel occasionally abandoned the strophic form to increase the affective quality of their music, and both used chromaticism in a dramatic fashion.[23] Some of the poems they chose to set have more resemblances to Herbert's meditative lyrics than to 'The Rose.'[24]

The publication of the airs ceased with John Attey's *The First Booke of Ayres* in 1622. This did not mean that the airs were no longer sung, but that, so far as the composers were concerned, the early baroque style had finally triumphed. Yet 'triumph' is perhaps too strong a word. That style, which developed and flourished in Italy from about 1580 to 1630, had been gradually introduced into England in the reign of James I, and the reign of Charles I may be called the 'formative period' of the English early baroque.[25] The new style was operatic in origin and its characteristics most closely related to poetry were its 'violent interpretation of the words, realized in the affective recitative in free rhythm,' and the fact that its 'forms were on a small scale and sectional.'[26] Despite the enthusiasm of Milton and other contemporaries, the music of the English early baroque composers does not seem satisfactory today, particularly in comparison with that of their English predecessors and successors or their Italian contemporaries. It was not until the end of the seventeenth century that English composers produced masterpieces in the middle baroque style. That development was directly reflected in the poetry of the time: the literary counterpart of the dramatic recitative was the rhapsodic movement of the 'Pindaric ode'; and, at the other extreme, the mechanical movement and triple rhythms of Dryden's lyrics are reflections of the increased strictness of measure in the popular triple-rhythm dances.[27] The songs of Herbert's lifetime did not go so far toward either the rhapsody or the anapestic dance: Herbert could hardly have imagined—or approved—the setting which Henry Purcell gave to 'Longing.'[28] Yet the general lines of development are significant. From the time of Sidney, with the efflorescence of 'trochaic rhythms, lines of seven and eleven syllables,' feminine endings, and stanzas of varying line lengths,[29] English poetry and English music moved together toward greater rhythmical complexity.

Although before 1640 Campion and other composers who set their own lyrics to music could admit a great deal of irregularity in the text and still frame their music congruently,[30] they usually chose texts in which the stanzas preserved a fairly uniform pattern; and pattern, for a poet-composer, concerned more than accents. Like Sidney's poetry, Campion's *Observations in the Art of English Poesy* (1602) indicates that the developing experimentation in music caused the poets to be increasingly conscious of the importance of duration as well as accent in English poetry. In his theory Campion failed to abide by the principle that the ear must pragmatically determine the duration of any English syllable within a specific context of meaning, but in practice he attempted to determine the natural sound of syllables as the basis for his measure. Unlike some of his contemporaries and successors, Campion 'was not interested so much in the musical representation of dramatic and impassioned speech as in copying in music the reading of verse that brought out its rhythmical structure': 'Campion's recognition that pauses as well as syllables must be counted to fill the time periods of a metrical pattern is a real contribution to prosody.'[31] 'What if a day,' 'When to her lute Corinna sings,' 'When thou must home to shades of underground,' and many other songs by Campion attest the validity of the poet-musician's perceptions. Although the musical settings are helpful, they are not absolutely necessary for intelligent reading. A careful attention to natural cadence and duration forces the reader to recognize, for example, that 'My sweetest Lesbia, let us live and love' is not written in lines of five equal stresses, but that in the first line the first syllable of 'Lesbia' and the word 'love' endure longer than any other syllables. A similar attention should make us .

recognize the force of the traditional musical 'Come away' which begins each stanza of Herbert's 'Dooms-day':

> Come away,
> Make this the day.
> Dust, alas, no musick feels,
> But thy trumpet: then it kneels,
> As peculiar notes and strains
> Cure Tarantulas raging pains.

The opening two lines of each stanza represent a different metrical pattern from the rest of the stanza. Despite their few syllables, each of these lines, with the pause which follows it, endures almost as long as any of the final lines. A similar effect contributes enormously to the success of 'Discipline,' in which the third line of each stanza dramatically disturbs the rhythm, and yet endures longer than a simple counting of accents would indicate:

> Love is swift of foot;
> Love's a man of warre,
> > And can shoot,
> And can hit from farre.

Such examples are everywhere in Herbert's poems.

In addition to the 'musical expression of the text,' the new music as well as the old was committed to the 'doctrine of affections and figures,' and to the 'intellectual and pictorial' 'representation of the word.'[32] Most of the vocal music of Herbert's time aspired to the condition of poetry. Thomas Morley, musically a reactionary, gave precise instructions for the musical expression of the text, including the dramatic use of harmony and rhythm, the rests allowed for the various marks of punctuation, and the pictorial representation of the meaning of the words: 'it will be thought a great absurditie to talke of heauen and point downwarde to the earth.'[33] The later composers exaggerated Morley's type of imitative practice. The various expressive conventions (such as the melismatic settings of words like 'adorning,' 'burning,' 'fire,' 'fury,' 'inspiring,' 'love,' 'mirth,' 'morning,' 'runs,' 'twining,' 'wounding,' 'wavering,' etc.[34])

suggested to the poets the use of certain words, phrases, and ideas because of their musical possibilities.[35]

Since the music and the poetry of the early seventeenth century developed together, each influenced the other in many ways. If the poet was concerned with musical values, 'neatness' became a necessity: the pattern of sound in the stanza and in the entire poem should be 'expressive' of the meaning within fairly wide limits of congruent patterning. Moreover, whether the poet was writing actual songs, song-like poems, or anti-musical 'spoken' poems, the tradition of the songs reinforced the fact that there was no one 'speech' for either poet or subject;[36] it offered many additional genres which a poet could use either simply or as parts of larger structures.

Herbert occasionally made dramatic use of a song as a section of a poem. In 'Easter,' 'Christmas,' and 'An Offering,' the first section is conceived as dramatic speech and the second as a song. Since the intent was to contrast the two modes, the songs in these poems represent the most rhythmically regular type of lyric. The second section of 'Easter' had appeared in an earlier version as a separate poem:

> I had prepared many a flowre
> To strow thy way and Victorie,
> But thou wa'st vp before myne houre
> Bringinge thy sweets along wth thee.
>
> The Sunn arising in the East
> Though hee bring light & th' other sents:
> Can not make vp so braue a feast
> As thy discouerie presents.
>
> Yet though my flours be lost, they say
> A hart can never come too late.
> Teach it to sing thy praise, this day,
> And then this day, my life shall date.[37]

Here the poem is not a song of triumph; it is a request to be taught to sing. The 'feast' seems required chiefly by the exigencies of the rhyme, and the final lines of the second stanza are flat. Standing alone the poem is slight, and rhythmically it is unsatisfactory as either song or speech. In the final version of the poem, the song is the evidence that the commands and prayers of the magnificent opening section of the poem have been answered. The poet has been taught to sing:

> I got me flowers to straw thy way;
> I got me boughs off many a tree:
> But thou wast up by break of day,
> And brought'st thy sweets along with thee.
>
> The Sunne arising in the East,
> Though he give light, & th' East perfume;
> If they should offer to contest
> With thy arising, they presume.
>
> Can there be any day but this,
> Though many sunnes to shine endeavour?
> We count three hundred, but we misse:
> There is but one, and that one ever.

In 'An Offering,' speech and song are contrasted even more obviously than in 'Easter':

> Come, bring thy gift. If blessings were as slow
> As mens returns, what would become of fools?
> What hast thou there? a heart? but is it pure?
> Search well and see; for hearts have many holes.
> Yet one pure heart is nothing to bestow:
> In Christ two natures met to be thy cure.
>
> O that within us hearts had propagation,
> Since many gifts do challenge many hearts!
> Yet one, if good, may title to a number;
> And single things grow fruitfull by deserts.
> In publick judgements one may be a nation,
> And fence a plague, while others sleep and slumber.

166

But all I fear is lest thy heart displease,
As neither good, nor one: so oft divisions
Thy lusts have made, and not thy lusts alone;
Thy passions also have their set partitions.
These parcell out thy heart: recover these,
And thou mayst offer many gifts in one.

There is a balsome, or indeed a bloud,
Dropping from heav'n, which doth both cleanse and close
All sorts of wounds; of such strange force it is.
Seek out this All-heal, and seek no repose,
Untill thou finde and use it to thy good:
Then bring thy gift, and let thy hymne be this;

            Since my sadnesse
            Into gladnesse
   Lord thou dost convert,
            O accept
            What thou hast kept,
  As thy due desert.

            Had I many,
            Had I any,
 (For this heart is none)
            All were thine
            And none of mine:
  Surely thine alone.

            Yet thy favour
            May give savour
  To this poore oblation;
            And it raise
            To be thy praise,
  And be my salvation.

The first four stanzas are written in a strangely asymmetrical rhyme scheme which establishes no rhythmical norm for the recurrence of the rhymes. The pattern of the 'hymn' insists on the recurrence of the rhymes, and the accents are placed with strict regularity. These obvious distinctions emphasize the contrasts in tone. The impatient authority of the imperative opening is followed by an ironical question, three direct questions in one line, an additional imperative with its 'reason,' and a statement of generalized truth. The lines are irregularly broken by heavy caesuras. The second stanza's meditation on the value of the heart, balancing and correcting the conclusion of the first stanza, contains, suitably, no full stops within the lines, and the light caesuras occur regularly after the second accent. The rhythm, imagery, and alliterative pattern of the fourth stanza's opening lines convey a heightened intensity. They are a statement of mystery and an incantation. The final lines of the first section descend to the level of ordinary speech. Throughout this part of the poem the illusion of an individual 'voice' is preserved. The trochaic pattern and elaborate rhyme scheme of the 'hymn' prevent its relapsing into fourteeners and give it some of its gaiety: with the turn and return after line 3 in each stanza, the poem has the movement of a dance. Here related rhymes and internal repetition serve to enrich the chime.

The imagery maintains the contrast between speech and song. The complexity of reference in the first section is remarkable even for Herbert.[38] Clarity is achieved by limiting the images to their illustrations of the bringing of the offering (stanza 1), its nature and number (stanzas 2 and 3), and the only manner in which it may be received (stanza 4). The three stanzas of the song are almost devoid of imagery, but they express the personal resolution of those three problems in the same order. The hymn is supposedly sung by the speaker of the opening section, with the instruction that it should be sung by the offerer—'you, parishioner,' 'you, reader.' The 'gladness' belongs both to speaker and hearer; the song establishes the formerly tentative identification of speaker and audience. The hymn is by definition a collective expression of personal truth. The various metaphorical frames of reference of the opening speech would not be suitable for a 'true' expression of each individual. In this 'hymn' metaphorical richness is assumed as background; the song is joyfully concerned with paradox. That parodox is available to the lyric because, with the background of Christian knowledge which Herbert assumed and with the specific knowledge furnished by the opening four stanzas, neither 'explanation' nor 'actualization' by metaphor is necessary. The hymn is intended as the joyful expression of one and all Christian hearts.

The distinction which 'An Offering' makes between speech and song provides no short-cut either to appreciation or classification of the other poems. There are many varieties of speech and music in Herbert's poetry, and the two modes are often not distinguishable. The speech of meditation may have more in common with the tone of the lute song than with the speech of dramatic direct address. Or, again, the bare language of allegorical narrative resembles the plain style of the hymn more closely than it resembles the intellectualized reasoning of didactic address. As Herbert indicated by the title of one poem, the dialogue needs only music to become a verse anthem. In most of the poems, however, one conception clearly predominates: they are speech modified by music, or song with some of the accents of speech. A close reader of *The Temple* is forced to recognize the claims of lyrics other than the dramatic 'conversational' poems so admired in recent years; he is likely to join in Campion's plea for aesthetic pluralism: 'Give beauty all her right, She's not to one form tied.' To George Herbert, song and poetry were related by more than metaphor:

> The shepherds sing; and shall I silent be?
>> My God, no hymne for thee?
> My soul's a shepherd too; a flock it feeds
>> Of thoughts, and words, and deeds.
> The pasture is thy word; the streams, thy grace
>> Enriching all the place.
> Shepherd and flock shall sing, and all my powers
>> Out-sing the day-light houres.
> Then we will chide the sunne for letting night
>> Take up his place and right:
> We sing one common Lord; wherefore he should
>> Himself the candle hold.
> I will go searching, till I finde a sunne
>> Shall stay, till we have done;

A willing shiner, that shall shine as gladly,
        As frost-nipt sunnes look sadly.
Then we will sing, and shine all our own day,
        And one another pay:
His beams shall cheer my breast, and both so twine,
Till ev'n his beams sing, and my musick shine.[39]

CHAPTER IX

Allegory and the Sonnet
A Traditional Mode and a Traditional Form

THE variety of forms and tones and genres which Herbert brought to the construction of *The Temple* may prove dazzling to the modern reader. Yet Herbert did not wilfully make things difficult. He did not pursue novelty for its own sake; rather, he sought to transform and to revitalize the conventional so as to make it freshly available to serious poetry. One can see both his attempt and his success in his handling of a traditional mode and a traditional form, allegory and the sonnet.

Although Herbert rejected both the style and subject of the conventional pastoral allegory, he did not abandon the popular Christian form. Allegory was as demanding in its requirements as it was rich in potentialities. With its at least two levels of meaning, it demanded a basically unfigurative language for clarity of communication; but within the general requirements of a narrative style the seventeenth-century writer had freedom. The possible points of view of the fictional narrator were manifold, and within a single point of view the poet could employ various voices. The relations between factual statement and allegorical significance could be varied from dramatic contrast to almost complete identity. Allegory did not have to be dull:

As I one ev'ning sat before my cell,
Me thoughts a starre did shoot into my lap.
I rose, and shook my clothes, as knowing well,
That from small fires comes oft no small mishap.
    When suddenly I heard one say,
    Do as thou usest, disobey,
    Expell good motions from thy breast,
Which have the face of fire, but end in rest.

I, who had heard of musick in the spheres,
But not of speech in starres, began to muse. ('Artillerie.')

Herbert often used allegorical passages to good effect in longer poems. Those poems which are totally allegorical are likely to prove among his most difficult for the modern reader.

'Humilitie' is difficult largely because we are unaccustomed to thinking in terms of the cardinal virtues, the natural passions, and the rule of reason:

> I saw the Vertues sitting hand in hand
> In sev'rall ranks upon an azure throne,
> Where all the beasts and fowl by their command
> Presented tokens of submission.
> Humilitie, who sat the lowest there
>   To execute their call,
> When by the beasts the presents tendred were,
>   Gave them about to all.

Even if we recognize the abstract identity of the actors, we may forget that they are engaged in an internal psychological drama and we may fail to recognize the chief point the poem makes: whereas Mansuetude, Fortitude, Temperance, and Justice when ruled 'by their law' of reason may be able to keep in control and make proper use of the natural passions (Anger the Lion, Fear the Hare, Desire the 'Turkie,' and the craft of the Fox), the natural virtues are themselves subject to 'the Crow bringing the Peacocks plume.' Before deceit and vanity (that combination of false light and darkness) the rule of reason is destroyed; the secular virtues are defenceless before the appeal to pride. Without the fifth and Christian virtue, 'Humilitie,' man becomes the slave of the 'beasts.' All this was more obvious to the seventeenth-century reader than it is to us. Yet Herbert presented his complex meanings with the utmost simplicity. The poem is written as the barest narrative of external action by an anonymous observer. The observer offers no opinion except for one remark which is also a statement of fact: 'And if the Fox had liv'd to rule their side, They had depos'd each one.' The climax is presented in the words of 'Humilitie':

Humilitie, who held the plume, at this
Did weep so fast, that the tears trickling down
Spoil'd all the train: then saying, *Here it is*
For which ye wrangle, made them turn their frown
Against the beasts: so joyntly bandying,
             They drive them soon away;
And then amerc'd them, double gifts to bring
             At the next Session-day.

The flat, understated narrative is maintained by sound and rhythm as well as diction. The poem is not a transparent fable, but an object for meditation. As in the vision tradition, the presentation is clear and factual; the significances of the vision are to be pondered and related both to the realms of abstract truth and the individual's life.

In contrast to 'Humilitie,' the narrator of 'The Pilgrimage' might be Bunyan's Christian. He is relating his own past experiences, and his attitude is all important:

I travell'd on, seeing the hill, where lay
          My expectation.
    A long it was and weary way.
    The gloomy cave of Desperation
I left on th' one, and on the other side
          The rock of Pride.

The weariness of the introductory past imperfect is sustained until the final stanzas. It often seems to prevent the continuation of either breath or thought in the short sentences and phrases of the narrative:

And so I came to Fancies medow strow'd
          With many a flower:
    Fain would I here have made abode,
    But I was quicken'd by my houre.
So to Cares cops I came, and there got through
          With much ado.

The poem is complex and certain details are obscure. William Empson has given an ingenious analysis of the third stanza,[1] and although some of his readings are improbable if the stanza is read within its context, the poem as a whole is unusually available to Empson's type of analysis: a recognition of the power of the inclusive event as well as the pun in allegory is necessary for its proper appreciation. The first stanza, however, with its 'cave of Desperation' and 'rock of Pride' (the Scylla and Charybdis of the Christian life) established without any ambiguity whatsoever for the seventeenth-century reader the central meaning of 'The Pilgrimage.' The subject was at least as old as the writings of St Paul. Any interpretations made on analogies to Herbert's biography are at best conjectures: 'Fancies medow,' 'Cares cops,' and 'the wilde of Passion' describe within the poem the characteristic landscape of the Christian's pilgrimage. The complexities derive from the many and witty ways in which the physical pilgrimage parallels the spiritual. In the final stanzas the 'narrator' abandons narration for the dramatic evocation of a specific scene, and the poem departs from traditional allegory. The traveller had reached the top of 'the gladsome hill, Where lay my hope, Where lay my heart,' and discovered only 'A lake of brackish waters on the ground':

> With that abash'd and struck with many a sting
> Of swarming fears,
> I fell, and cry'd, Alas my King!
> Can both the way and end be tears?
> Yet taking heart I rose, and then perceiv'd
> I was deceiv'd:

> My hill was further: so I flung away,
> Yet heard a crie
> Just as I went, *None goes that way*
> *And lives*: If that be all, said I,
> After so foul a journey death is fair,
> And but a chair.

We have not been led directly from the vales of Sin to the Heavenly City on the Hill. The hill which the pilgrim had thought would provide his goal has furnished only tears; the first hill was not off the path, but his true hill was 'further,' and it could only be reached by death. There is a temptation

to identify the first hill biographically with Herbert's career
as priest, but the poem does not require such an interpretation. Christian allegory was valued largely because it was
true for every man, and the first hill clearly represents within
the poem that state of grace or service which the Christian
may falsely hope can assure him of continuous beatitude on
this earth. The pilgrim has not reached the end of his
journey at the end of the poem, for no man can describe the
end except by means of a dream; but in his willingness to
lose his life, we are assured that he will find it. The final two
lines contain the only true metaphor in the poem. With the
image of the 'chair,' with the homely and ordinary rest
which it represents, the poem abandons allegory for simple,
metaphorical spiritual statement.

In 'Peace' and 'Love unknown,' Herbert departed even
further from traditional allegory, and both poems derive
much of their vitality from the use of two contrasting
speakers. In the first twenty-one lines of 'Peace' the speaker
addresses the personified title of the poem and describes his
search, but he constantly shifts between direct address,
narrative, and quotations of others and of his own thoughts:

> Sweet Peace, where dost thou dwell? I humbly crave,
> Let me once know.
> I sought thee in a secret cave,
> And ask'd, if Peace were there.
> A hollow winde did seem to answer, No:
> Go seek elsewhere.
>
> I did; and going did a rainbow note:
> Surely, thought I,
> This is the lace of Peaces coat:
> I will search out the matter.
> But while I lookt, the clouds immediately
> Did break and scatter.

The narrator's fanciful reaction to the rainbow and his
belief that Peace must dwell at the root of such 'A gallant
flower' as 'The Crown Imperiall' both skilfully delineate
his character and contribute to the reader's pleasure. The

last half of the poem, however, is a direct quotation of the words of the 'rev'rend good old man,' whom the first speaker met in his search. Herbert desired symmetry for the full question and answer which is the underlying structure of the poem, yet he did not wish the poem to fall apart; he achieved his effect by constructing the poem in seven stanzas and dividing it at the mid-point of the fourth stanza. In the 'good old man's' narrative concerning the 'Prince of old' and the 'twelve stalks of wheat' the conversational rhythms change to a prevailingly regular iambic, and the surface of the poem becomes extraordinarily simple. The simplicity is only on the surface, for the narrative's frame of reference includes the Prince-Priest Melchisedec, who lived at 'Salem' (the former name of Jerusalem meant 'Peace,' and the city was a type of the Church Militant and Triumphant) and 'brought foorth bread and wine' (Gen. xiv. 18), the type of Christ; and the 'twelve stalks of wheat' involve the twelve tribes, the twelve apostles, and primarily that 'bread of life' which is Christ and His message. The 'story' finished, the poem ends with the address of the 'old man' to the narrator, and, incidentally, to the reader:

> Take of this grain, which in my garden grows,
> And grows for you;
> Make bread of it: and that repose
> And peace, which ev'ry where
> With so much earnestnesse you do pursue,
> Is onely there.

The language is still simple, but in sound and rhythm and meaning the poem has become the sacramental invitation.[2] As nearly as any single poem in *The Temple*, 'Peace' indicates Herbert's range. It moves from wit to ritual, from conversation to mystery. It is so nimble that we should have to forgive a medieval allegorist if he failed to recognize his distant progeny. With all its disparate elements the poem is a freshly created whole.

'Love unknown' is a triumph in tone. The occasion for Coleridge's ironical remark concerning 'the characteristic fault of our elder poets,' namely, 'the conveying the most

fantastic thoughts in the most correct and natural language,'
the poem has chiefly concerned commentators on the score
of its 'fantastic thought,' organized around three emblematic
incidents: the heart is seized from an offering of 'a dish of
fruit'; when the narrator attempts to offer 'a sacrifice out of
my fold,' his heart is thrown into 'A boyling caldron,'
'AFFLICTION'; finally, returning home in the hope 'to sleep
out all these faults,' the narrator discovers 'that some had
stuff'd the bed with thoughts, I would say *thorns*.' The
religious meaning of the allegory is not especially obscure.
Herbert has prevented misinterpretation by the remarks of
the 'Friend' after each episode ('*Your heart was foul, I fear*';
'*Your heart was hard, I fear*'; '*Your heart was dull, I fear*'),
followed by the narrator's admissions ('Indeed 'tis true')
and explanations of how the charges apply.

The matter of these episodes is predominantly biblical,[3]
but similar matter is usually dull in Quarles's poems. It is
the manner which makes the poem. The opening lines
establish the narrator's tone:

> Deare Friend, sit down, the tale is long and sad:
> And in my faintings I presume your love
> Will more complie then help.

The narrator gives fair warning of his garrulity (the poem
contains seventy lines) and of his emotional state. He does
not really expect help, but he wants to complain and he
wants an audience. He is breathless, and with his excited
insistence that the full extent of his sorrow be realized by
his auditor he shows a particular fondness for the paren-
thetical phrase:

> A Lord I had,
> And have, of whom some grounds, which may improve,
> I hold for two lives, and both lives in me.
> To him I brought a dish of fruit one day,
> And in the middle plac'd my heart. But he
> (I sigh to say)
> Lookt on a servant, who did know his eye
> Better then you know me, or (which is one)
> Then I my self.

It is the second typographical parenthesis which admits the
reader to the fiction: the external dialogue is an image of the
interior dialogue between the natural and the spiritual man.
The establishment of this fact does not break the dramatic
framework: the poem continues as a dialogue between two
friends whose individuality extends to their speech rhythms
and language, but Herbert insists that the reader recognize
the fiction.

The speech of the narrator is one of Herbert's most successful approximations of conversational tone. For most of
the poem Herbert has used a succession of lines rhymed as
quatrains, but the poem is not arranged in stanzas. The
overriding enjambment and the practice of ending the
sentences at the caesuras prevent any realization of the
quatrain pattern in the narrator's speech. The sound and
rhythm give the effect of an extraordinarily flexible dramatic
blank verse:

> But you shall heare. After my heart was well,
> And clean and fair, as I one even-tide
> > (I sigh to tell)
> Walkt by my self abroad, I saw a large
> And spacious fornace flaming, and thereon
> A boyling caldron, round about whose verge
> Was in great letters set AFFLICTION.
> The greatnesse shew'd the owner. So I went
> To fetch a sacrifice out of my fold,
> Thinking with that, which I did thus present,
> To warm his love, which I did fear grew cold.
> But as my heart did tender it, the man,
> Who was to take it from me, slipt his hand,
> And threw my heart into the scalding pan;
> My heart, that brought it (do you understand?)
> The offerers heart.

The regular metrical pattern of the 'Friend's' gnomic
speech provides a measure for the narrator's freedom. The
Friend brings the poem to a firm and patterned conclusion.
With the resolution of the poem's questions, the integrity
of the lines is established:

ALLEGORY AND THE SONNET

Mark the end.
The Font did onely, what was old, renew:
The Caldron suppled, what was grown too hard:
The Thorns did quicken, what was grown too dull:
All did but strive to mend, what you had marr'd.
Wherefore be cheer'd, and praise him to the full
Each day, each houre, each moment of the week,
Who fain would have you be new, tender, quick.

Allegory, modulating to parable or exemplum or simple metaphor, was a method which Herbert used in many forms. Herbert's sixteen sonnets (seventeen if one considers 'Love [I]' and 'Love [II]' as two sonnets rather than one poem) are the only sizeable group of poems in which he used the same external form. The extraordinary innovator in verse lengths and rhyme schemes seems to show an unexpected conservatism in the sonnet. Herbert did not even attempt the Petrarchan octave, the favourite form of both Sidney and Donne; except for 'Josephs coat' with its one unrhymed line, he was content with two simple patterns. 'Sinne (I),' 'Avarice,' the first part of 'Christmas,' 'The Holdfast,' 'The Sonne,' and 'The Answer' are in the Shakespearean pattern; the final six lines shift to *e f f e g g* in 'The Sinner,' 'Redemption,' 'H. Baptisme (I),' 'Prayer (I),' the double sonnet 'Love,' 'The H. Scriptures (I)' and 'II,' and the two early sonnets printed by Walton. The conventionality is, however, only external. Many of these poems are so unconventional that we hardly recognize them as sonnets. By Herbert's day the sonnet had hardened to a conventional form which seemed to defy originality. But Herbert put the form to new uses, and showed that it was still capable of greatness.

For all their debt to Sidney, the two poems Herbert wrote when he was seventeen already show the direction of his experiments with the sonnet. They use the rhyme scheme which was to be Herbert's favourite, *a b a b c d c d e f f e g g*.·

The advantage of that pattern was that it could be used to achieve the formal effects of nearly all the conventional sonnet schemes: the first eight lines could be treated either as two quatrains or an octave; and the last six lines might be constructed as a sestet, two tercets, or a quatrain and a couplet. But Herbert was not satisfied with imitating the conventional effects. 'My God, where is that ancient heat towards thee' violates every traditional rule. In view of Herbert's later practice, what might be attributed to youthful brashness seems to be deliberate experimentation:

> My God, where is that ancient heat towards thee,
>> Wherewith whole showls of *Martyrs* once did burn,
>> Besides their other flames? Doth Poetry
> Wear *Venus* Livery? only serve her turn?
> Why are not *Sonnets* made of thee? and layes
>> Upon thine Altar burnt? Cannot thy love
>> Heighten a spirit to sound out thy praise
> As well as any she? Cannot thy *Dove*
> Out-strip their *Cupid* easily in flight?
>> Or, since thy wayes are deep, and still the same,
>> Will not a verse run smooth that bears thy name?
> Why doth that fire, which by thy power and might
>> Each breast does feel, no braver fuel choose
>> Than that, which one day Worms may chance refuse?[4]

The poem is a self-conscious and satirical declaration of independence from the traditional style as well as subject-matter of the Elizabethan sonneteers. It is also a formal declaration. The five heavy caesuras marked by the questions within the lines destroy the flow usually intrinsic to the effect of a sonnet, and overriding enjambment prevents the realization of any one of the expected formal divisions: *flight*, the first *e* rhyme, gives a ninth line to what should be the octave, and although the tenth and eleventh lines form a couplet, the last three lines are a lonely tercet containing the questioned conclusion.

Herbert may have realized that his breaking up of the individual lines in this poem had almost destroyed the *raison d'être* for his form; at any rate, he never again introduced such quantities of full stops within the lines of a sonnet. In contrast to his usual practice of making every external formal element mirror internal logic and meaning, however, Herbert continued to violate frequently the traditional formal divisions of his sonnets. In 'H. Baptisme (I),' for example, the organization of the thought neatly reverses the positions of octave and sestet. The first section of 'Josephs coat' is nine lines in length, and it is followed by a tercet and a couplet. 'The H. Scriptures (I)' seems to be divided neatly into two sections of seven lines each. This technical experimentation is fascinating, but it is never done *in vacuo*. Whether Herbert used or violated traditional schemes, he created individual speech and form. The poems range from the courtly wit of the opening quatrain of 'The Sonne' to the controlled agony of 'The Answer.'

The sonnets 'Redemption,' 'Prayer (I),' and 'The Answer' have almost nothing in common, except that they are three of Herbert's best poems. 'Redemption' gives Herbert's allegorical account of the granting of the Covenant of Grace. The traditional mode and the traditional form make for an untraditional poem:

> Having been tenant long to a rich Lord,
>   Not thriving, I resolved to be bold,
>   And make a suit unto him, to afford
> A new small-rented lease, and cancell th' old.
> In heaven at his manour I him sought:
>   They told me there, that he was lately gone
>   About some land, which he had dearly bought
> Long since on earth, to take possession.
> I straight return'd, and knowing his great birth,
>   Sought him accordingly in great resorts;
>   In cities, theatres, gardens, parks, and courts:
> At length I heard a ragged noise and mirth
>   Of theeves and murderers: there I him espied,
>   Who straight, *Your suit is granted*, said, & died.

For this dramatic narrative the conventional two quatrains and two tercets give structural firmness. The simple language of allegory is sustained until the effective 'ragged noise and mirth,' a metaphorical expansion which grants added drama to the final bare line. It is somehow fitting that Herbert should have made one of his most radical dislocations of the iambic line within the opening of a sonnet, but throughout the poem the sound and rhythm continue to maintain the fiction of the 'unpoetic' narrator who recounts his observations of physical fact. The richness of the poem derives in large part from the relations between that timely fiction and the timeless reality which it represents: the speaker is both one man in the present and all mankind from the Fall to the Crucifixion; the search is the search of the Jews until Calvary and it is also the search of every man who wishes to be a Christian; the discovery was made by humanity at one moment in the past, but it is also made by individuals at every moment, present and future.

'Prayer (I),' a sonnet without statement, is an achievement in suggestion:

> Prayer the Churches banquet, Angels age,
>   Gods breath in man returning to his birth,
>   The soul in paraphrase, heart in pilgrimage,
>   The Christian plummet sounding heav'n and earth;
> Engine against th' Almightie, sinners towre,
>   Reversed thunder, Christ-side-piercing spear,
>   The six-daies world transposing in an houre,
> A kinde of tune, which all things heare and feare;
> Softnesse, and peace, and joy, and love, and blisse,
>   Exalted Manna, gladnesse of the best,
>   Heaven in ordinarie, man well drest,
> The milkie way, the bird of Paradise,
>   Church-bels beyond the starres heard, the souls bloud,
>   The land of spices; something understood.

'Prayer (I)' is a poem rather than a series of metaphorical appositives because of its strict formal patterning. The first two quatrains build a crescendo and diminuendo of evocation, from the peace of the banquet through the violent war to the 'kinde of tune'; and the sestet moves from 'Softnesse' to the 'land of spices' with a continuous heightening of the bliss of communion. The last three lines, with their 'definition' of that state of being which surpasses knowledge and logic, depend not only on the pattern of ideas and imagery of which they are a part, but also on the subtle changes of the rhythm and the dislocation of the language: the rhythmical daring of 'Church-bels beyond the starres heard' is matched by the phrase's startling ambiguity of reference. The peace of 'The land of spices; something understood' is both an abandonment of metaphor and its final crowning. Never before had the sonnet been put to such use in English.

Differing completely from 'Redemption' and 'Prayer (I)' in conception, language, and rhythm, 'The Answer' is equally successful:

> My comforts drop and melt away like snow:
> I shake my head, and all the thoughts and ends,
> Which my fierce youth did bandie, fall and flow
> Like leaves about me: or like summer friends,
> Flyes of estates and sunne-shine. But to all,
> Who think me eager, hot, and undertaking,
> But in my prosecutions slack and small;
> As a young exhalation, newly waking,
> Scorns his first bed of dirt, and means the sky;
> But cooling by the way, grows pursie and slow,
> And setling to a cloud, doth live and die
> In that dark state of tears: to all, that so
>   Show me, and set me, I have one reply,
>   Which they that know the rest, know more then I.

F. P. Wilson has perceptively suggested that 'rest' in the final line means not only 'the rest of Herbert's life story summarized in the poem, but also "the freedom from toil or care associated with the future life."'[5] Within the context of the poem, the 'reply' must be a statement in the midst of his desolation of the speaker's dependence on the will of God, and they who know the 'rest'—the end of the story and the final bliss—know both the nature of that reply and its truth and depth. Like 'Affliction (I)' and 'The Crosse,' 'The Answer' is more personal than most of Herbert's poems; the speaker's experiences are not typical but individual, and more than any of the other sonnets, this poem suggests that Herbert may have read Shakespeare with profit. The direct yet courtly statement, the metaphorical complexity of lines 4 and 5, and the long development of the 'young exhalation' are reminiscent of the former master's technique. Yet formally the sonnet is not at all Shakespearean. In the manner in which it is paragraphed, the poem looks forward to Milton, that other great seventeenth-century experimenter who finally and firmly broke through the Elizabethan conventions as to what a sonnet must be and do.

Herbert's uses of the allegorical genre and the sonnet form show that if idiosyncrasy was not one of his ideals, neither was simple traditionalism. Lesser poets, in Herbert's day and ours, are 'traditional'; Herbert and the major poets use the traditional and 'make it new.'

CHAPTER X

Conclusion

WE can fully realize Herbert's poetic achievement
—or almost any one poem in *The Temple*—only
within the light of the ideas, beliefs, and conventions of early seventeenth-century England. The same
convictions which restricted Herbert's poetry to the service
of religion gave him extraordinary freedom as a poet, for
all the genres and tones and forms yet known were too few
to praise God properly, and any subject provided potentially
important content for a poem. Puns, music, love, joy,
history, law, farming, business, medicine, the Court, the
windows of the church, the way a bird drinks, the sufferings
of the poet and the sufferings of Christ on the Cross, all
could be used in his poems, not because the poet created
their significances, but because God had created them
significant. 'Invention' was the poet's most important task,
but Herbert understood that word to mean the discovery of
God's truth. Yet this does not mean that the poems can or
should be viewed as bits of archeological evidence. When a
reader has understood the poems within their cultural context, he is likely to discover that they become more rather
than less relevant to his own life in a different world.

Yet both the understanding and the discovery are difficult
today. To those whose lives have been largely formed by a
secular culture, many of Herbert's conceptions seem obscure
or incomprehensible. Most of us are not accustomed to
thinking of religion and poetry in Herbert's terms. The
secularization of English culture began before Herbert's
birth, but in his lifetime that culture was still predominantly
Christian, and religion was generally recognized, verbally at
least, as the most vital issue for man. The violence of the
Civil War which was partly undertaken in the name of
religion contributed to the establishment of a secular state
and the decline of traditional Christianity. Of course Chris-

tianity did not die: the vitality of various religious traditions and groups has been manifested continually throughout the past three centuries. But religion shared in the gradual compartmentalization of life in general. Since Herbert's time we have had religion as reason or common sense, religion as enthusiasm and evangelicalism, religion as nature worship, as ritualism, as aestheticism, as ethics, as progress, as the social gospel, as institutionalism, and as a theory of history. While few of these are wholly irrelevant, none provides a satisfactory substitute for the wholeness of an earlier age's Christianity, either for the poet or for other men.

The advantages of the earlier age for poetry have been frequently noted. Both the solipsist and the sceptic find it difficult to write poetry: the greatest poetry is the product of the poet's conviction that he has experienced knowledge of more than himself. In an age in which solipsism and scepticism have often appeared the most likely philosophical positions, the poets and literary critics have been properly concerned with 'objectivity,' 'aesthetic distance,' 'escape from personality,' 'the objective correlative'; today the word 'myth' is one of the commonest literary coins, possessing various valuations. For however personal his material, the good poet, like the creator of tragedy, must possess some 'frame of reference within which to make actual his dramatic conflicts,'[1] some criteria of good and evil, some principles of organization by which individual experience acquires coherence and meaning and by which it can be given an existence and reality beyond formless autobiography. The modern poet, forced to create a cosmos before he creates a language for its articulation, has found the problem complex. His invented 'myths' have often served as the final symbols of his isolation rather than of his community. For Herbert, Christianity provided the means of giving order and universal significance to his personal experience. His poetry reinforces the belief that valuable poetic objectivity cannot be gained by attempts to 'escape from personality' by means of technical literary devices; it comes only from a fulfilment of personality through a belief in a reality larger than the personal. Yet such a fulfilment cannot be willed. Good contemporary poetry will continue to stem from the realities and order which a poet has experienced, not from those which he may have desired.

For a new generation of poets who are attempting to achieve an order and significance beyond personality, Herbert's example may prove more useful than Donne's. But it is an infinitely more difficult example and a more dangerous one. With Herbert, in contrast with Donne, our final impression is not of the brilliant surfaces, of the delightful logical gymnastics, or of a powerful personality engaged in dramatizing its conflicts and its vitality; it is, rather, an impression of astonishing simplicity. And true simplicity cannot be imitated (the attempt results only in the mawkish); it must be earned.

The simplicity is the simplicity of the spirit; it is the reverse of naïveté. It is the impression left by the few who are most successful in the almost impossible search to know what they are and to recognize unflinchingly what they feel. Herbert was what he believed all men to be,

> A wonder tortur'd in the space
> Betwixt this world and that of grace. ('Affliction [IV].')

He knew his deepest and most consistent desire: to live a life at one with the will of God. But he was equally ready to recognize the reality of his momentary experience. He believed that the true state of man was 'Giddinesse':

> O what a sight were Man, if his attires
> Did alter with his minde;
> And like a Dolphins skinne, his clothes combin'd
> With his desires!

> Surely if each one saw anothers heart,
> There would be no commerce,
> No sale or bargain passe: all would disperse
> And live apart.

No man is always a philosopher, and the poet forgets that fact at the peril of his poetry. But as Herbert rarely deceived himself about his momentary emotions, he was also rarely blinded by them. He observed and judged and recorded them in the light of a lifetime of observations and of convictions beyond the ephemeral. In 'The Crosse' he described personal failure and agony with a chilling precision:

> To have my aim, and yet to be
> Further from it then when I bent my bow;
> To make my hopes my torture, and the fee
> Of all my woes another wo,
> Is in the midst of delicates to need,
> And ev'n in Paradise to be a weed.

There was no honest consolation for that experience; the poet could only submit to it as before a renewal of the mystery of the Crucifixion. But man cannot live long in such a condition; if he lives, it is from a 'resurrection' of vitality within him. It is an inevitable part of the form of *The Temple* —and at least symbolically of Herbert's experience—that 'The Flower' follows 'The Crosse':

> How fresh, O Lord, how sweet and clean
> Are thy returns! ev'n as the flowers in spring;
> To which, besides their own demean,
> The late-past frosts tributes of pleasure bring.
> Grief melts away
> Like snow in May,
> As if there were no such cold thing.

> Who would have thought my shrivel'd heart
> Could have recover'd greennesse?

Herbert did not succumb before torment: he was one of those who 'are the trees, whom shaking fastens more' ('Affliction [V]'). But his continuous desire was for that life, 'Straight as a line,' which 'ever tends to thee,'

> To thee, who art more farre above deceit,
> Then deceit seems above simplicitie. ('A Wreath.')

The continuous prayer was, 'Give me simplicitie, that I may live.'

It is only superficially a paradox that simplicity of spirit should be the primary quality of the poetry which has been too well known recently as 'conceited' and difficult. There may have been many individuals who have achieved such simplicity, such fidelity to experience, without much knowledge of the ways of the world, but we have no way of knowing. We can only partially judge of such things when they are communicated to us by an artist who has also achieved an anything but simple technical mastery of his craft. It is inconceivable that a poet should possess a mastery of language adequate to convey such a quality without a knowledge of the ways of men. The ways of language are determined by the ways of men. To define with clarity, to obtain his desired effects, the religious poet above all must know the ways in which language can destroy as well as create experience. He must know the traditions of social life as well as literature, the ways in which men constantly exhaust ideas and expressions until, changed in all true signification, they become the inexplicable, the cliché. He must possess the 'wit' capable of seeing with multiple vision if he is to avoid the bathetic and the melodramatic, the words which seem too easy or too extreme. It was essential for Herbert to know the ways in which

> The wanton lover in a curious strain
> Can praise his fairest fair;
> And with quaint metaphors her curled hair
> Curl o'er again.   ('Dulnesse.')

Such knowledge was not only necessary to present his major experience; it was also a part of that experience. For Herbert, like most men, did not constantly fluctuate between the extremes of agony and ecstasy. The middle way is also the way inhabited longest, and the marvellous wit and playfulness of 'The Quip' or 'The British Church' are as essential to *The Temple* as either 'The Crosse' or 'The Flower.' The wit is evidence of Herbert's knowledge that language, like man, has constantly to be renewed in order to stay alive.

With nimbleness, intelligence, and sensitivity, and with total devotion to his craft and his experience, Herbert was able to create poems which derive from his 'baroque' age, but which also live apart from it. However quickly we may be distracted, at the moment when we read his greatest poems we can only recognize with Rilke the immediate imperative of the greatest art: 'You must change your life.'[2]

'MR HERBERT'S TEMPLE & CHURCH MILITANT EXPLAINED AND IMPROVED'

IN 'Mr Herbert's Temple & Church Militant explained and improved,' George Ryley annotated and paraphrased every poem in *The Temple*. The neglect of Ryley's work is unfortunate, for Ryley's largely theological commentaries often provide the key to many of the passages and poems which are difficult for the modern reader of Herbert. Ryley's MS., dated March 24th, 1714/15 (Bodleian, MS. Rawlinson D 199; my references are to the copy made in 1904 by A. F. Parker for G. H. Palmer, Houghton Library, Her 2.3), was noticed by George Herbert Palmer, but Palmer made little use of it in his edition of *The English Works* (1907): 'Ryley's aims and my own are so divergent that I have been able to quote him less often than I should like, especially as I obtained a copy of his manuscript only after my notes were practically complete' (II, 6n). Palmer was not particularly interested in theology, but a close reading of Ryley's commentary early in his studies might have prevented his 'chronological' rearrangement of the poems. Herbert's definitive editor, F. E. Hutchinson, dismissed Ryley's work with the remark, 'it has no authority for the text, which, where it is cited, evidently follows a late edition; and the comments lack originality' (*Works*, p. lvi). But Ryley did not even quote the texts of most of the poems, and he remarked on p. 2, 'I don't pretend to an exactness and especially not in the form of the quotations used here, for they were generally made from absent authors, which my liberal friends have often supplied me with. The uttermost I please myself with is that a tollerable sence is put upon every poem, & there are not many that have escaped a genuine denudation.' On the theological level Ryley almost makes good his boast.

Ryley's commentary must, however, be used with due

allowance for his intentions, his beliefs, and his knowledge. In his 'Praemonitio' he stated his purpose succinctly: 'The whole design of this undertaking being to gratifie 2 or 3 of my friends who desired a better acquaintance with the Divine Poet, I look't upon my self as happily freed from studying to be elaborate, & chose to write only what occur'd to my first tho'ts under each poem.' Ryley's 'first tho'ts' were better than most of his contemporaries' third ones. He did not assume that his friends had much knowledge of Renaissance poetry, but he did expect them to be well versed in divinity. In addition to his countless biblical citations, Ryley elucidated passages by references to the works of 'Mr Calvin,' Matthew Henry, John Reynolds, Richard Baxter, Bunyan, Alexander Ross, and Edward Stillingfleet. Ryley was also well read in the science of his day. His citations extend from Sir Thomas Browne's *Vulgar Errors* (1646) and Samuel Clarke's *Geography* (1657)—both of which had been reprinted in the 1670's—to such impressive volumes of the Newtonian era as John Ray's *The Wisdom of God manifested in the Works of the Creation* (1691), Nehemiah Grew's *Cosmologia Sacra, or a Discourse of the Universe, as it is the Creature and Kingdom of God* (1701), and William Derham's *Physico-Theology, or a Demonstration of the Being and Attributes of God from his Works of Creation*, published in 1713, just before Ryley wrote his notes on Herbert. The modern reader may need to be reminded that these last three works were written by scientists of distinction, and continued to enjoy great popularity during the first half of the eighteenth century. Grew became Secretary of the Royal Society in 1677. Ray's and Derham's volumes, each of which ran through twelve editions before 1760, were used by William Paley at a later date.

Like John Reynolds and Emerson, Ryley occasionally forced a 'modern' theological interpretation on Herbert's text, but he was usually content to relate what he found there. He effaced himself so thoroughly that, despite the significant volumes of 'nonconformity' in his reading, it is impossible to determine whether he was an extremely low member of the Church of England or a moderate Dissenter, perhaps a

Presbyterian. The most promising evidence in the manuscript proves inconclusive: on pages 321 and 378 Ryley
used 'our' before a reference to the Church of England, but
in each case the adjective might imply nationality rather
than conformity, and in one of the passages his purpose was
to show that both he and Herbert disagreed with 'the
Constitution of our Diocesan Church of England' in their
belief that the 'power of the keys' belonged to all priests
rather than only to the 'highest orders of Metropolitan.'
Although Ryley's attitude toward the ritual obviously
differed greatly from Herbert's, he found nothing to which
he specifically objected in the poems. In his comment on
the poem 'Church Monuments,' p. 106, he stated his
general premise, 'A good man is ready to spiritualize every
thing he meets with.' Ryley could, therefore, consider a
meditation on a suspect rite profitable if it firmly emphasized
symbolic significance rather than inherent power. He became
enthusiastic about nearly every poem in *The Temple*.

Ryley was fond of both Horace and Prior, and his lament
for the condition of divine poetry in his comment on
'Jordan (I)' (p. 87) shows literary perspicuity: 'Now few
have appeared in the dress of Divine poets, that are truely
qualified with a *native genius* for it: Herbert & Milton & a
few short handed ones have grac't the stage, such as
Reinolds, &c. Yet there is room enough for more. What
might we have promised ourselves if * Dryden, Rochester,
Tate, Brown, & many more, that have been not only
translaters but authors of the finest tho'ts in another dress,
had applyd themselves to Divine subjects, instead of either
indifferent, or immoral ones. On the other hand, many have
appeared in the field of poesie to treat of Divine subjects,
so wretchedly poor & flatt, that it has allmost nauseated
politer genius with not only their performance but the subjects themselves.' Yet Ryley's knowledge of literature was
not extensive, and when he complained of obscurities in

* 'Cowley' is written and cancelled before 'Dryden,' probably because,
on second thought, Ryley remembered that Cowley had contributed to
divine poetry. 'Religio Laici' and 'The Hind and the Panther' did not,
evidently, qualify.

Herbert's poetry he showed a literary naïveté which is refreshing after much of the traditional comment on *The Temple*. For the obscurities which perplexed him were neither those which modern readers find in Herbert nor those which the usual eighteenth-century critic condemned. Ryley had never heard of the 'bird of Paradise,' he thought 'purling' meant 'bitter,' and he conjectured that the unknown word 'knell' was West Country dialect for 'cell,' but he rarely had difficulty with an entire poem, and he was unconscious that Herbert used 'conceits'—not because he was well schooled in Renaissance poetry, but because his close knowledge of the Bible and traditional theology made Herbert's ideas and language seem most natural.

APPENDIX B

BACON AND HERBERT

GEORGE HERBERT and Francis Bacon had more in common than is generally recognized. The poems and letters which Herbert addressed to Bacon show a close knowledge of what the Lord Chancellor had written. In the short 'Ad Autorem Instaurationis Magnae' (*Works*, p. 435), Herbert celebrated Bacon's 'killing' of the ancients, 'so splendidly and agreeably' that they must consider burial as a gift. His comment in 'In Honorem Verulamij' (*Works*, pp. 436-37) was more flattering and more specific:

> Who passes yonder? his is not a face
> Of every day. You know not him? then hear.
> The Prince of Theories, the High Priest of Truth,
> Lord of Induction, and of Verulam,
> Master of the Universe, but not of Arts;
> The Pine-tree of Profundity and Grace;
> Nature's particular Augur, Chronicle
> Of Science, Courier of Experiment;
> Equity's standard-bearer; he that found
> Poor Science chained from undergraduate hope,
> And set her free; *Promus* of Light; that drove
> Before him all our Phantoms and our Clouds;
> Colleague o' the Sun; and Square of Certitude;
> The Sophist's scourge; the literary Brutus,
> Ending the tyrannies of Authority;
> Of Thought and Sense stupendous Arbiter,
> The Reason's whetstone; of Physics very Atlas,
> To whom the Stagirite bowed his giant strength;
> A Noah's Dove, who in old age perceiving
> No place nor rest for's Art, chose for himself
> Thus to return to his maternal Ark.
> The text of Subtilty, the child of Time,
> His mother Truth; the Hive of Honey'd Wit;

Of earth and life the only Hierophant;
The axe of Error: grain of mustard-seed,
Bitter to others, growing to itself—
But my wit droops. Aid me, Posterity!*

The subsequent development of certain aspects of Bacon's thought may distort our picture of Bacon himself. But Bacon was no more the agnostic who demanded that all style should conform to the criteria of the Royal Society than he was Shakespeare or, as Emerson called him, 'the purple' modern. Whether as Lord Chancellor or as the advocate of the new learning, Bacon seems to have been chiefly concerned with power. Yet in his early years George Herbert was also concerned with power, and with his penchant for reading 'charitably,' Herbert probably took Bacon's bows to traditional morality at their face value. Herbert would not have been particularly disturbed by Bacon's attack on poetry as a source of knowledge, since the attack was limited to that secular and pagan poetry which Herbert had, verbally at least, rejected as wearing '*Venus* Livery.' Herbert followed Bacon's advice in forming his collection of 'wisdom' concerning good morals and good manners, *Outlandish Proverbs*, and he shared the desire of Bacon and the age for a 'practical divinity' which excluded the controversial and the overly speculative. He would have agreed completely with Bacon's description of

> that divine state of mind, which religion and the holy faith doth conduct men unto, by imprinting upon their souls charity, which is excellently called the bond of perfection, because it comprehendeth and fasteneth all virtues together . . . if a man's mind be truly inflamed with charity, it doth work him suddenly into a greater perfection than all the doctrine of morality can do, which is but a sophist in comparison of the other . . . only charity admitteth no excess. For so we see, aspiring to be like God in

* I quote Edmund Blunden's translation from *ESEA*, XIX (1934), pp. 35-36. The 'Fugator Idolum' of line 12 is an obvious reference to Bacon's 'Idols.' 'Promus' may refer to Bacon's 'A Promus of Formularies and Elegancies,' a work existing only in manuscript during Herbert's lifetime.

power, the angels transgressed and fell; *Ascendam, et ero similis altissimo*: by aspiring to be like God in knowledge, man transgressed and fell; *Eritis sicut Dii, scientes bonum et malum*: but by aspiring to a similitude of God in goodness or love, neither man nor angel ever transgressed, or shall transgress. (*The Advancement of Learning, Works*, III, 343.)

Herbert seems to have been undisturbed by the discoveries of the new science. He accepted, I believe, Bacon's chief theses in so far as 'learning' was concerned; having accepted them, he could devote himself to the problems of religion and poetry with comparative freedom. Bacon had called religion the 'most sovereign' of the medicines which could be applied to the will of man (*Helps for the Intellectual Powers, Works*, VII, 100). He had said that 'the imperfections in the conversation and government of those which have chief place in the church have ever been principal causes and motives of schisms and divisions' (*An Advertisement Touching the Controversies in the Church of England, The Letters and the Life* [London, 1861-74], I, 80. Cf. Walton's report, *Lives*, p. 304, of Herbert's principal 'cure for the wickedness and growing Atheism of our Age.') He had also said that 'a feeling Christian will express in his words a character either of zeal or love' (*An Advertisement, Letters and Life*, I, 76). He had stated that poetry was to be used in dealing with the affections, rhetoric in religion. However different the two men were in spirit, Bacon's expressions foreshadow Herbert's to a remarkable degree.

ABBREVIATIONS USED IN NOTES

B	MS. Tanner 307 in the Bodleian Library
DNB	*Dictionary of National Biography*
ELH	*English Literary History*
ESEA	*Essays and Studies by Members of the English Association*
Gardiner, *History*	Samuel R. Gardiner, *History of England from the Accession of James I to the Outbreak of the Civil War: 1603-1642*, 10 vols. (rev. ed.; London, 1883-1884)
JEGP	*Journal of English and Germanic Philology*
MLN	*Modern Language Notes*
NED	*New English Dictionary*
PQ	*Philological Quarterly*
RES	*Review of English Studies*
SP	*Studies in Philology*
W	MS. Jones B 62 in Dr Williams's Library

NOTES TO CHAPTER I

1. F. E. Hutchinson describes fifteen editions and three variants in *The Works of George Herbert*, 2nd ed. (Oxford, 1945), pp. lvi-lxii. Since Hutchinson's and all modern editions of *The Temple* have alphabetical tables of the poems, I have omitted page references to specific poems of Herbert. For much of the material in the following pages I am indebted to Hutchinson's essay on Herbert's 'Contemporary and Later Reputation,' *Works*, pp. xxxix-l, as well as to Arthur H. Nethercot's more general studies: 'The Reputation of the "Metaphysical Poets" during the Seventeenth Century,' *JEGP*, XXIII (1924), 173-98; 'The Reputation of the "Metaphysical Poets" during the Age of Pope,' *PQ*, IV (1925), 161-79; 'The Reputation of the "Metaphysical Poets" during the Age of Johnson and the "Romantic Revival,"' *SP*, XXII (1925), 81-132; 'The Term "Metaphysical Poets" before Johnson,' *MLN*, XXXVII (1922), 11-17.

2. See 'A Stepping Stone to the Threshold of Mr Herbert's Church-Porch,' *The Works of George Herbert* (London, 1859), II, 298.

3. *The Works*, ed. L. C. Martin (Oxford, 1914), II, 391.

4. *Henry Vaughan: A Life and Interpretation* (Oxford, 1947), pp. 102-03.

5. See, e.g., Vaughan's 'Retirement,' *The Works*, II, 462-63. Here the 'throne of azure' seems to be taken from Herbert's 'Humilitie,' and 'Keeping close house' reflects the 'keep house unknown' of 'The Flower.' 'And would not see, but chose to wink' applies to God the phrase which Herbert applied to the rebellious soul in 'The Collar': 'While thou didst wink and wouldst not see.' 'Love-twist' derives directly in meaning and form from the 'silk-twist' of 'The Pearl.' In the final stanza of 'Retirement,' 'school . . . heraldry . . . Thy true descent' are lifted bodily from 'Church-monuments,' and the dramatic final words, 'I will,' imitate the 'My Lord' of 'The Collar.' There are also other possible reminiscences of Herbert's 'Affliction (I),' 'The H. Communion,' 'Love (II),' and 'Frailtie.' But 'Retirement' is not singular in the number of its borrowings; it reminds us of Herbert because, despite some looseness and awkwardness, it imitates Herbert's tone and logical structure.

6. Thirty-three of the thirty-six chapters begin with the words, 'The Countrey Parson.' Chapter i begins with 'A Pastor,' chapter ii with 'Of Pastors,' and chapter x with 'The Parson.'

7. *The Lives*, ed. G. Saintsbury ('World's Classics'; London, 1927), p. 288.

8. See John Butt, 'Izaak Walton's Methods in Biography,' *ESEA*, XIX (1934), 67-84.

9. *A Letter to B. O. the Publisher of Mr Herberts Country Parson. From T. B.* (London, 1672).

10. *The Works* ('Bohn's Library'; London, 1901-03), II, 345.

11. *Ibid.*, II, 358.

12. Occasionally imitation of Herbert made for good verse. For 'Peace' (in *Prison Pietie*, 1677), Samuel Speed retained the title of the Herbert poem he closely imitated, but his poem possesses a rough distinction of its own. Ralph Knevet, whose 'To the Honorable Sir Robert Paston's Lady; A Gallery to the Temple' is still largely in manuscript (Brit. Mus. Add. MS. 27447), seems to me the most interesting of Herbert's avowed disciples after Vaughan. L. Birkett Marshall printed ten poems from Knevet's collection in *Rare Poems of the Seventeenth Century* (Cambridge, 1936), pp. 126-40.

13. *Poems Upon Several Occasions* (London, 1697), pp. 83-89. Baker's poem is full of the most extravagant praise of Herbert: Herbert is, in fact, the hero who, single-handed, rescued poetry from the pagans and defeated the 'infernal Pow'rs.' But there is hardly a phrase to indicate that Baker had read Herbert's poetry; his language and versification show him a poor if striving disciple of Cowley.

14. See Hutchinson, *Works*, p. xliv. Bryan quoted three poems in full and parts of seven others in his *Dwelling with God* (1670), a volume used by Bunyan.

15. See, e.g., Baxter's 'Divine Love's Rest' and 'Self-Denial,' *Poetical Fragments*, pp. 61-62, 65-74.

16. See Thomas H. Johnson, 'Edward Taylor: A Puritan "Sacred Poet,"' *The New England Quarterly*, X (1937), 318; and *The Poetical Works of Edward Taylor* (New York, 1939), p. 16.

17. For a just discussion of Taylor's achievement see Kenneth B. Murdock, *Literature & Theology in Colonial New England* (Cambridge, Mass., 1949), pp. 152-72.

18. *A View of Death: or, The Soul's Departure from the World. A Philosophical Sacred Poem, with a Copious Body of Explanatory Notes,*

and Some Additional Composures (London, 1725), p. 31n. The title
poem was first published in 1709. Reynolds may have learned of
Herbert through his father's friend, Richard Baxter, or through his
own friend, Matthew Henry, the son of that Philip Henry (1631-96)
who was named for his godfather and George Herbert's patron, Philip
Herbert, fourth Earl of Pembroke—see *DNB*.

19. *A View of Death*, pp. 111-12. Reynolds carefully footnoted his
many specific references to Herbert's poems in this 142-line poem.

20. *A View of Death*, preface.

21. *Ibid.*, p. 70n. The same lines from Herbert were quoted for a
similar purpose by A. O. Lovejoy, *The Great Chain of Being* (Cambridge, Mass., 1936), p. 60.

22. *A View of Death*, pp. 61n-63n.

23. *Ibid.*, pp. 37, 55.

24. *Ibid.*, p. 49.

25. 'John Wesley and George Herbert,' *The London Quarterly and
Holborn Review*, CLXI (1936), 439.

26. Preface to *Poetical Fragments*.

27. Quoted by Hutchinson, *Works*, p. xlvii, from *Memoirs of the
early life of William Cowper, written by himself* (1816), pp. 26-27.

28. *The Complete Works*, ed. W. G. T. Shedd (New York, 1884),
III, 439. The poems referred to are 'Sinne (I),' and 'Love unknown.'
Coleridge also quoted 'Vertue.'

29. *Miscellaneous Criticism*, ed. T. M. Raysor (Cambridge, Mass.,
1936), p. 250.

30. Coleridge's 'Notes' were first published in Pickering's edition
of Herbert's *Works* (London, 1835-36), II, 379-82.

31. *Miscellaneous Criticism*, p. 244.

32. Preface to *The Poems of George Herbert*, etc. ('Canterbury
Poets'; London, 1885), p. xxviii.

33. Preface to *The Temple*, 4th ed. of 1633 facs. (London, 1883),
pp. viii, xxii, xxiv. Shorthouse believed that Herbert 'has that religious
sympathy with flowers which is a note of the true Church.'

34. (Boston and New York, 1874), p. vii. Norman A. Brittin has
evaluated the debt of Emerson's poetry to Herbert in 'Emerson and
the Metaphysical Poets,' *American Literature*, VIII (1936), 1-21.

35. *The Journals*, ed. E. W. Emerson and W. E. Forbes (Boston
and New York, 1909-14), V, 5.

36. *Collected Poems*, ed. Carl Bode (Chicago, 1943), pp. 81-82, 89-91.

37. Emerson, *Works*, IX, 359, 510n. The mistake was easy to make, for Emerson's poem derives from Herbert's 'Sinne (I),' the sonnet which Coleridge had quoted in *Biographia Literaria*.

38. Poem No. 232, *Bolts of Melody*, ed. M. L. Todd and M. T. Bingham (New York and London), p. 125.

39. In his *Journal* for Sept. 15th, 1831 (II, 415), Emerson wrote: 'I often make the criticism on my friend Herbert's diction, that his thought has that heat as actually to fuse the words, so that language is wholly flexible in his hands and his rhyme never stops the progress of the sense. And, in general, according to the elevation of the soul will the power over language always be, and lively thoughts will break out into spritely verse.'

40. 'Charity,' *The Poetical Works*, ed. W. M. Rossetti ('Globe Library'; London, 1924), pp. 84, 465n.

41. *Ibid.*, pp. 234, 339. Eleanor W. Thomas comments on the Herbertian quality of 'Good Friday' in *Christina Georgina Rossetti* (New York, 1931), p. 195. Comparison of 'Up-Hill' with Herbert's 'Love (III)' is inevitable.

42. William E. Addis's judgment is quoted by G. F. Lahey, *Gerard Manley Hopkins* (London and New York, 1938), p. 19.

43. *The Correspondence of Gerard Manley Hopkins and Richard Watson Dixon*, ed. C. C. Abbott (London, 1935), pp. 23-24, 98; see also *The Letters of Gerard Manley Hopkins to Robert Bridges*, ed. C. C. Abbott (London, 1935), p. 88. Emerson's publicly expressed preference for Herbert was so decided that the partisans of Vaughan took offence. See *The Letters of Ralph Waldo Emerson*, ed. R. L. Rusk (New York, 1939), VI, 32n, 59-60.

44. W. H. Gardner discusses Hopkins's poetic 'keepings' from Herbert in *Gerard Manley Hopkins (1844-1889): A Study of Poetic Idiosyncrasy in Relation to Poetic Tradition* (London, 1944-49), I, 127, 170-72, 184. Hopkins may have learned from Herbert the use of such typical devices as 'the epithet of three elements,' and there are echoes in his poems from Herbert's 'Bitter-sweet,' 'Paradise,' 'The Flower,' and 'The Church-porch.'

45. (Boston and New York, 1905), 3 vols. A revised edition appeared in 1907, and a one-volume edition in 1916.

46. 'George Herbert,' *Shelburne Essays: Fourth Series* (New York and London, 1906), p. 69.

47. *The English Works*, I, xii.

48. The edition of James Russell Lowell and Charles Eliot Norton appeared in 1895 and that of E. K. Chambers in 1896. Gosse's *Life and Letters* came in 1899.

49. For a condensed and critical view of Donne's modern reputation see Douglas Bush, *English Literature in the Earlier Seventeenth Century: 1600-1660* (Oxford, 1945), pp. 135, 526. Theodore Spencer and Mark Van Doren, *Studies in Metaphysical Poetry: Two Essays and a Bibliography* (New York, 1939), provide an accurate measure of the extraordinary quantity of writings, scholarly and critical, concerning 'metaphysical poetry' from 1912 to 1938.

50. See Merritt Y. Hughes, 'Kidnapping Donne,' *Essays in Criticism: Second Series* (Berkeley, 1934), pp. 61-89, and Rosemond Tuve, *Elizabethan and Metaphysical Imagery: Renaissance Poetic and Twentieth Century Critics* (Chicago, 1947), *passim*.

51. *Metaphysical Lyrics*, pp. xxii, xiv.

52. *Ibid.*, p. xvi.

53. Introduction to *The Poetical Works of George Herbert*, ed. C. C. Clarke (London, 1863).

54. The specific references in this paragraph have been confined to George Williamson, *The Donne Tradition* (Cambridge, Mass., 1930), pp. 100-09, and Joan Bennett, *Four Metaphysical Poets: Donne, Herbert, Vaughan, Crashaw* (Cambridge, 1934), pp. 50-66, as typical and influential expressions of the prevailing attitude. While a detailed study of Herbert's modern reputation would include many more figures and some interesting variations of opinion, these pages state the central formulations which were echoed most often in casual references to Herbert.

55. *Metaphysical Lyrics*, p. xliv.

56. In *Puritan and Anglican: Studies in Literature* (London).

57. The MS. of the lectures is in Houghton Library, Harvard University.

58. I find myself in general agreement with the attitude expressed long ago by Edward Dowden in *New Studies in Literature* (London, 1902), p. 92: 'I do not believe in the existence of this so-called "metaphysical school."' The literary term metaphysical, whether defined by 'spirit' or style, has lost whatever descriptive value it may once have possessed. Rarely used with much precision from Dryden on, it has in the last thirty years been loosely applied to various

qualities and poems. Poets classified as 'metaphysical' have included Dante, Lucretius, Browning, and Wordsworth. Those essays and anthologies which have attempted to confine the term to a specific school in seventeenth-century England have rarely included identical figures as members of the 'school': Mark Van Doren used the adjective according to the statistical evidence of his bibliography when he remarked, 'By metaphysical poetry I mean the poetry of the seventeenth century.' The conception of the 'metaphysical conceit' offers small aid, since there is as little agreement in the definition of the noun as of the adjective: catachresis was used before Donne; the 'structural metaphor' has never been unknown to English poetry; and the degree of 'shock,' 'fantasticality,' or 'incongruity' in a metaphor can be measured only by a sense, possibly mistaken, of the poetic norm at any one period of time. Finally, thought and emotion are 'fused' to a greater or lesser degree in all good poetry. It would, therefore, seem in the interest of precise communication to avoid the word 'metaphysical' whenever possible. The following words, among others, convey most of the meanings intended by the term in the past: 'great,' 'passionate,' 'disillusioned,' 'sceptical,' 'intellectual,' 'rational,' 'philosophical,' 'theological,' 'sensual,' 'sensuous,' 'conversational,' 'anti-poetic,' and 'rough.' Perhaps most useful, since it is so awkward it would not be abused, is 'Donne-like.'

59. *Spectator*, CXLVIII (1932), 360-61.

60. 'George Herbert,' *American Review*, VII (1936), 249-71. A revised version of the essay (from the final page of which I quote) is printed in Warren's *Rage for Order: Essays in Criticism* (Chicago, 1948), pp. 19-36.

61. Hutchinson's edition first appeared in 1941. His earlier essay in *Seventeenth Century Studies Presented to Sir Herbert Grierson* (Oxford, 1938), pp. 148-60, is also helpful. Knights's excellent essay appeared in *Scrutiny* in 1944 and is reprinted in his *Explorations* (London and New York, 1947), pp. 129-48. Tuve's 'On Herbert's "Sacrifice,"' *The Kenyon Review*, XII (1950), 54-75, was a section of *A Reading of George Herbert* (London and Chicago, 1952). Other recent essays which throw light on Herbert's poetry include Helen C. White's chapters on Herbert in *The Metaphysical Poets: A Study in Religious Experience* (New York, 1936); Albert McHarg Hayes's 'Counterpoint in Herbert,' *SP*, XXXV (1938), 43-60; and Rosemary Freeman's 'George Herbert and the Emblem Books,' *RES*, XVII (1941), 150-65. A revised form of the last essay is included in Freeman's *English Emblem Books* (London, 1948), pp. 148-72.

NOTES

NOTES TO CHAPTER II

1. It was to Walton's purpose to indicate that Magdalene Herbert's family, the Newports, 'for their Loyalty, have suffered much in their Estates'—*Lives*, pp. 260-61.

2. Since Herbert earned his right to be an heir of classical, Christian, and Renaissance traditions, one can easily discover parallels to his imagery, ideas, and even language in the works of almost any sixteenth- or seventeenth-century writer; but Sidney, Donne, Bacon, Southwell, and William Herbert, Earl of Pembroke, seem to be the only 'modern' writers whose work Herbert used in a significant fashion. It is sufficient to indicate here that Donne's influence was by no means so preponderant as most modern critics have assumed. Donne's relations, both personal and literary, were closer with Magdalene Herbert and Edward Herbert (the ward of Donne's unwilling father-in-law, Sir George More) than with George Herbert, twenty years his junior. Herbert knew Donne's poetry, but he rarely borrowed from it. In his 'In Sacram Anchoram Piscatoris,' Herbert addressed Donne as the eloquent and religious Dean of St Paul's rather than as the poet. 'A Parodie,' occasionally regarded as the most obvious evidence of Herbert's discipleship to Donne, is derived from 'Soul's joy when I am gone,' but that poem was almost certainly written by William Herbert rather than by Donne. (See Grierson's comment in *The Poems of Donne*, II, cxxv-cxxvi. Although the editing of Pembroke's poems in 1660 was notoriously careless, the younger John Donne, the editor, would hardly have attributed to William Herbert a poem written by his father.) In the life and writings of George Herbert there is as little evidence of simple literary discipleship as there is of literary naïveté.

3. The pages which immediately follow are based on Hutchinson's meticulous biography in Herbert's *Works*, pp. xxi-xxxix. In this entire chapter my debt to Hutchinson is enormous. I have also found suggestive A. G. Hyde's *George Herbert and His Times* (London and New York, 1906).

4. See *Memoriae Matris Sacrum*, Poem ii, ll. 61-65. The *Memoriae Matris Sacrum*, in conjunction with Walton's *Life* and Donne's funeral sermon, almost inevitably arouses speculation today concerning the psychological relationship between Herbert and his mother. The literary critic without professional psychiatric training, however, can hardly hope for a greater success in medical diagnosis than the

psychiatrist ignorant of literary conventions usually achieves in literary criticism.

5. John Donne, *A Sermon of Commemoration of the Lady Dāuers . . . Together with other Commemorations of Her; By her Sonne G. Herbert* (London, 1627), p. 131.

6. Charles, the fourth son, had published verse (in Zouch's *The Dove*) before his death at New College, Oxford, in 1617. Thomas Herbert, the youngest son, was identified in the *DNB* as the 'probable author' of a number of political pamphlets in inferior verse published in 1641, and G. H. Palmer accepted the attribution. The Herbert name was, however, a common one. One line in *An Answer to . . . Mercuries Message* (p. 5), 'No Canterburnian I, though Kentish borne,' makes it certain that the Thomas Herbert who wrote the pamphlets was not Magdalene Herbert's son.

7. Donne, *A Sermon of Commemoration*, pp. 132-33, 145-46, 156-58.

8. Letter of 1619, *Works*, pp. 471-73.

9. For Chauncy's early life see Samuel Eliot Morison, *The Founding of Harvard College* (Cambridge, Mass., 1935), pp. 89-91, 371. The careers of Chauncy and Herbert were closely parallel from 1606 until 1623. Herbert was one year in advance of Chauncy at both Westminster and Trinity. The two scholars ranked second in the *Ordo Senioritatis* in successive years, both became fellows of Trinity in 1614, and both became lecturers. In 1619 each contributed Latin verses to the official Cambridge volume on the death of Queen Anne. At the granting of the degrees to the Spanish and Austrian ambassadors, Feb. 27th, 1623, Herbert gave one oration and Chauncy the valedictory. While Herbert left Cambridge within the following year, Chauncy remained in residence until 1626, the year in which Herbert took deacon's orders.

10. William and Philip as well as Edward Herbert were glad to acknowledge the relationship: see, e.g., William Herbert's letter to Edward in *Old Herbert Papers at Powis Castle and in the British Museum* (London, 1886), p. 121. William and Philip were godfathers to Sir Henry Herbert's son William, when Lady Danvers (Magdalene Herbert) was godmother—see Sir Henry's MS. note printed in *Epistolary Curiosities . . . Consisting of Unpublished Letters, of the Seventeenth Century, Illustrative of the Herbert Family*, ed. Rebecca Warner (Bath, 1818), p. 3.

11. Gardiner's estimate (*History*, VI, 29) is based on the subsidy payments of 1625.

12. The impressive list of William Herbert's friends or protégés includes Donne, Daniel, William Browne, Massinger, Ben Jonson, and Chapman. Davidson's *Poetical Rhapsody* was dedicated to William. The dedication of the Shakespeare First Folio provides the most famous evidence of the Pembrokes' reputation as literary patrons.

13. See Morison, *The Founding of Harvard College*, pp. 79-91, 360. Thomas Neville, Master of Trinity until 1615, was one of the chief opponents of Baro and Barrett in the 1590's; he officially preserved Trinity's Calvinist orthodoxy. His successor, John Richardson, was known in some circles as an Arminian, but his years at Trinity were fairly peaceful.

14. Hyde, *George Herbert and His Times*, p. 156; cf. Walton, *Lives*, pp. 270, 275. Not until after Laud's visitation of 1635 were matters corrected.

15. Sept. 1619. *Works*, pp. 369-70.

16. See *Works*, pp. 587-88, 590-92.

17. Hutchinson cites references to and borrowings from the following: Aristotle, Cassienus Bassus, Cato, Chrysostom, Cicero, Columella, Erasmus, Galen, Herodotus, Homer, Horace, Juvenal, Lucian, Menander, Ovid, Persius, Philo Judaeus, Plato, Plutarch, Seneca, Suetonius, Terence, Virgil, Xenophon. Doubtless the list could be expanded. In the poems, most of which are concerned with religious subjects, Herbert 'used' Horace, Ovid, and Virgil most often.

18. Cf. letter of June, 1620, *Works*, pp. 462-63.

19. Townsend went to France as Edward Herbert's companion in 1608-09. Carew accompanied Herbert to Paris, March 13th, 1619, as secretary to the new ambassador.

20. See Herbert's letter of Dec. 26th, 1618, *Works*, pp. 367-69, and Hutchinson's note, p. 579. For Harley's later activities, see *DNB*. Harley was on various Parliamentary committees, including one which prepared the order to prohibit the wearing of the surplice, and one empowered to gather information about (and destroy) 'idolatrous monuments' in Westminster Abbey and the London churches. He took down the cross in Cheapside and sold the mitre and crossier staff in St Paul's.

21. *The Autobiography of Lord Herbert of Cherbury*, ed. Sidney Lee (New York, n.d.), p. 134n. Boswell had established at the Synod of Dort his right to judge of orthodoxy.

22. *DNB*. Among contemporaries, however, Thorndike was better known as the advocate of a conciliatory 'primitive' form of

church government in which, so 'that as without the Bishop nothing to be done, so the Bishop to do nothing without advice of his Presbyters'—see Thorndike's *Of the Government of Churches; A Discourse Pointing at the Primitive Form* (Cambridge, 1641), p. 207.

23. Concerning the friendship Hutchinson, *Works*, p. xxvi, quotes from *The Fairfax Correspondence*, ed. G. W. Johnson (1848), I, 64. Fairfax became a Fellow of Trinity in 1608. At the Restoration, when there were objections to his name and his long residence at Nun Appleton, Fairfax voluntarily withdrew from his living.

24. Hutchinson's note in the 1945 edition of *Works* (p. viii) was the first modern notice of Herbert's election to Parliament. Although Philip was Earl of Montgomery, his brother William was more concerned with matters of state at the time and 'commanded numerous seats in the House of Commons' (Gardiner, *History*, VI, 30). Sir Henry Herbert was elected to succeed his brother George in 1626.

25. Perhaps unjustly, one searches for a political motive for Williams's slightest action. The 1624 appointment might be accounted for by the fact that Herbert had just attended his first session of Parliament. After several months of tense disagreement with Buckingham, Williams was dismissed as Lord Keeper, Oct. 25th, 1625, and exiled to his diocese. The 1626 institution may have been a politic reminder of his continued good will to the Earls of Pembroke and Montgomery, as well as to the then unemployed Edward, Lord Castle-Island.

26. Sir Henry's duties included supervising the dramatic productions at Court and granting licences for other plays. Unlike Sir John Danvers and Lord Herbert of Cherbury (but like Lord Herbert's sons), Sir Henry remained loyal to the King during the Civil War; his loyalty, however, seems to have been based on personal and political rather than ecclesiastical considerations. In a letter written while he was with Charles during the First Bishops' War (early June, 1639, *Epistolary Curiosities*, pp. 20-25), Sir Henry clearly stated his respect for the Covenanters and regret at the English policy. His conclusion that 'The quarrell began among the women; and ther the fyer burnes still, not to be putt out, but in putting them out' seems to be a scarcely veiled reference to the bishops.

27. May 6th [1627 ?]. The letter may have been written upon Herbert's ordination the year before. Hutchinson's assumption, *Works*, p. xxx, that Herbert made a Latin speech at the installation of Buckingham as Chancellor, July 13th, 1626, is based on Mede's account of the proceedings, printed in J. B. Mullinger, *The University of*

Cambridge (Cambridge, 1911), III, 672-73. But Mede mentioned only 'the orator,' and by 1626 either Thorndike or Creighton may have been thus referred to casually.

28. See Hutchinson, *Works*, p. xxxiv. The Court was not at Wilton or Salisbury, and Laud and Philip Herbert were on bad terms at the time.

29. Hutchinson, *Works*, p. xxxiv; cf. Gardiner, *History*, VII, 133. The election occurred two days after Philip succeeded to the title on the death of his brother William, the former Chancellor.

30. Hutchinson, *Works*, pp. xxxvi, 583. Some slight substantiation of Aubrey's statement is furnished by Herbert's letter of December 10th, 1631, and his visit to Lady Anne Clifford, Countess of Pembroke, at Wilton in October 1632. See *Works*, pp. 376-77, and *The Ferrar Papers*, ed. B. Blackstone (Cambridge, 1938), p. 267.

31. Gardiner, *History*, VII, 132, and H. R. Trevor-Roper, *Archbishop Laud: 1573-1645* (London, 1940), p. 111. After his sermon at Whitehall in March 1630, Davenant escaped punishment from the Privy Council by promising 'a judicious silence for the future.' According to the visitation report a few years after Herbert's death, the church ornaments at Salisbury Cathedral 'had been sold forty years ago, and . . . surplice and hood were "now scarce seen once a quarter"' (see Trevor-Roper, *Laud*, p. 192; cf. Gardiner, *History*, VIII, 108). Since Herbert loved to attend services there, however, one must assume that the music under Davenant's direction was excellent.

32. Herbert's letter to Sir John Danvers, March 18th, 1618, *Works*, pp. 364-65.

33. *Works*, pp. 367-69, 365-66, 434, 596.

34. *Lives*, p. 275.

35. See Hutchinson, *Works*, pp. liii-lvi, lxvii. Of the 164 poems in *The Temple*, 69 which do not refer to Herbert's being priest are found in MS. Jones B 62 in Dr Williams's Library, Gordon Square, London. It may be assumed that these poems were written before his ordination in 1630.

36. Letter to Sir John Danvers, Oct. 6th, 1619, *Works*, p. 370.

37. *Lives*, pp. 289-90 (reversed italics). For this 'speech' one suspects that Walton used his gift for reconstruction with some memory for his subject's writings: Herbert's poem 'Dotage' seems particularly to the point here. But Walton's circumstantial introduction

('And the same night that he had his Induction, he said to Mr *Woodnot* . . .') convinces one of the passage's general truth.

38. Lord Herbert's remark, *Autobiography*, p. 11, may indicate slight annoyance that his brother was 'little less than sainted' 'around Salisbury' as well as his pride in the Herbert temperament.

39. Walton, *Lives*, p. 270.

40. Lord Herbert, *Autobiography*, p. 43, and Magdalene Danvers's letter of May 12th, 1614, *Old Herbert Papers*, pp. 85-86. The prospects of Herbert's other brothers also seemed good at the time. Richard Herbert was engaged in the wars as the time-honoured method of advancement, and Thomas, who had distinguished himself at Juliers in 1610, had, along with Sir Thomas Roe, visited the Great Mogul at Surat in 1617. Henry was acquiring polish in Paris.

41. See Herbert's letters of 1618-19, *Works*, pp. 363-67, 369-70.

42. See *Old Herbert Papers*, pp. 87-89; for a later date, see pp. 118, 121, and *passim*.

43. Herbert had secured the support of Sir Francis Nethersole, Sir Benjamin Rudyerd, John Richardson, Sir John Danvers, and, it seems, the Earl of Pembroke (*Works*, pp. 369-70, 580).

44. Hutchinson, *Works*, p. xxvii, quotes Hacket's account from *Scrinia Reserata* (1693), I, 175.

45. May 20th, 1620, *Works*, pp. 458-59. For James's reaction, see Walton, *Lives*, pp. 270-71.

46. See Gardiner, *History*, IV, 56-107. Bacon submitted to the Lords a general confession, April 22nd, and one more detailed, April 30th. He was sentenced May 3rd. From the title of the poem Hutchinson concludes, *Works*, p. 597, that it was written 'between 27 Jan. 1620/21, when Bacon was created Viscount St Alban, and the following 1 May when he was deprived of the Great Seal.'

47. Hutchinson quotes a contemporary account, *Works*, p. 600.

48. Gardiner, *History*, V, 128-29.

49. *History*, VII, 266-67.

50. 'Triumphus Mortis' is No. xxxii of *Lucus*, *Works*, pp. 418-21. 'Inventa Bellica,' first printed by Pickering, seems to be a revision, but the manuscript is lost. Edmund Blunden's abbreviated translation of 'Inventa Bellica' was printed in *ESEA*, XIX (1934), 37-39.

51. 'Triumphus Mortis,' ll. 34-35.

52. Herbert's Oration, ll. 10-11, *Works*, p. 449.

53. Blunden's translations of the final line of 'Inventa Bellica.'

54. Gardiner, *History*, V, 176-235, is my primary source for the session.

55. The reference in *Ferrar Papers*, p. 58, to their 'having but once had personall Conference each with other' must refer to the years after Ferrar was at Little Gidding.

56. Pembroke, Williams, and Hamilton, along with Lodovic Stuart, were members of the Commission for Spanish affairs, and they had opposed Buckingham's plan for war with Spain the month before the session opened. By the time Parliament convened (after a postponement because of Stuart's death), Pembroke had been appeased, and his defence of Buckingham's conduct procured from Parliament an almost unanimous vote of approval. But Pembroke and Hamilton were again in opposition to Buckingham in April for his plan to send Bristol to the Tower, and again in September for his willingness to agree to France's demands concerning the English Catholics.

57. Modern scholars have shown that Sandys and the Ferrars were inefficient in their management, and that, political considerations aside, the welfare of the colony and the 'business issue' justified the dissolution. I am concerned here, however, only with how matters would have appeared to the step-son of Sir John Danvers, a close friend of the Ferrars and of that 'Arthur Wodenoth' who wrote 'An Account and Observation taken by A. W., a true friend and Servant to Sir John Danvers and the Parliament-interest, containing a great part of his more Publick Transactions concerning the Plantation of Virginia'—see Wesley Frank Craven, *Dissolution of the Virginia Company: The Failure of a Colonial Experiment* (New York, 1932), pp. 16-19. Woodnoth's account, written about 1644, was printed in *A Short Collection of the Most Remarkable Passages from the originall to the dissolution of the Virginia Company* (London, 1651).

58. *Ferrar Papers*, pp. 22-23. Middlesex opposed the Spanish war, and it seems certain that Buckingham and Charles instigated the impeachment because of that impolitic action; but the 'above one hundred Parl: men, that was of the Virginia Company' (John Ferrar's estimate, *Ferrar Papers*, p. 22) were glad to lend their support.

59. *DNB*.

60. Craven, *Dissolution of the Virginia Company*, pp. 319n-320n, quotes Sir Francis Nethersole's account. They attributed their difficulties to the 'malign influence' of the Spanish Ambassador as well as to Middlesex and Nathaniel Rich.

61. On May 28th, James scolded the assembly in such language that the Commons refused to enter his speech on the records. On the final day he flatly refused to pass the bill for enforcing the recusancy laws, made a few witticisms on the bill for the proper observance of the Sabbath, expressed his anger at the impeachment of Middlesex, and indicated that, since the Parliament had failed to indicate that the recovery of the Palatinate was one of the objects of its grants, he would place his own marginal notation of that aim on the subsidy bill. The final feeling among most members of Parliament was astonishment as well as anger.

62. *Ferrar Papers*, p. 26. Ferrar's old friend and business associate, Sir Edwin Sandys, approved of the decision.

63. Edward Herbert was recalled at Louis's request; but his just warning concerning France's motives and probable actions in the English alliance had earned him the enmity of Charles and Buckingham. His serious financial troubles date from this time, since he was never recompensed for many of his expenses as ambassador. In May of 1626 he was still writing to Charles to complain of 'the most publique disgrace that ever minister in my place did suffer.' His later career is largely a record of desperate attempts to regain favour—attempts which included his defence of the expedition to the Isle of Rhe after Buckingham's death, and his flattering biography of Henry VIII. Favour actually came only a few years before the outbreak of the war; but when his castle was besieged, Herbert quickly made terms with Parliament.

64. For the session, see Gardiner, *History*, V, 336-74, 397-432. Charles's answer to Parliament's new accusations against Richard Montague (the appearance of *Apello Caesarem* had increased the anger, evident in 1624, at the Arminian author of *A New Gag for an Old Goose*) was to make Montague his chaplain. At the end of the session all of Parliament's suspicions were stated openly: there were renewed protests against the imprisonment of members of Parliament, an expression of the fear that English ships had been sent to fight French Protestants, and a full-scale attack on Buckingham's foreign policy. In Sir John Eliot's words, 'We have had no fruit yet but shame and dishonour over all the world.' After Buckingham's unsatisfactory defence, the attack became even more specific. Buckingham was charged with one-man rule: he would neither ask nor accept counsel. Throughout the session, Pembroke and Williams were continually at odds with Charles and Buckingham. Pembroke was too important to be alienated, and a reconciliation was effected in the following

September. Williams, however, was dismissed in disgrace on October 25th.

65. Walton, *Lives*, pp. 276-77.

66. Hutchinson, *Works*, p. 587. In his will George Herbert described Lawley as 'A Merchant of London.' The grant seems to have been in partial recognition of the clamorous claims of Sir Edward for recompense of his services as ambassador, as well as an indication that the other two men deserved some consideration.

67. Herbert, 'Affliction (I).'

68. 'The Priesthood.'

69. In *A Priest to the Temple*, *Works*, pp. 274-75, Herbert defined his attitude toward wealth more carefully than did many of his contemporaries and successors: 'Lastly, riches are the blessing of God, and the great Instrument of doing admirable good; therfore all are to procure them honestly, and seasonably, when they are not better imployed. Now this reason crosseth not our Saviours precept of selling what we have, because when we have sold all, and given it to the poor, we must not be idle, but labour to get more, that we may give more, according to St *Pauls* rule, *Ephes*. 4. 28. *I Thes*. 4. 11, 12. So that our Saviours selling is so far from crossing Saint *Pauls* working, that it rather establisheth it, since they that have nothing, are fittest to work.'

70. 'Submission.'

71. Cf. Malcolm Mackenzie Ross, 'George Herbert and the Humanist Tradition,' *The University of Toronto Quarterly*, XVI (1947), 169-82.

72. W. J. Courthope, *A History of English Poetry* (London and New York, 1895-1910), III, 116.

NOTES TO CHAPTER III

1. Barnabas Oley's preface to *Herbert's Remains* (1652). The remainder of this paragraph is based on the following: *Ferrar Papers*, pp. 27, 55; Henry Collett, *Little Gidding and its Founder* (London, 1925), pp. 21, 31, 46; Gardiner, *History*, VII, 262-64; Hyde, *George Herbert and His Times*, p. 221n.

2. *Ferrar Papers*, p. 63.

3. *Documents Illustrative of English Church History*, comp. Henry Gee and W. J. Hardy (London, 1910), p. 509.

4. *English Devotional Literature (Prose), 1600-1640* (Madison, 1931), p. 187; see also p. 52 and Wilbur K. Jordan, *The Development of Religious Toleration in England* (Cambridge, Mass., 1932-40), II, 115n. In reading the theological literature of the first half of the seventeenth century, one needs to keep in mind certain semantical distinctions. Every religious writer thought himself a member of the 'catholic' Church, and the use of the work 'catholic' furnishes no clue to theological opinion. The Roman Catholics were assured that the Council of Trent had established the true, 'primitive' catholic doctrine, and Calvinists, Lutherans, and Anabaptists were equally sure that theirs was the truly 'catholic' religion, purified from the 'innovations' of Rome. The appeal to antiquity was universal. So far as I know, no theologian ever admitted to being an 'innovator': the word has an entirely pejorative sense. 'Primitive,' by analogy, is a word of praise, although a distinction can be made between the 'primitive' of Anglicans and Lutherans who looked to the Church of the first four centuries and that of the Presbyterians and 'sectarians' who tended to look more exclusively at the Bible or at the writings of Calvin. In England 'Arminianism' (as well as 'Puritanism') was almost always a term of opprobrium, and even Montague denied that he was an Arminian. 'Arminian' was originally applied to the followers of those doctrines condemned at the Synod of Dort in 1619, by which Arminius modified the strict Calvinist theory of predestination. In England, however, the word came to be used as a loose equivalent of 'un-orthodox.' It was often applied to those who placed unusual emphasis on St James's 'Faith without works is dead.' Sir Francis Knollys used the word with some precision when he called Arminians 'free-wyll men and justiciaries or justifiers of themselves,' but Parliament's resolution of 1629 against 'Popery, or Arminianism, or heterodoxy' is more typical. The word came to be applied to advocates of ritual or the episcopacy, whatever their theology. I have restricted my use of the word in accordance with the definition given by Edward L. Cutts, *A Dictionary of the Church of England* (London, n.d.), to the members of the *theologically* 'Anglo-Catholic school of reaction against the prevalent Calvinism in England in the seventeenth century.'

5. W. Fraser Mitchell, *English Pulpit Oratory from Andrewes to Tillotson: A Study of its Literary Aspects* (London, 1932), p. 203.

6. Quoted in *Anglicanism*, ed. P. E. More and F. L. Cross (London and Milwaukee, 1935), p. xlviii.

7. In its Resolutions on Religion of 1629, the Parliamentary committee claimed to act as the conservative defender of the Elizabethan settlement. Although the Resolutions may have exaggerated the number of Arminians in high office by that time, the trend was unmistakable.

8. 'The King's Majesty's Declaration to His Subjects Concerning Lawful Sports to be Used,' issued originally by James I in 1618 and reissued with additional comments by Charles I, Oct. 18th, 1633, Gee and Hardy, *Documents*, p. 531.

9. William Holden Hutton, *William Laud* (Boston and New York, 1895), p. 85.

10. Mario Praz, *Studies in Seventeenth Century Imagery* (London, 1939), I, 131n. It need hardly be added that Quarles gave no credit line.

11. See Mitchell, *English Pulpit Oratory*, pp. 202-03, and White, *English Devotional Literature*, pp. 71 ff.

12. In *A Priest to the Temple, Works*, pp. 246, 259, Herbert's comments on the position of the table and the method of receiving Communion, two of the chief points of dissension at the time, echoed the vagueness of the Elizabethan compromise: 'the Pulpit, and Desk, and Communion Table, and Font should be as they ought, for those great duties that are performed in them'; while 'he that sits, or lies, puts up to an Apostle,' yet 'Contentiousnesse in a feast of Charity is more scandall than any posture.'

13. Melville's poem was published in David Calderwood's *Parasynagma Perthense*; Hutchinson reprints it in *Works*, pp. 609-14. Herbert's *Musae Responsoriae | Ad Andreae Melvini Scoti | Anti-Tami-Cami-Categoriam* was first published by James Duport in his *Ecclesiastes Solomonis* (Cambridge, 1662). For the date of composition, see Hutchinson's comment, *Works*, pp. 587-88.

14. Hutchinson, *Works*, p. 588.

15. *Works*, p. 386.

16. 'De Autorum enumeratione,' *Works*, p. 398.

17. 'In Monstrum vocabuli *Anti-Tami-Cami-Categoria,' Works*, p. 386, suggests 'Anti-furi-Puri-Categoria' and 'Anti-pelvi-Melvi-Categoria' as equivalents of Melville's 'monstrous' word.

18. In 'De impositione manuum,' *Works*, p. 397, Herbert dismissed Melville's objection to the 'laying on of hands' with a pun: 'Quantò Impositio melior est Imposturâ!' In 'De rituum vsu,' pp.

395-96, he insisted that the Puritans, in their desire to strip the Bride of Christ, wished to leave her as vulnerable to the Devil as the naked British were to Caesar. 'De annulo coniugali,' p. 396, argues that if one believes a symbol for eternity unsuitable for an earthly marriage, he may consider the wedding ring, like the rainbow, a sign that good weather is in store—in the lawful marriage bed.

19. *Works*, p. 392.

20. 'De Signaculo Crucis,' *Works*, p. 389. Comparison with Donne's 'The Crosse' is almost inevitable.

21. 'De Purificatione post puerperium,' *Works*, pp. 389-90.

22. 'Ad Seren. Regem,' *Works*, p. 402.

23. 'De Textore Catharo' and 'De labe maculísque,' *Works*, pp. 392-93.

24. 'Ad Melvinum,' *Works*, pp. 400-01.

25. 'Ad Seren. Regem,' *Works*, p. 402. The Puritans were not the only recipients of Herbert's criticism. In one of his most pointed epigrams in *Lucus* ('Papae titulus *Nec Deus Nec Homo*,' *Works*, p. 412) he remarked, 'Let us cease to search for the Antichrist; the Pope is neither God nor man: and Christ was both.' Herbert developed that idea in 'The Church Militant,' ll. 205-20, where Rome was not only 'Antichrist,' but the 'Western *Babylon*' as well. His remarks are not surprising, for most of Herbert's contemporaries in England shared such opinions of Rome.

26. *Lives*, p. 273. The letter with the aphorisms has never been traced.

27. 'Briefe Notes relating to the dvbious and offensive places in Valdesso's *Considerations*,' *Works*, p. 313; see Hutchinson's comment, pp. 566-68. Herbert's notes were sent to Ferrar, Sept. 29th, 1632. An apologetic censure by Dr Thomas Jackson accompanied their publication with Ferrar's translation of the *Considerations* (Oxford, 1638). The anonymous editor of a second edition published at Cambridge in 1646 carefully eliminated a reference to the Pope, but also strangely censored the sentence I have quoted. This passage is followed by a comment on Valdesso's statement, 'Neither *Pharaoh*, nor *Iudas*, nor those who are *vessels of wrath*, could cease to be such.' Herbert remarked, 'This doctrine however true in substance, yet needeth discreet, and wary explaining.' The 'explanation' would probably involve a thorough exegesis of the relation of the 'Covenants' to predestination.

NOTES

28. *Works*, pp. 190-98. Since the poem is in *W*, it was probably written before 1630; but the final version shows thorough revision, supposedly made after 1630. I cannot agree with Hutchinson's judgment (p. 543) that 'All the internal evidence points to an early date for the inception of the poem.' The references to Spain and France (ll. 89, 265, 241-46) seem rather historical than either 'complimentary' or 'depreciatory,' and Herbert's comments in *A Priest to the Temple* show that he did not lose interest in the religious possibilities of the Colonies with the dissolution of the Virginia Company in 1624. The stylistic differences between 'The Church Militant' and the other poems in *The Temple* might be caused by the requirements of genre rather than by the overweening influence of Donne on the young poet. New England readers appreciated the theology of the poem as well as Herbert's declaration that 'Religion stand on tip-toe in our land, Readie to passe to the *American* strand' (ll. 235-36).

29. Bodleian, MS. Rawlinson D 199. I have read and refer to the manuscript copy made in 1904 by A. F. Parker for G. H. Palmer, Houghton Library, Her 2.3. In my quotations I have modernized the abbreviations. For further discussion of Ryley's work see my Appendix A.

30. Houghton MS., p. 28. 'The Church' is the title given to all the poems in *The Temple* except the introductory 'The Dedication,' 'The Church-porch,' and 'Superliminare,' and the concluding 'The Church Militant' and 'L'Envoy.'

31. Walton, *Lives*, p. 314.

32. Commentary on 'Dulnesse,' p. 217.

33. Pp. 327-28.

34. Commentary on 'Assurance,' p. 306. In *The New England Mind: The Seventeenth Century* (New York, 1939), Perry Miller has given an extensive account of the development of the doctrine of the Covenant in colonial New England. As Miller indicates in his appendix on 'The Federal School of Theology,' pp. 502-05, 'The Covenant of Grace was, of course, an old catchword in theology, which had long served as a descriptive for the scheme of redemption.' In 'H. Baptisme (I)' ('In you Redemption measures all my time'), Herbert seems to relate that sacrament to the Covenant of Grace in a manner similar to Richard Hooker's: 'baptism implied "a covenant or league between God and man," wherein God bestows remission of sins, "binding also himself to add in process of time" sufficient grace for the attainment of life hereafter.' Herbert's usual

use of the conception, however, goes far beyond reference to the sacrament of baptism to include the entire way of salvation which God's providence has predestined. Miller's discussion of 'The Covenant of Grace,' pp. 365-97, as it was developed by Perkins, Ames, and Preston, is relevant to an understanding of the theological background of Herbert's belief.

35. P. 43.

36. Cf. Ryley's comment, pp. 194-98.

37. 'The Author's Prayer before Sermon,' *Works*, p. 288.

38. Walton, *Lives*, p. 314.

39. *Works*, pp. 204-05.

40. In Herbert's letter 'To his Mother, in her sickness,' May 29th, 1622, *Works*, p. 373, he wrote, 'For my self, *dear Mother*, I alwaies fear'd sickness more then death, because sickness hath made me unable to perform those Offices for which I came into the world, and must yet be kept in it.'

41. *Works*, p. 254.

42. 'The Author to the Reader,' *Works*, p. 224.

43. *Works*, pp. 262-63. The arguments for the 'Schismatick' centre on the necessity of authority: 'whether things once indifferent, being made by the precept of Authority more than indifferent, it be in our power to omit or refuse them.'

44. According to Hutchinson, *Works*, pp. 563-64, Herbert's personally composed public prayers for before and after the sermon were allowed by a liberal interpretation of Canon lv (1604).

45. *Works*, pp. 246-47.

46. 'In Mundi sympathiam cum Christo,' the final poem of *Passio Discerpta*, *Works*, p. 409, makes specific mention of Plato:

> Non moreris solus: Mundus simul interit in te,
> Agnoscítque tuam Machina tota Crucem.
> Hunc ponas animam mundi, Plato: vel tua mundum
> Ne nimium vexet quaestio, pone meam.

47. 'The H. Communion,' from *W*, *Works*, p. 200.

48. See Hutchinson, *Works*, pp. 566-68. Valdés is known in England by the Italianized form of his name, 'Valdesso.' The original Spanish version of *The Considerations* was never printed. The work first appeared in an Italian translation (Basel, 1550) and later in French (Lyons, 1563; Paris, 1565).

49. 'A Copy of a letter written by *Mr George Herbert* to his friend the Translator of this Book,' Sept. 29th (1632), *Works*, p. 305.

50. *Works*, p. 318.

51. P. 307.

52. P. 308. My italics.

53. P. 308.

54. Pp. 308-09.

55. Pp. 315-16.

56. P. 315.

57. P. 316.

58. P. 313.

59. 'Consideration 32,' *Works*, p. 309.

60.
> Intellectus adultus Angelorum
> Haud nostro similis, cui necesse,
> Vt dentur species, rogare sensum:
> Et ni lumina ianuam resignent,
> Et nostrae tribuant molae farinam,
> Saepe ex se nihil otiosa cudit.
> A nobis etenim procul remoti
> Labuntur fluuij scientiarum:
> Si non per species, nequimus ipsi,
> Quid ipsi sumus, assequi putando.
> Non tantum est iter Angelis ad vndas,
> Nullo circuitu scienda pungunt,
> Illis perpetuae patent fenestrae,
> Se per se facili modo scientes,
> Atque ipsi sibi sunt mola & farina.

No. xxiv, ' In Angelos,' *Lucus, Works*, p. 415.

61. *The American College Dictionary* (New York and London, 1947).

NOTES TO CHAPTER IV

1. See Kenneth B. Murdock's discussion in *Literature & Theology in Colonial New England*, pp. 8-29. I owe a great deal to his comments on Herbert, pp. 21-27.

2. *Spiritual Exercises*, ed. Orby Shipley (London, 1870), p. 24.

3. *Lives*, p. 278.

4. *Ferrar Papers*, p. 34. For the symbolic design of the chapel at Little Gidding, see p. 28.

5. *Lives*, p. 301.

6. *L'Esthétique de Saint Augustin et ses sources* (Brno, 1933), p. 199. I am reminded of Paul Oskar Kristeller's admonition concerning the historical impropriety of the word 'aesthetic' in such a context. In their use of the word, however, Svoboda, and Katherine E. Gilbert and Helmut Kuhn in *A History of Esthetics* (New York, 1939), pp. 129-30, 155-60, are conscious of Baumgarten's invention of 1750 and of the fact that 'art' meant something quite different to the ancients and the men of the Middle Ages from what it usually means today. Yet thinkers before the Renaissance were immensely concerned with the definition and the meaning of 'beauty,' and their conceptions of beauty, while never confined to the productions of men's hands, were relevant to such productions. If we clearly understand the modernity of the ideas of an isolated group of 'fine arts' and a particular 'psychology of the artist,' the use of the word 'aesthetic' in itself should cause no misconceptions.

7. Augustine, *The Confessions*, tr. Pusey, Book X, Chap. xxxiv.

8. Cf. Herbert's 'Sinne (II).'

9. *Confessions*, Book X, Chap. xxxiii.

10. *The Anatomy of Melancholy*, ed. Floyd Dell and Paul Jordan-Smith (New York, 1938), p. 95. Burton's quotation is hardly fair: in *The Confessions*, Book I, Chap. xvi, Augustine was condemning the teaching of erotic pagan poetry to the young.

11. Herbert, 'The Pulley.'

12. *Of the Laws of Ecclesiastical Polity*, Book V, Sect. lviii.

13. 'George Herbert and the Emblem Books,' *RES*, XVII, 151.

14. See, e.g., the sections of Byrd's 'Magnificat' and Morley's 'Out of the Deep' printed in Edmund H. Fellowes's *English Cathedral Music from Edward VI to Edward VII* (London, 1941), pp. 77, 84.

15. Walton, *Lives*, p. 314.

16. Sermon X, April 9th, 1615, from *Ninety-Six Sermons, Works* (Oxford, 1841-54), II, 347-48. The entire sermon provides an interesting analogue to Herbert's thought.

17. *The Metaphysical Poets*, pp. 167-68.

18. Hutchinson, *Works*, pp. lv-lvi, summarizes the changes in order: 'the first sixteen poems in *W* are in nearly the same order as in *B*, but . . . after them there are only nine instances of two poems in the same consecutive order in *W* and *B*, until the group of nine *W* poems at the end of *B*. There are no *W* poems in *B* between No. 79, "Obedience" and the final group beginning with No. 156, "The

Elixir.'" See Hutchinson's listing of the poems in *W* and his general discussion, pp. liii-lv, lxx-lxxiv.

19. The sequence of poems which I discuss is found in *Works*, pp. 44-61.

20. 'George Herbert,' *Spectator*, CXLVIII, 360-61.

21. 'The Temple explained and improved,' p. 376.

22. *A Priest to the Temple, Works*, p. 283.

23. See 'Sepulchre.'

24. *The Metaphysical Poets*, p. 183.

25. 'The Familie.'

26. 'Man.'

27. *Rage for Order*, p. 30.

28. See Herbert's 'Grief.'

NOTES TO CHAPTER V

1. Bennett, *Four Metaphysical Poets*, p. 50.

2. The letter is printed by Hutchinson, *Works*, pp. 470-71. I quote from Grosart's translation, *The Complete Works in verse and prose of George Herbert* (London, 1874), III, 475-77.

3. Quoted from Tenison's preface to *Baconiana* (1679) in Bacon's *Works*, ed. J. Spedding, R. E. Ellis, and D. D. Heath (London, 1857-1859), I, 420.

4. Quoted from Tenison's preface by Hutchinson, *Works*, p. xl n.

5. Bacon's *Translation* is printed in his *Works*, VII, 265-86. I quote from Hutchinson's unmodernized transcription of the dedication in Herbert's *Works*, p. xl.

6. Bacon died in the year following the appearance of his *Translation*, and Herbert's 'In obitum incomparabilis... Baronis Verulamij,' the slight but graceful elegiac tribute which was Herbert's contribution to *Memoriae Francisci Baronis de Verulamio Sacrum* (London, 1626), is additional evidence of the two men's friendship. See *Works*, p. 438, for Herbert's poem, and pp. xxx, 599, for Hutchinson's comments. For a further discussion of the relationship between Bacon and Herbert, see my Appendix B.

7. Cf. Karl Wallace, *Francis Bacon on Communication & Rhetoric or: The Art of Applying Reason to Imagination for the Better Moving*

of the *Will* (Chapel Hill, 1943), p. 183. Bacon's practice followed his theory: it is a mistake to picture him as the inveterate proponent of the 'Attic' versus the Ciceronian style, of the *genus humile* rather than the *genus grande*. Wallace, pp. 153-54, contrasts the 'artificial, balanced periods' of Bacon's speeches for the revels at Gray's Inn and his letters to royalty with 'the free-running, conversational narrative of the *New Atlantis*.' *The Essays* and *The Advancement of Learning* provide contrasts to both.

8. *Advancement of Learning, Works*, III, 302.

9. *Ibid.*, 409.

10. Quoted by Wallace, p. 31, from *De augmentis*, vi, 3, *Works*, IV, 456.

11. Quoted by Wallace, p. 96, from preface to *Wisdom of the Ancients, Works*, VI, 698.

12. *Lives*, p. 295.

13. *A Priest to the Temple, Works*, pp. 234-35.

14. *Works*, p. 255.

15. Pp. 233, 275.

16. P. 228.

17. P. 257.

18. *Loc. cit.*

19. This and the quotations which follow are taken from chapter vii, 'The Parson Preaching,' *Works*, pp. 232-35.

20. *Works*, p. 279.

21. P. 278.

22. P. 279.

23. Letter of 1618, *Works*, p. 366.

24. In *A Priest to the Temple, Works*, pp. 231-32, Herbert described in detail the parson's emotions and art when he engaged in public prayer.

25. *Works*, p. 206.

26. Cf. Southwell, 'The Author to his Loving Cousin,' *The Poetical Works*, ed. W. B. Turnbull (London, 1856), pp. 1-2.

27. 'Ephes. 4.30. *Grieve not the Holy Spirit, &c.*'

28. A glance at Herbert's revisions of the poem, *Works*, pp. 102-03, should discredit the theory that he intended to reject 'art.'

29. 'Prayer (II)' which follows 'Jordan (II)' describes the accessibility of God when the individual ceases the 'search':

> Of what an easie quick accesse,
> My blessed Lord, art thou ! how suddenly
> May our requests thine eare invade !
> To show that state dislikes not easinesse,
> If I but lift mine eyes, my suit is made:
> Thou canst no more not heare, then thou canst die.

30. *A Priest to the Temple, Works*, p. 238.

31. 'Conversations with Drummond,' *Selected Works of Ben Jonson*, ed. Harry Levin (New York, 1938), p. 992.

32. Austin Warren, *Rage for Order*, p. 29.

33. 'Divinitie.'

34. Herbert expected his readers to recognize his paraphrase of the 'First and greatest Commandment,' Luke x. 27. The relationship of that command to 'love God' with the impossibility of its fulfilment ('*O, could I love!*') and God's loving justification of faith causes the poem to expand in meaning to include the whole plan of salvation. Yet the immediate subject is the composition of 'A true Hymne,' and these lines apply equally to that subject. Herbert and his contemporaries would not consider the poem an example of 'human ingenuity,' but a recognition of the ingenious manner in which the basic relationship between the soul and God extends to each activity of the Christian life.

35. From 'The Church Militant' it seems obvious that Herbert had no objections to such references in an extended narrative or description—or, more obviously, in the epic. In short poems addressed to God and 'attended' by all, a large number of classical references would be as improper as in the prayers of 'The Country Parson.'

36. 'Easter' and 'Easter-wings' are in *W*, and 'The Dawning' is not. The final lines of the first stanza of 'The Dawning' derive from the prayer of 'Easter-wings,' 'With thee Let me combine And feel this day thy victorie,' and the opening lines of the second stanza look back to the opening of 'Easter':

> Rise heart; thy Lord is risen. Sing his praise
> Without delayes,
> Who takes thee by the hand, that thou likewise
> With him mayst rise.

37. See, e.g., 'The Sonne,' a sonnet built upon a pun. Ryley's commentary, p. 336, summarizes the biblical background: 'which

imploys [*sic*] he was *born of a woman*, that he chased away the darkness of the former ages, & *brought life & immortality to light*, 2 *Tim.* 1.10; and that he was fruitfull, *for he saw his seed, & will bring many sons to glory. Is.* 53.10. *Heb.* 2.10.' The references to the culmination of light and fruit in the 'Son' are almost endless. Probably of importance to Herbert were Mal. iv. 2 and Rev. xxii. 5: 'But vnto you that feare my Name, shall the Sunne of righteousness arise with healing in his wings,' and 'And there shalbe no night there; and they need no candle, neither light of the sunne, for the Lorde God giueth them light.'

NOTES TO CHAPTER VI

1. *NED*, Sb. 2.

2. In his *Hieroglyphicorvm Collectanea, ex Veteribvs et Neotericis Descripta* ('In hoc postrema editione recognita & expurgata'; Lvgdvni, 1626), p. 7, Giovanni Pierio Valeriano summarized the general usage: 'Ad hieroglyphica accedunt emblemata, symbola, insignia, quaemuis nomine differant, reipsa multi modis conuenir videntur.'

3. Quoted in *NED*, 'Hieroglyphically,' 2, from 'Sermon I' (1642) in *A Discourse Concerning the True Notion of the Lord's Supper* (London, 1670), p. 210.

4. 'Meditatio tertia,' *Hadassa: or The History of Qveene Ester* (1621), *The Complete Works*, ed. A. B. Grosart (Edinburgh, 1880-81), II, 50.

5. Matt. xvi. 16-18. I give the Protestant interpretation of the passage.

6. 1 Cor. x. The marginal reading for 'ensamples,' v. 11, is 'Or, Types.'

7. George Ryley, 'The Temple explained and improved,' pp. 315-16, summarizes the biblical allusions: 'Joseph's Coat was of *many colours*; very beautifull; and it was a token of his father's peculiar affection. *Gen.* 37.3. . . . This poem speaks the language of the prophet, *Is.* 61.10, *I will greatly rejoice in the Lord, &c.* for he hath *cloathed me with the garments of salvation*, and of the Apostle, 2 Cor. 6.10, *As sorrowfull, yet always rejoicing.*'

8. Ps. cii. 11; Isa. xl. 6; 1 Pet. i. 24.

9. 'Against' and 'fall' are used ambiguously. 'Against' means both 'in preparation for' and 'in opposition to,' and 'fall' means both physical collapse and 'fall' into sin. These ambiguities are characteristic of Herbert's use of the device. Neither is at all recondite: 'against' in the sense of 'in preparation for' often carried something of the meaning of 'in opposition to,' and 'the fall' of man and angels had traditionally equated physical and moral movement.

10. *Primitivism and Decadence: A Study of American Experimental Poetry* (New York, 1937), pp. 10, 123.

11. On the rare occasions when a stanza ends with a colon or semicolon, modern usage would often require a period.

12. The third example is st. 5 of 'The Bag.' Here the comma after line 30, 'And straight he turn'd, and to his brethren cry'd,' is strong, since it precedes the two stanzas of direct quotation.

13. *Works*, p. 499.

14. *Works*, p. 65. In *B* the line begins a new page.

15. The only significant change which Herbert made after the version in *W* was to introduce 'crumbled' in line 22 for the less effective 'broken.'

16. In the twenty-four lines the sound of *t* occurs 59 times; *th* and *th*, 36; *s* and *z*, 51; *sh*, 15; *n*, 35; *d*, 27.

17. Grierson, *Metaphysical Lyrics*, pp. 231-32.

18. Douglas Bush has remarked that in the first stanza describing the 'type,' the consonants *l*, *m*, and *r* predominate; in the second concerning the 'natural man,' *p*, *st*, *t*, *z*, and *s*; and in the final stanza the two patterns of consonants are united.

19. 'The Pulley.'

20. Hutchinson, *Works*, p. 538, summarizes the relevant passages from Exod. xxviii.

21. Cf. 'The Priesthood.'

22. See Kenneth B. Murdock's discussion and quotations in *Handkerchiefs from Paul* (Cambridge, Mass., 1927), pp. liv-lvi.

23. In the discussion which follows I am indebted to Miss Margaret Church's 'The Pattern Poem' (Doctoral thesis, Radcliffe College, 1944), the most useful discussion of the history and development of the European pattern poem which I have found. Miss Church's Appendix C, pp. 240-427, 'includes copies of all the pattern poems discussed in the text with the exception of several *carmina quadrata* by P. Optatianus Porfirius and Hraban Maur.'

24. Church, p. 161, cites the comments of Nashe, 'Have with you . . .,' *The Works*, ed. R. B. McKerrow (London, 1900), III, 67; Harvey, *Letter-Book*, ed. E. J. L. Scott (Westminster, 1884), pp. 100-01; and Jonson, *The Works*, ed. F. Cunningham (London, 1816), III, 320, 470, 488.

25. Except for one 'lozenge,' 'On God's Law,' in the *Divine Fancies* of 1632, all of Quarles's patterns, like his emblems, were published after 1633. If there was any influence, it was Herbert who influenced Quarles.

26. See Church, pp. 297 ff. English composers of altars before Herbert included Richard Willis (1573), Andrew Willet, and William Browne of Tavistock (in *The Shepherd's Pipe*, 1614). Willet's shapes were printed at the beginning of Sylvester's *Bartas His Devine Weekes & Workes* (1605-08). It seems safe to assume that Herbert, rhetorician, classicist, and poet by profession, knew the poems of the 'Greek Anthology' as well as current practice. Arthur Woodnoth's letter to Nicholas Ferrar shortly before Herbert's death, *Ferrar Papers*, pp. 268-69, makes doubtful the hypothesis that Italian poetry directly influenced Herbert: 'Sauonorola in Latine he hath of the Simplicity of Chr: Religion and is of great esteme wth him. He sayth he doth Vnderstand Italian a lyttle.' Hutchinson notes, *Works*, pp. 564-65, that Herbert's translation of Luigi Cornaro's *Treatise of Temperance and Sobrietie* was based not on the original (Padua, 1558) but on Lessius's Latin version (Antwerp, 1613, 1614, 1623). A 'lyttle' understanding of Italian would have sufficed for the translations in *Outlandish Proverbs*. Unlike Ferrar, Crashaw, and Milton, Herbert never went to Italy.

27. Hutchinson, *Works*, p. 26, notes that in *W* the word 'onely' has been corrected to 'blessed.' The change is a poetic improvement, but the original word substantiates my interpretation of the poem.

28. Cf. the references cited by Cameron Mann, *A Concordance to the English Poems of George Herbert* (Boston and New York, 1927). For 'sacrifice,' see 'The Church-porch,' ll. 6, 275; 'The Sacrifice' throughout and especially l. 19; 'Mattens,' l. 3; 'Providence,' l. 14; 'Love unknown,' l. 30. For 'altar' see 'Love (I),' l. 21 and the first of the 'Sonnets to his Mother,' l. 6. At first reading chapter vi, 'The Parson Praying,' of *A Priest to the Temple* (*Works*, pp. 231-32) seems to provide an exception to Herbert's customary use of 'altar.' After a description of the parson's actions 'when he is to read divine services,' Herbert adds, 'This he doth, first, as being truly touched and amazed with the Majesty of God, before whom he then presents himself;

yet not as himself alone, but as presenting with himself the whole Congregation, whose sins he then beares, and brings with his own to the heavenly altar to be bathed, and washed in the sacred Laver of Christs blood.' Despite the familiar imagery, there is no reference here to the Eucharist. The 'altar' and 'the sacred Laver of Christs blood' are truly *in* heaven. Reading 'divine services' to Herbert did not imply administering the Holy Communion. In chapter xxii (p. 259), Herbert notes that the Country Parson celebrates the Communion 'if not duly once a month, yet at least five or six times in the year. . . . And this hee doth, not onely for the benefit of the work, but also for the discharge of the Church-wardens, who being to present all that receive not thrice a year; if there be but three Communions, neither can all the people so order their affairs as to receive just at those times, nor the Church-Wardens so well take notice who receive thrice, and who not.'

29. Herbert may have sacrificed accuracy to symmetry as part of his image of 'A *broken* altar.' The altars of both Dosiados and Richard Willis followed the pattern of two short lines, longer for four, much shorter for eight, and longer for five at the base (see Church, p. 46). The first two short lines which Herbert omits represent the slab (sometimes identified as the altar proper) on which the sacrifice takes place. The opening phrase of Herbert's poem makes attractive the conjecture that his pattern is intended to convey both the perfect ordering of the ideal spiritual altar and the fact that this altar is not constructed for the ancient blood-sacrifice. Such a significance is, however, perhaps too recondite for Herbert to have intended his audience to grasp it. And against such an interpretation is the fact that 'An Altare and Sacrifice to Disdaine' in *A Poetical Rhapsody* had been symmetrical (four long lines, twelve short, four long) without iconographical significance. See *A Poetical Rhapsody (1602-1621)*, ed. H. E. Rollins (Cambridge, Mass., 1931), I, sig. I₃ᵛ.

30. *Works*, p. 484.

31. See Bennett, *Four Metaphysical Poets*, p. 66.

32. As Lloyd Frankenberg has pointed out, *Pleasure Dome: on reading modern poetry* (Boston, 1949), pp. 172-79, Cummings continually writes such poems; the fact that his patterns are based on individual and spontaneous gestures or situations or personalities rather than on symmetrical and abstract forms has disguised the fact from some readers. John L. Sweeney, *The Selected Writings of Dylan Thomas* (New York, 1946), p. xxi, has suggested that the pattern of Thomas's 'Vision and Prayer' may have been inspired by 'Easter- .

wings.' As Theodore Spencer once remarked, the formal effects of James Joyce's *Ulysses* are directly related to the tradition of George Herbert's poetry.

33. *The Defence of Poesy, The Miscellaneous Works*, ed. William Gray (Boston, 1860), pp. 69-70.

NOTES TO CHAPTER VII

1. 'Counterpoint in Herbert,' *SP*, XXXV, 43-60.

2. Hayes, p. 48.

3. On pp. 53-54 Hayes gives a statistical table of his classifications of Herbert's 127 stanzaic poems into 'Seven Types.'

4. The counterpoint of two or more musical voices is not truly analogous to the poetic 'counterpoint' of rhyme and metrical patterns. A stricter, but still general, parallel to musical counterpoint would be the interweaving of ideas or images in a poem (as in Eliot's *Four Quartets*), while the musical parallel to Herbert's practice would be the placing of related cadences after an irregular number of measures. Hayes's attempt to relate Herbert's experiments to a desire to eliminate the 'disparity' between a 'contrapuntal music' and a 'non-contrapuntal' verse (p. 58) is unjustifiable. It was no accident that most of the madrigals had fairly simple 'harmonic' texts, since metrical regularity was desirable if four or more voices were to repeat the phrases at varying intervals, respond to and imitate each other, ornament and 'express' the text, and still preserve coherence. The subtleties of a contrapuntal text would be lost in such a process. Herbert's practice may be relevant to the more harmonic lute song, in which one voice clearly carried the air, and the rhythmical subtleties of the text could be heard.

5. Hayes listed no poems by Sidney as 'contrapuntal' or 'approximately contrapuntal.' His tabulations, p. 59, were based on the Muses Library edition of Sidney (London, 1922), which included neither *The Psalmes* nor all the poems from the *Arcadia*. Hayes's suggestion, pp. 48-51, that Herbert was inspired to experiment by Donne and Puttenham is questionable. Although three of Donne's poems ('A Valediction: of my name, in the window,' 'Witchcraft by a Picture,' and 'A Jeat Ring sent') 'can be strictly classified as contrapuntal,' Hayes himself pointed out how greatly Herbert and Donne differed

in their stanzaic practice: 'Herbert had great care for the coherence
of his stanzas; Donne, very little. The average Herbert stanza is
shorter than Donne's . . . and it is held together by interlocking rimes.
The average Donne stanza is a shapeless group of quatrains, couplets,
and triplets, held together only by the thought.' (Judged by Puttenham's rule that the rhymes must 'Entertangle,' 'Only 6 of Donne's
49 "Songs and Sonets" hold together . . . but 82 out of 127 by
Herbert.') In chapter xi of *The Arte of English Poesie* Puttenham
described but disapproved of 'contrapuntal' stanzas. It is, moreover,
hardly safe to assume that any poet who knew Elizabethan and
Jacobean poetry must necessarily have known Puttenham's work.

6. Theodore Spencer gave the best modern discussion of Sidney's
poetry in 'The Poetry of Sir Philip Sidney,' *ELH*, XII (1945), 251-
278. Spencer noted, p. 254, that of the 43 psalms which were Sidney's,
'With the exception of psalms vii and xii, both of which are in terza
rima, each psalm is translated in a different stanza form.'

7. Of those attributed to Sidney, xx, xxiii, xxxiii, xxxviii, xxxix,
and xli; of those attributed to the Countess of Pembroke, lxxxii, cii,
ciii, cix, cxix-*c*, cxix-*d*, cxix-*n*, cxix-*r*.

8. Psalm xxxviii, *The Psalmes of David translated by Sir Philip
Sidney and the Countess of Pembroke* (London, 1823), p. 66.

9. Psalm cii, p. 187. Similarities are not, of course, merely the
result of Sidney's and Mary Herbert's use of 'counterpoint.' These
poems are translations of the Psalms (by far the most influential
volume of poetry for Herbert), written by poets who were experiment-
ing with rhetorical and rhythmical effects. Herbertian passages occur
frequently:

> Alas! how long, my God, wilt thou delay me?
> Turn thee, sweete Lord, and from this ougly fall,
> My deere God, stay me. (Psalm vi, p. 7.)

> Behold me, Lord; let to thy hearing creep
> My crying;
> Nay, give me eyes and light, lest that I sleep
> In dying. (Psalm xiii, p. 19.)

10. *The Psalmes* were not published until the nineteenth century,
but, as Donne's complimentary poem indicates, they were known
during the period in manuscript. They were likely to be known by a
relative who was also a religious poet.

11. Hayes, p. 44.

12. Hayes, p. 56.

13. Part of the insistence of the song derives from the fact that it can be 'sung' as four-stress rhyming couplets; the point is that the breaking of the line and the introduction of the counterpointed rhymes increase the music. The stanzaic pattern is $a^7 b^3 a^4 b^7 c^3 b^4$, with no variations for three stanzas. The c of one stanza becomes the a rhyme of the following stanza. In the concluding stanza the c line is eliminated (for 'Who hath made of two folds one'), and the couplet pattern established.

14. The final lines of the first two stanzas rhyme; also of stanzas 3 and 4.

15. 'Yet through these labyrinths, not my groveling wit' is technically a permissible pentameter line, with the medial syllables of both 'labyrinths' and 'groveling' elided. Yet the first five of the theoretically ten syllables are either accented or long, and the constant conjunctions of consonants throughout the line require pauses which slow the movement. Perhaps it was the editor's conviction that the line was impossibly long which caused the 1633 emendation of 'these' to 'the.' The greater precision of 'these' and a recognition of what happens rhythmically in the rest of the line justify Hutchinson's acceptation, *Works*, p. 89, of the MS. readings of *B* and *W*.

16. One cannot divorce the masterly movement from the complex meanings conveyed by it. In st. 2, e.g., 'voluntarie' serves as a hesitating polysyllabic contrast to the prevailing monosyllables. The 'bed-graves' are 'voluntarie' in that the boys enter the beds willingly and without constraint. But in anticipation of the 'musick' of line 2 of the following stanza, something of the related sense of the musical 'voluntary' seems intended: these beds are improvised graves, and they serve as preludes to the graves. 'Convey' implies not only 'to bear to the final destination,' but also has the overtone of enslavement, 'to carry away secretly.' 'Bound for' indicates the proposed destination, but following the previous 'bindes' it also implies the fated and 'involuntary' chains in which the young passengers make the voyage.

17. The following stanzas show a similar care in their closely woven sound patterns. The apparently simple $a b a b c c$ rhyme scheme becomes complicated. The 'feares-eares' c rhyme of st. 1 is transmuted to the 'sphere-there' b rhyme of st. 2. The b rhyme of st. 3 ('board-word') becomes the c rhyme of st. 4 ('Lord-sword'). The simple long e ('thee,' 'be,' 'me') is the c rhyme of st. 2, the a of st. 3, and the b of st. 4.

NOTES TO CHAPTER VIII

1. *Lives*, p. 269. One suspects that Walton's 'quotation' is partially derived from Herbert's 'Church-musick.'

2. P. 303.

3. P. 307. Mr Bostock supplied for Herbert during those absences.

4. Pp. 316-17. Walton customarily quoted Herbert's poems from memory. In the first quotation the opening exclamation is not part of 'The Thanksgiving,' ll. 39-40, and Walton has turned two lines into three. In 1670 Walton freely changed ll. 3-4 of 'Sunday,' st. 5 (see *Works*, p. 76). In 1675, however, the quotation was accurate except that Heaven still had a 'dore' rather than a 'gate.'

5. Fellowes, *English Cathedral Music*, pp. 15-16, 18.

6. *A Priest to the Temple*, ch. xiv, *Works*, p. 248. No group had a monopoly on the singing of Psalms. Fellowes notes, p. 18, that settings of the metrical Psalms were sung in cathedrals as early as 1562, and harmonized versions were in use until the Restoration.

7. 'William Barton in the second edition (1645) of *The Book of Psalms in metre*, "Printed by Order of Parliament," introduced Herbert's version, with a few changes, but without naming the author. As there were many subsequent editions, Herbert's version must have become widely known'—Hutchinson, *Works*, p. 537. Herbert's poem was also sung in the Established Churches of the Restoration. *Psalms & Hymns in Solemn Musick of Fovre Parts on the Common Tunes to the Psalms in Metre: Used in Parish-Chvrches* . . . (London, 1671) was dedicated to William Sancroft, owner of the Bodleian MS. of *The Temple* and later Archbishop of Canterbury. John Playford quoted Herbert's 'Antiphon (I)' in the preface, and on p. 26 printed 'The 23d Psalme' by 'G. H.' to be sung to 'Canterbury tune.'

8. 'Three Musical Parson-Poets of the xviith Century,' *Proceedings of the Musical Association* (Fifty-fourth session; Leeds, 1928), pp. 93-113. The note on 'The Pearl' occurs on pp. 95-96.

9. Cf. No. 57 of Samuel Daniel's *Delia*, set as No. 14 of John Daniel's *Songs for the Lvte Viol and Voice* (1606):

> If any pleasing relish here I use,
> Then judge the world her beauty gave the same.

See *English Madrigal Verse: 1588-1632*, ed. E. H. Fellowes (Oxford, 1920), p. 402.

10. Herbert scrapped the earlier concluding lines of the stanza, found in *W* (*Works*, p. 89):

> Where both their baskets are wth all their store,
> The smacks of dainties and their exaltation:
> What both y[e] stops and pegs of pleasure bee:
> The ioyes of Company or Contemplation
> Yet I love Thee.

The 'baskets' and 'smacks' are only distracting, and the 'stops and pegs' focus attention on the musical metaphor at the expense of what the poem is saying. In the new version the expansion of meaning in 'brass' relates the musical imagery directly to the senses and furnishes the occasion for the direct statement of the final lines.

11. Manfred F. Bukofzer, *Music in the Baroque Era: From Monteverdi to Bach* (New York, 1947), p. 365. The convention persisted into the age of well-tempered tuning.

12. Fellowes, *English Cathedral Music*, p. 92.

13. Naylor, *op. cit.*, pp. 96-97.

14. Hutchinson, *Works*, p. 489.

15. Herbert was not a professional composer, and although he may have written some of his settings for the 'Musick-meeting' at Salisbury, probably most of his compositions were merely remembered for his own use. Publication would hardly have been considered during his lifetime. Walton states (*Lives*, p. 321), however, that 'many of Mr *Herberts* private Writings' were lost in the burning of Highnam House.

16. The study of the interrelations between poetry and music in the English Renaissance has only been begun. Bruce Pattison's *Music and Poetry of the English Renaissance* (London, 1948) marks a beginning for the Elizabethan period, and it has proved immensely helpful for a reader of my limitations. But Pattison's scope is so great that the fruitfully detailed examination of specific settings in relation to specific poems is still, largely, to be made. Edmund H. Fellowes's various works and editions are invaluable as sources, but Fellowes's chief concern is music rather than poetry. Manfred F. Bukofzer's *Music in the Baroque Era* is European in scope and only incidentally concerned with English music before Purcell, but it offers the most illuminating account of the transition from Renaissance to baroque music which I have discovered.

17. Hyde, *George Herbert*, pp. 36 ff., gives an account of music at Westminster during Herbert's years there. John Holmes was com-

poser and organist at Salisbury from 1602-10, and Thomas Lawes (d. 1640), the father of Henry and William Lawes, was 'in all probability the person who was a vicar-choral at Salisbury'—*DNB*.

18. Bukofzer, p. 199.

19. *Ibid.*, p. 198.

20. See, e.g., No. 1 in 'Coperario's' *Songs of Mourning* (1613), with Thomas Campion's thoroughly 'contrapuntal' text (*English Madrigal Verse*, p. 385). In *Mottects or Grave Chamber Music* (1630), Martin Peerson set thirteen of Fulke Greville's *Caelica* sonnets. Sonnet No. 86, 'O false and treacherous Probability,' is particularly 'unmusical'—by nineteenth-century standards (*English Madrigal Verse*, p. 170).

21. Pattison, *Music and Poetry of the English Renaissance*, pp. 68, 86, states that Byrd's volume did not contain true madrigals. Byrd had originally written his songs 'for solo voice and string quartet, after the English manner,' as he pointed out in his preface: 'Heere are diuers songs, which being originally made for Instruments to expresse the harmonie, and voyce to pronounce the dittie, are now framed in all parts for voyces to sing the same.' But the new Italian madrigals were popular, and Byrd published his songs in the madrigal form. Although the madrigal is the best known genre of the period today, Pattison notes (p. 149) that it 'always remained an Italian form and influenced English poetry only incidentally.' 'Most of the poetry of the period was strophic and intended to be set to airs.'

22. Pattison, pp. 37, 120, describes how Ronsard as well as the Italians helped establish the literary tradition of the air. Ronsard claimed, 'Premiere j'ay dit la façon D'accorder le luth aux Odes,' and in the *Abrégé de l'art Poétique* he assumed the identity of poetry and song: 'car la Poesie sans les instrumens ou sans la grace d'une seule ou plusieurs voix, n'est nullement aggréable, non plus que les instrumens sans estre animez de la melodie d'une plaisante voix.'

23. The text of No. xv in Daniel's *Songs* (*English Madrigal Verse*, p. 405) provides a poetic commentary on the practice:

> Can doleful notes to measured accents set
> Express unmeasured griefs that time forget?
> No, let chromatic tunes, harsh without ground,
>   Be sullen music for a tuneless heart;
> Chromatic tunes most like my passions sound,
>   As if combined to bear their falling part.
> Uncertain certain turns, of thoughts forecast
> Bring back the same, then die, and dying last.

24. See, e.g., No. xii from John Dowland's *A Pilgrimes Solace* (1612) and No. xvii from John Daniel's *Songs for the Lvte Viol and Voice* (1606), *English Madrigal Verse*, pp. 448-49, 406.

25. Bukofzer, pp. 71, 180-82, 199, outlines the development. Elements of the new style had appeared in the second generation of madrigalists and lutanists. The style made a dramatic appearance in Jonson's masques in 1617. In *Vision of Delight*, 'the introductory speech, "Let your shows be new and strange" was sung, fittingly enough, in *stylo recitativo*,' and in *Lovers Make Men*, 'the whole masque was sung after the Italian manner, *stylo recitativo*, by Master Nicholas Lanier, who ordered and made both the scene and the music.' William Child's *First Set of Psalms* (1639), 'written for three voices and continuo, is the first important document of the Italian influence on English church music,' although 'Porter, Child (1606-1697), Portman, and the brothers Lawes' had already appeared in the Anthem Book of 1635.

26. Bukofzer, p. 17.

27. Cf. Pattison, pp. 180-81.

28. Purcell's setting was included in Henry Playford's *Harmonia Sacra* (London, 1688), the most important late seventeenth-century collection of music for private devotion. Herbert hardly conceived of the fourteen stanzas of 'Longing' as a lyric, but Purcell selected the most dramatic stanzas of direct lament (Nos. 1, 2, 4, 5, 6, 7, 14) and omitted the meditative stanzas which evaluate the experience and give shape to the poem. Purcell took full advantage of the opportunities for dramatic expression in the text. The music imitates all the important phrases: 'doubling knees,' 'cries,' 'grones,' 'sighs,' 'ascend,' 'My thoughts turn round, And make me giddie,' 'I fall,' 'Let not the winde Scatter my words,' 'Behold, thy dust doth stirre, It moves, it creeps, it aims at thee,' etc. In the attempt to delineate the affections of the text, the music abandons the poetic rhythm of the lines, and the formal function of the stanzas. Herbert's text sounds as if it were either a dramatic prose monologue or an ode by a follower of Cowley.

29. Pattison, pp. 178-79. The extreme variations in line lengths of the madrigals were satirized by Lyly and Jonson. The nine 'ditties' and two madrigals of Lord Herbert of Cherbury, however, show that the practice did not end with the Elizabethans.

30. Pattison, pp. 149-50.

31. Pattison, pp. 134, 130. Pattison's discussion of the *Observations*,

pp. 128-36, is one of the most valuable sections of his study. I am greatly indebted to it in my remarks.

32. Bukofzer notes, pp. 4-5, that although the early baroque theorists claimed these practices as inventions, in reality they developed Renaissance conventions: 'The two periods actually operated under the same principle, but they differed fundamentally in the method of its application. The renaissance favored the affections of restraint and noble simplicity, the baroque the extreme affections, ranging from violent pain to exuberant joy.'

33. Morley's most condensed discussion occurs in *A Plaine and Easie Introduction to Practicall Musicke* (Shakespeare Association Facs. No. 14; London, 1937), pp. 177-78. The violence with which he attacked musical offenders and critics indicates that many of his rules were already threatened in 1597, but his book was popular enough to be reprinted in 1608.

34. Pattison's list, pp. 108-09, could be almost indefinitely extended, and similar lists might be made of words and ideas used with other devices.

35. The poets must also have found in the music another stimulus toward the delights of hieroglyphic form. Bukofzer, p. 388, describes the relation of music to the emblem: 'The *locus descriptionis* depicted extra-musical ideas by means of metaphorical and allegorical figures and similes which, according to baroque thinking, were as essential to music as they were to the emblems, in which pictorial and figurative meaning were inseparable. Not by accident do emblematic books of the time contain music, as does for example Majer's *Atlanta fugiens*.' The volume was published in 1618.

36. With our contemporary concern for psychological reconstruction we may overlook the fact that Donne's 'Breake of Day' was written for the voice of a woman; the fact was not overlooked by the lutanists nor was it considered extraordinary. Donne's practice is often in opposition to musical tradition; yet Walton's account, *Lives*, p. 62, of Donne's causing 'A Hymne to God the Father' 'to be set to a most grave and solemn Tune,' and the surviving settings of some of the secular poems indicate that we should take the title *Songs and Sonets* fairly seriously. In *The Poems*, II, 54-56, 252-53, Grierson printed settings for 'Song: Goe and catch a falling starre,' 'Breake of Day,' and 'A Hymne to God the Father,' taken from Egerton MS. 2013 and Corkine's *Second Book of Ayres* (1612). The composer of 'A Hymne to God the Father' was 'John Hilton (d. 1657), organist to St Margaret's Church, Westminster.' The settings which Grierson

printed were transcribed and 'conjecturally corrected by Mr Barclay Squire'; John Murray Gibbon's notations of the melodic lines for Donne's poems and others in *Melody and the Lyric: from Chaucer to the Cavaliers* (London and New York, 1930) seem more authentic.

37. *Works*, p. 42.

38. The heart is originally a gift which is examined for 'holes.' It is then desired to be capable of 'propagation,' and it is assured that the 'single' can be 'fruitfull.' Law and the nation are introduced, for one heart (like David's) can both represent a nation and 'fence' it from a plague. The 'divisions' and 'partitions' into which lusts and passions 'parcell out thy heart' point the negative side of multiplicity and, in conjunction with the previous vegetative imagery and the 'fence,' fleetingly raise the image of enclosures. In the final stanza the 'holes' and 'partitions' become 'wounds' for which only the 'balsome' 'All-heal' (the balm of Gilead, the medicine of the Great Physician whose own blood is his balsam) furnishes a cure (cf. Jer. viii. 22). That the healing balsam is 'Dropping from heav'n' parallels and contrasts with ordinary balsam which 'drops' from trees or plants, and suggests the image of the dropping manna, that type of Christ, the 'true bread from heaven' (John vi. 32-35). The image of the sacrament is invoked in relationship to its significance.

39. 'Christmas,' part two. The *mélange des sens* of the final line is probably derived from the traditional and valued ambiguity of the Latin word 'clarus': 'clear,' 'bright,' 'shining,' 'loud,' 'distinct,' 'intelligible,' 'honorable,' 'glorious.'

NOTES TO CHAPTER IX

1. *Seven Types of Ambiguity* (rev. edn.; London and New York, 1947), pp. 129-31.

2. See Rosemary Freeman, 'George Herbert and the Emblem Books,' *RES*, XVII, 158-59.

3. David's psalm of repentance (Ps. li) seems the most important single source. Within it are the rejection of the old offerings (Herbert's fruit and lamb parallel Cain and Abel's offerings as well as the later ritual Hebrew offerings), and the prayer for purgation, for the creation of a clean heart, and for the renewal of the spirit. The Mosaic type of the rock is the source of Christ's spiritual drink in 1 Cor. x. 4. God's deprival of sleep and the command to watch and forbear sleep

occur in Job, in Christ's words at Gethsemane, in 1 Thess. v. 6, and elsewhere. The parallels of such traditional materials are endless. Herbert may have known specific emblems which pictured his episodes, but one does not need to assume such knowledge.

4. *Works*, p. 206.

5. Quoted by Joan Bennett in a review of Hutchinson's edition of Herbert, *RES*, XVII (1941), 352.

NOTES TO CHAPTER X

1. F. O. Matthiessen, *American Renaissance: Art and Expression in the Age of Emerson and Whitman* (New York, 1941), p. 179.

2. 'Du musst dein Leben ändern.'—'Archaïscher Torso Apollos,' M. D. Herter Norton's *Translations from the Poetry of Rainer Maria Rilke* (New York, 1938), pp. 180-81.

INDEX

INDEX